SECOND EDITION

SHORT VERSION # English ESSENTIALS

*What
everyone
needs to know
about grammar,
punctuation,
and usage*

John Langan

TP

INSTRUCTOR'S EDITION

Townsend Press Reading Series
Groundwork for College Reading with Phonics
Groundwork for College Reading
Ten Steps to Building College Reading Skills
Ten Steps to Improving College Reading Skills
Ten Steps to Advancing College Reading Skills
Ten Steps to Advanced Reading

Townsend Press Vocabulary Series
Vocabulary Basics
Groundwork for a Better Vocabulary
Building Vocabulary Skills
Building Vocabulary Skills, Short Version
Improving Vocabulary Skills
Improving Vocabulary Skills, Short Version
Advancing Vocabulary Skills
Advancing Vocabulary Skills, Short Version
Advanced Word Power

Other Reading and Writing Books
Clear Thinking and Writing
English Essentials
English at Hand
The Reading-Writing Connection
The Advanced Reading-Writing Connection
Voices and Values: A Reader for Writers

Supplements Available for Most Books
Instructor's Edition
Instructor's Manual and Test Bank
Online Exercises

Copyright © 2015 by Townsend Press, Inc.
Printed in the United States of America
9 8 7 6 5 4 3 2 1

ISBN (Student Edition): 978-1-59194-462-1
ISBN (Instructor's Edition): 978-1-59194-463-8

Book design: Barbara Solot
Cover design: Hal Taylor
Photography credits: Front cover, from top down and then from left to right: © Image Source/Superstock;
© Media Bakery; © Asia Images Group Pte Ltd/Alamy; © PhotoAlto/Superstock; © OLJ Studio/Alamy;
© Andres Rodriguez/Alamy; © Fancy Collection/Superstock; © Vladimir Gjorgiev/Shutterstock;
© Mike Kemp/Media Bakery; © Steve Hamblin/Alamy.

Send book orders and requests for desk copies or supplements to:
Townsend Press Book Center
439 Kelley Drive
West Berlin, New Jersey 08091

For even faster service, contact us in any of the following ways:
By telephone: 1-800-772-6410
By fax: 1-800-225-8894
By e-mail: cs@townsendpress.com
Through our website: www.townsendpress.com

Contents

PART THREE Writing and Proofreading

PART FOUR For Reference

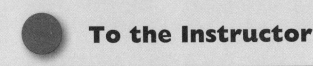

To the Instructor

About the Book

Several features make this book different from other grammar texts on the market:

1   Ease of use.

- Part One focuses on fourteen grammar and punctuation skills that students most need to write well. Once students master the basics, they can go on to Part Two, which includes secondary information about a number of skills. The materials in Parts Three and Four may be introduced at any time during the course.

   It is better to learn a step at a time than to risk confusion by trying to learn everything at once. For example, dependent-word fragments are the subject of one chapter; other common types of fragments appear in a second chapter. The most common homonyms are covered in Part One; other homonyms follow in a "More about Homonyms" section in Part Two.

- Each skill is explained in a one-page review that students can read and understand fairly quickly. Once they have grasped this basic material, they can go on to learn more about the skill and practice using the skill.

- Explanations are written in simple, familiar language, with a real emphasis on clarity and a minimum of grammatical terminology.

- The book is written in a friendly and helpful tone of voice—one that never condescends to students, but instead treats them as adults.

2   Abundant practice. The book is based on the assumption that students learn best when clear explanations are followed by abundant practice. For each chapter in Part One, there is a practice activity followed by four full-page tests. The last two tests are designed to resemble standardized tests and permit easy grading.

3   Engaging materials. Lively and engaging examples and practice materials will help maintain student interest throughout the book.

4   Reasonable price. The low cost of the book makes it an attractive consumable. It can be be given outright to students for marking up, writing answers, tearing out pages, and the like. Teachers will no longer have to spend valuable time preparing handouts for use in class.

5 Helpful supplements. The following supplements are available at no charge to instructors adopting the book:

- A combined *Instructor's Manual and Test Bank* that includes teaching hints, diagnostic and achievement tests, a full answer key, and a bank of additional mastery tests.

- Online exercises for each chapter in Part One. Users of the book can access these exercises by visiting the Townsend Press website and clicking on "Learning Center."

In short, *English Essentials* is designed as a core worktext that will both engage the interest of today's students and help them truly master the skills they need for writing well.

Changes in the Second Edition

A new Part Three. This section begins with a chapter on the basics of writing, followed by twenty writing assignments, some with sample student paragraphs. It also includes a chapter on proofreading techniques as well as ten proofreading tests.

An expanded Part Four. This section now contains material on spelling tips along with dictionary use and parts of speech.

Revised and updated practice sentences and tests. Content throughout Parts One and Two of the book has been refreshed, including more than one hundred new practice items.

Acknowledgments

I am grateful to several colleagues who helped me with the revision of *English Essentials, Short Version*. Maggie Sliker looked at thousands of photographs before finding just the right ones for the cover of the book. At Townsend Press, Barbara Solot has once again cheerfully accepted a design challenge; her clear and inviting full-color design makes the book appealing to both instructors and students. And finally, I would like to thank my long-time editor, Janet Goldstein, for her help with every phase of work on this second edition. A baseball fan, Janet knows what it takes to provide a strong finish to a game. She always delivers.

John Langan

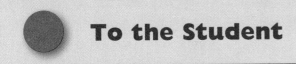

To the Student

As the title of the book suggests, it is about English *essentials*—meaning the most important and most needed writing skills. This book will help you quickly master practical skills that you'll use every day.

How quickly? Glance at one of the one-page reviews that open each of the chapters in Part One of the book. That page will contain basic information about a particular skill. Once you understand the basics, you can turn to the pages that follow to practice that skill. In some cases, you can also refer to Part Two to learn other useful information about the skill.

Here is what is covered in the book:

PART ONE: Fourteen Basic Skills.

Look at the table of contents on page iii for a list of the fourteen grammar and punctuation skills presented in Part One. These are the most basic skills that you need to write well.

Then turn to the first page of "Subjects and Verbs." You will notice that the basic information about subjects and verbs is presented on one page. Ideally, in just a minute, you should be able to review the basic information about subjects and verbs.

Now turn to the other five pages in the chapter. You'll see they are made up of a practice activity followed by four tests. The last two tests are designed to resemble standardized tests, and you or your teacher can easily grade them.

PART TWO: Extending the Skills.

Look again at the table of contents on pages iii and iv. Part Two presents some topics not included in Part One. It also includes additional information about many of the topics presented in Part One. For example, one section presents "More about Commas," adding to the basic comma rules presented in Part One.

PART THREE: Writing and Proofreading.

In this part, you'll find a detailed explanation of the writing process, including everything from prewriting to revising and editing. This section also includes twenty writing topics, proofreading suggestions and practice, and ten proofreading tests.

PART FOUR: For Reference.

For reference purposes, this part of the book provides a complete and handy guide to parts of speech as well as spelling tips and guidelines for dictionary use.

A FINAL WORD

English Essentials has been designed to benefit you as much as possible. Its format is inviting, its explanations are clear, and its practice material and tests will help you learn through doing. *It is a book that has been created to reward effort,* and if you provide that effort, you can help yourself master the basic rules of English. I wish you success.

John Langan

Subjects and Verbs

Basics about Subjects and Verbs

Every complete sentence contains a **subject** and a **verb**.

SUBJECTS

The **subject** of a sentence is the person, place, thing, or idea that the sentence is about. The subject can be called the "who or what" word. To find the subject, ask yourself, "Who or what is this sentence about?" or "Who or what is doing something in this sentence?"

For example, look at the following two sentences:
- People applauded.
- Gloria wrote the answers on the board.

People is what the first sentence is about; they are the ones who applauded. So *people* is the subject of the first sentence. The second sentence answers the question, "Who is doing something in the sentence?" The answer is *Gloria*. She is the person who wrote the answers on the board. So *Gloria* is the subject of the second sentence.

A subject will always be a noun or a pronoun. A **noun** is the name of a person, place, thing, or idea. A **pronoun** is a word—such as *I, you, he, she, it, we,* or *they*—that stands for a noun.

VERBS

Many **verbs** express action; they tell what the subject is doing. You can find an **action verb** by asking, "What did the subject do?" Look again at these sentences:
- People applauded.
- Gloria wrote the answers on the board.

You remember that *people* is the subject of the first sentence. What did they do? They *applauded*. *Applauded* is the verb in the first sentence. *Gloria* is the subject in the second sentence. What did Gloria do? She *wrote*, so *wrote* is the verb in the second sentence.

Some verbs do not show action; they are called **linking verbs**. Linking verbs like *is, are, was,* and *were* join (or link) the subject to something that is said about the subject. For example, in the sentence *Gloria is a teacher*, the linking verb *is* connects the subject *Gloria* with what is said about her—that she is a teacher.

> ### NOTES
> **1** Some verbs consist of more than one word—a **helping verb** plus the main verb. Here are some examples of verbs containing more than one word:
> - Gloria has written the answers on the board.
>   The verb is *has written*.
> - The balloons were drifting slowly to earth.
>   The verb is *were drifting*.
>
> **2** The verb of a sentence never begins with *to*. For example:
> - Gloria is going to write the answers on the board.
>   The verb of the sentence is *is going*. It is not *write* or *to write*.
> - The balloons seemed to hang in the air.
>   The verb of the sentence is *seemed*. It is not *hang* or *to hang*.

A Note on Prepositional Phrases

The subject of a sentence is never part of a prepositional phrase. A **prepositional phrase** is a group of words that begins with a preposition and ends with a noun. Common prepositions are *about, after, as, at, before, between, by, during, for, from, in, into, like, of, on, outside, over, through, to, toward, with,* and *without.* As you look for the subject of a sentence, it may help to cross out any prepositional phrases that you find. Here are examples:

The coffee ~~from the leaking pot~~ stained the carpet.

One ~~of my classmates~~ fell asleep ~~during class.~~

The woman ~~on that motorcycle~~ has no helmet.

The cracks and booms ~~during the thunderstorm~~ were terrifying.

A Note on Helping Verbs

As already mentioned, many verbs consist of a main verb plus one or more helping verbs. Helping verbs are shown below:

Forms of **be:**	be, am, is, are, was, were, being, been
Forms of **have:**	have, has, had
Forms of **do:**	do, does, did
Special verbs:	can, could, may, might, must, ought (to), shall, should, will, would

Subjects and Verbs: PRACTICE

In each sentence below, cross out the prepositional phrases. Then underline the subject of each sentence once and the verb of each sentence twice.

1. <u>Dogs</u> ~~at the animal shelter~~ <u><u>wait</u></u> ~~for a good home~~.

2. The frozen <u>fish</u> ~~on the counter~~ <u><u>defrosted</u></u> quickly.

3. My computer's <u>screen</u> <u><u>went</u></u> blank ~~without warning~~.

4. The <u>kitchen</u> ~~in my parents' house~~ <u><u>smells</u></u> ~~like vanilla and cinnamon~~.

5. A very large <u>truck</u> <u><u>stalled</u></u> ~~on the bridge~~.

6. The <u>orange</u> ~~in the refrigerator~~ <u><u>has</u></u> purple spots.

7. <u>Everyone</u> <u><u>cried</u></u> ~~at one point~~ ~~during the movie~~.

8. Several sad-looking <u>puppies</u> <u><u>huddled</u></u> ~~in the small cage~~.

9. Two young <u>boys</u> ~~from the neighborhood~~ <u><u>were playing</u></u> catch ~~in the alley~~.

10. ~~By the end of the day,~~ <u>we</u> <u><u>had sold</u></u> ~~between 350 and 400 tickets~~.

Name _____   Section _____   Date _____

Subjects and Verbs: TEST 1

For each sentence, cross out any prepositional phrases. Then underline the subject <u>once</u> and the verb <u>twice</u>. Remember to include any helping verb(s).

NOTE To help in your review of subjects and verbs, explanations are given for the first three sentences.

1. A <u>family</u> ~~of ducks~~ <u><u>waddled</u></u> ~~toward the pond~~.

   Of ducks and *toward the pond* are prepositional phrases. The sentence is about a *family (of ducks)*; what they did was *waddled*.

2. <u>Ramona</u> <u><u>loves</u></u> to post messages ~~on her friends' Facebook walls~~.

   Since *post* has a *to* in front of it, it cannot be the verb of the sentence.

3. Many park <u>visitors</u> <u><u>have complained</u></u> ~~about the new regulations~~.

   Have complained (*complained* plus the helping verb *have*) is what the sentence says the park visitors did.

4. The <u>pot</u> ~~of vegetable soup~~ <u><u>simmered</u></u> gently ~~on the stove~~.

5. Your digital <u>camera</u> <u><u>takes</u></u> very clear pictures ~~in all kinds of locations~~.

6. ~~After the study session~~, <u>we</u> <u><u>decided</u></u> to go ~~to an all-night diner for a late meal~~.

7. The summer <u>concert</u> <u><u>was canceled</u></u> ~~with only one day's notice~~.

8. The <u>coffee</u> ~~from the leaking pot~~ <u><u>left</u></u> a stain ~~on the white carpet~~.

9. A German <u>shepherd</u> <u><u>was waiting</u></u> patiently ~~outside the drugstore~~.

10. The curious <u>child</u> <u><u>stared</u></u> silently ~~at the man in the Santa Claus suit~~.

Name _____   Section _____   Date _____

Score: (Number right) _____ x 10 = _____ %

Subjects and Verbs: TEST 2

For each sentence, cross out any prepositional phrases. Then underline the subject <u>once</u> and the verb <u>twice</u>. Remember to include any helping verb(s).

1. The <u>candles</u> ~~on the table~~ <u><u>smell</u></u> ~~like vanilla~~.

2. The <u>people</u> ~~in my family~~ <u><u>speak</u></u> two languages.

3. The clean <u>clothes</u> ~~on the line~~ <u><u>were soaked</u></u> ~~in the sudden thunderstorm~~.

4. ~~Without a word~~, <u>Hugh</u> <u><u>raced</u></u> ~~out of the house~~ and ~~into the front yard~~.

5. <u>Teams</u> ~~of cheerleaders~~ <u><u>yelled</u></u> ~~on opposite sides of the gym~~.

6. Sofia's <u>boyfriend</u> <u><u>is</u></u> good ~~with cars~~.

7. <u>I</u> <u><u>work</u></u> ~~at the computer lab~~ ~~between classes~~.

8. Huge <u>mounds</u> ~~of dirt~~ <u><u>surround</u></u> the construction site.

9. The <u>tiles</u> ~~on the bathroom floor~~ <u><u>look</u></u> gray ~~in the dim light~~.

10. For more than fifty years, <u>movies</u> ~~about dinosaurs~~ <u><u>have been</u></u> popular ~~with audiences~~.

Name _____ Section _____ Date _____

Score: (Number right) _____ x 10 = _____ %

Subjects and Verbs: TEST 3

Read the sentences below. Then, in the space provided, write the letter of the correct answer to each question.

● The movie audience shrieked with laughter during the hilarious scene.

___A___ **1.** In the sentence above, the subject is
   a. audience.   **b.** laughter.   **c.** scene.

___A___ **2.** In the sentence above, the verb is
   a. shrieked.   **b.** laughter.   **c.** during.

● A solution to the problem suddenly popped into my head.

___C___ **3.** In the sentence above, the subject is
   a. problem.   **b.** head.   **c.** solution.

___A___ **4.** In the sentence above, the verb is
   a. popped.   **b.** suddenly.   **c.** head.

● During the long bus trip from Baltimore to Florida, many passengers slept.

___C___ **5.** In the sentence above, the subject is
   a. bus.   **b.** many.   **c.** passengers.

___C___ **6.** In the sentence above, the verb is
   a. During.   **b.** many.   **c.** slept.

● For his birthday dinner, Will plans to have a pizza with pepperoni, mushrooms, and onions.

___C___ **7.** In the sentence above, the subject is
   a. dinner.   **b.** birthday.   **c.** Will.

___A___ **8.** In the sentence above, the verb is
   a. plans.   **b.** have.   **c.** to have.

● After my final exam, I can forget about school for a week.

___B___ **9.** In the sentence above, the subject is
   a. exam.   **b.** I.   **c.** school.

___B___ **10.** In the sentence above, the verb is
   a. can.   **b.** can forget.   **c.** forget.

Name _____ Section _____ Date _____

Score: (Number right) _____ x 10 = _____ %

Subjects and Verbs: TEST 4

Read the sentences below. Then, in the space provided, write the letter of the correct answer to each question.

● During the hot, dry summer, the farmers worried about their crops.

___C___ **1.** In the sentence above, the subject is
    a. summer.   **b.** crops.   **c.** farmers.

___C___ **2.** In the sentence above, the verb is
    a. During.   **b.** about.   **c.** worried.

● Drops of icy rain began to fall on the basketball players.

___A___ **3.** In the sentence above, the subject is
    a. Drops.   **b.** rain.   **c.** players.

___B___ **4.** In the sentence above, the verb is
    a. icy.   **b.** began.   **c.** fall.

● As a result of my father's illness, my family in the past two months has lived a nightmare.

___C___ **5.** In the sentence above, the subject is
    a. illness.   **b.** result.   **c.** family.

___B___ **6.** In the sentence above, the verb is
    a. lived.   **b.** has lived.   **c.** has.

● To catch the bus to school, Maya awakens before sunrise.

___A___ **7.** In the sentence above, the subject is
    a. Maya.   **b.** bus.   **c.** sunrise.

___C___ **8.** In the sentence above, the verb is
    a. catch.   **b.** to catch.   **c.** awakens.

● Tracy has been sending romantic texts to her boyfriend during computer lab.

___A___ **9.** In the sentence above, the subject is
    a. Tracy.   **b.** boyfriend.   **c.** texts.

___B___ **10.** In the sentence above, the verb is
    a. has.   **b.** has been sending.   **c.** sending.

2 Irregular Verbs

Basics about Irregular Verbs

Most English verbs are **regular**. That is, they form their past tense and past participle by adding *-ed* or *-d* to the basic form, as shown here:

Basic Form	Past Tense	Past Participle
ask	asked	asked
raise	raised	raised

Some English verbs are **irregular.** They do not form their past tense and past participle by adding *-ed* or *-d* to the basic form of the verb. Instead, their past tenses and past participles are formed in other ways. Here are some of the most common irregular verbs.

Basic Form	Past Tense	Past Participle	Basic Form	Past Tense	Past Participle
become	became	become	go	went	gone
begin	began	begun	grow	grew	grown
break	broke	broken	have	had	had
bring	brought	brought	hide	hid	hidden
catch	caught	caught	is	was	been
choose	chose	chosen	keep	kept	kept
come	came	come	know	knew	known
do	did	done	leave	left	left
drink	drank	drunk	read	read	read
drive	drove	driven	see	saw	seen
eat	ate	eaten	shake	shook	shaken
feel	felt	felt	spend	spent	spent
find	found	found	take	took	taken
forget	forgot	forgotten	tell	told	told
get	got	got, gotten	write	wrote	written
give	gave	given			

A word about helping verbs Sometimes the verb of a sentence consists of more than one word. In these cases, the main verb will be joined by one or more **helping verbs**. Look at the following sentence:

> I **should have gone** to bed earlier last night.

In this sentence, the main verb is *gone*. The helping verbs are *should* and *have*. Other common helping verbs include *be, can, could, do, has, may, must, will,* and *would.* (For a longer list of helping verbs, see page 4.)

When you use the above chart, keep these two points in mind:

1 If the verb in your sentence does **not** have a helping verb, choose the past tense form.

I **ate** a bacon, lettuce, and tomato sandwich.

2 If the verb in your sentence **does have** a helping verb, choose the past participle.

I **had eaten** a bacon, lettuce, and tomato sandwich.

NOTE If you think a verb is irregular, and it is not in the above list, look it up in your dictionary. If it is irregular, the principal parts will be listed. See "Dictonary Use," page 267.

Irregular Verbs: PRACTICE

For each sentence below, fill in the correct form of the verb in the space provided.

broke, broken   1. When I _____*broke*_____ my leg, my friends scribbled cheerful messages on the cast.

spended, spent   2. Nathan _____*spent*_____ most of his teenage years dressed in black and alone in his bedroom.

catched, caught   3. The kindergarten teacher _____*caught*_____ chicken pox from one of her students.

went, gone   4. The sign on the barbershop door said, "Closed. I have _____*gone*_____ fishing."

wrote, writed   5. Before he was famous, the horror author Stephen King taught high-school English and _____*wrote*_____ short stories and novels at night.

done, did   6. I _____*did*_____ everything I could to keep my grandmother comfortable when she was sick.

bringed, brought   7. Seven people _____*brought*_____ potato salad to the church picnic, and only one person made a dessert.

chose, choosed   8. Although she was close to winning $100,000, the game-show contestant lost it all when she _____*chose*_____ the wrong answer to the final question.

shook, shaked   9. Rick made a huge mess when he _____*shook*_____ up a bottle of ketchup without realizing that the cap was off.

eaten, ate   10. My friend stuck to his diet for six days. Then he _____*ate*_____ an entire gallon of ice cream and a bag of Snickers in fifteen minutes.

A Note on Three Problem Verbs

Three common irregular verbs that confuse many writers are *be, do,* and *have.* Here are the correct present tense and past tense forms of these three verbs.

	Present Tense		**Past Tense**	
Be	I am	we are	I was	we were
	you are	you are	you were	you were
	he, she, it is	they are	he, she, it was	they were
Do	I do	we do	I did	we did
	you do	you do	you did	you did
	he, she, it does	they do	he, she, it did	they did
Have	I have	we have	I had	we had
	you have	you have	you had	you had
	he, she, it has	they have	he, she, it had	they had

Name _____ Section _____ Date _____

Irregular Verbs: TEST 1

Each of the items below contains **two** errors in irregular verbs. Find the errors and cross them out. Then, in the spaces provided, write the correct forms of the verbs.

NOTE To help you master irregular verbs, explanations are given for five of the sentences.

1. Once I ~~seen~~ a hawk dive from the top of a tall tree to capture a field mouse. The bird ~~catched~~ the tiny creature in its claws and flew back to its perch.

>   **a.** _____ *saw* _____
>
>   **b.** _____ *caught* _____

Use the past tense of the irregular verb *see* for the first correction needed.

2. Our neighbors have always ~~gave~~ their little children household chores. This month, their son sets the table, and their daughter does some dusting. Last month, they both ~~done~~ some weeding in the backyard.

>   **a.** _____ *given* _____
>
>   **b.** _____ *did* _____

Use the past participle of the irregular verb *give* for the first correction needed.

3. My aunt ~~be~~ a big fan of Elvis Presley. Every time she hears "Love Me Tender," she becomes misty-eyed. Last year, she and my uncle ~~gone~~ on a trip to Graceland, Elvis's home. While there, she bought "Elvis Lives" bumper stickers for herself and all her friends.

>   **a.** _____ *is* _____
>
>   **b.** _____ *went* _____

Use the past tense of the irregular verb *go* for the second correction needed.

4. It is dangerous to shake a baby. Many babies who have been ~~shook~~ have suffered brain injuries. The adults who ~~done~~ this seldom meant to cause such harm.

>   **a.** _____ *shaken* _____
>
>   **b.** _____ *did* _____

Use the past tense of the irregular verb *do* for the second correction needed.

5. I was determined not to forget anything I needed at the store. I sat down and ~~writed~~ a long shopping list. Feeling proud of myself, I went to the store. Then I realized I had ~~forgotted~~ the list.

>   **a.** _____ *wrote* _____
>
>   **b.** _____ *forgotten* _____

Use the past participle of the irregular verb *forget* for the second correction needed.

Name _____ Section _____ Date _____

Score: (Number right) _____ x 10 = _____ %

Irregular Verbs: TEST 2

Each of the items below contains **two** errors in irregular verbs. Find the errors and cross them out. Then, in the spaces provided, write the correct forms of the verbs.

1. It really can be more fun to give than to receive. Yesterday I ~~gived~~ my sister a ring of mine that she has always loved. When she saw what I had ~~gave~~ her, her face lit up.

   a. _____ *gave* _____

   b. _____ *given* _____

2. In the winter, I drink about a quart of orange juice a week. But last week, when it was so hot, I ~~drinked~~ that much in a day. Once all the orange juice was ~~drank~~, I started in on ice water and cold soda.

   a. _____ *drank* _____

   b. _____ *drunk* _____

3. I was angry that my friend ~~taked~~ the money that was lying on the dresser. She didn't know it was mine, but she ~~knowed~~ it wasn't hers.

   a. _____ *took* _____

   b. _____ *knew* _____

4. The teacher ~~becomed~~ impatient with the students who had forgotten their homework. "I thought you had ~~growed~~ up by now," he complained.

   a. _____ *became* _____

   b. _____ *grown* _____

5. Three people had ~~saw~~ the robbery take place, but no one ~~be~~ sure what the robber looked like.

   a. _____ *seen* _____

   b. _____ *was* _____

Name _____ Section _____ Date _____

Score: (Number right) _____ x 10 = _____ %

Irregular Verbs: TEST 3

Read each sentence below. Then choose the correct verb, fill in the blank, and write the letter of your choice in the space provided in the margin.

___D___ **1.** Sandy has ___gone___ to a counselor every week since her parents' divorce.
    a. went   **c.** go
    b. wented   **d.** gone

___C___ **2.** My grandmother has ___written___ our family history.
    a. writed   **c.** written
    b. wrote   **d.** write

___B___ **3.** Our neighbors ___drove___ us crazy when they first moved in, but now we're good friends.
    a. drived   **c.** driven
    b. drove   **d.** droved

___B___ **4.** How long have you and Stephanie ___known___ each other?
    a. knew   **c.** knowed
    b. known   **d.** knewed

___C___ **5.** The lucky woman who ___caught___ the home run ball got it autographed by the famous baseball player.
    a. catched   **c.** caught
    b. catch   **d.** caughted

___D___ **6.** In the middle of dinner, Stacy gasped, "I ___forgot___ I was supposed to baby-sit tonight!"
    a. forget   **c.** forgotted
    b. forgotten   **d.** forgot

___B___ **7.** Trying to avoid catching a cold, everyone in the family ___took___ extra vitamin C every day last winter.
    a. take   **c.** taked
    b. took   **d.** tooked

___C___ **8.** The kindergarten teacher was not thrilled when Keith ___brought___ a live worm to class.
    a. bring   **c.** brought
    b. brang   **d.** bringed

___C___ **9.** The boss ___told___ everyone to plan to work late Thursday night.
    a. tell   **c.** told
    b. telled   **d.** tolded

___A___ **10.** Only the people who had ___seen___ the first movie understood the sequel.
    a. seen   **c.** seed
    b. saw   **d.** sawed

Name _____   Section _____   Date _____

Score: (Number right) _____ x 10 = _____ %

Irregular Verbs: TEST 4

Read each sentence below. Then choose the correct verb, fill in the blank, and write the letter of your choice in the space provided in the margin.

___C___   **1.** Last July, Ivan ____*became*____ an American citizen.
    a. become   **c.** became
    b. becomed   **d.** becamed

___D___   **2.** The tiny, cute puppy has ____*grown*____ into a ninety-pound monster.
    a. grow   **c.** growed
    b. grew   **d.** grown

___A___   **3.** Last night, Natalie ____*spent*____ nearly four hours on homework.
    a. spent   **c.** spended
    b. spends   **d.** spend

___D___   **4.** Most people who traveled to Alaska during the Gold Rush ____*found*____ little or no gold.
    a. finded   **c.** find
    b. founded   **d.** found

___B___   **5.** My father has ____*done*____ everything he can to keep our car in good shape.
    a. did   **c.** do
    b. done   **d.** doned

___B___   **6.** I had ____*forgotten*____ to do the assignment.
    a. forget   **c.** forgot
    b. forgotten   **d.** forgetted

___C___   **7.** My family had ____*eaten*____ the whole pie before I got home.
    a. eat   **c.** eaten
    b. ate   **d.** eated

___A___   **8.** The millionaire businessman ____*left*____ all his money to charity.
    a. left   **c.** lefted
    b. leave   **d.** leaved

___D___   **9.** Juanita has ____*chosen*____ the color gray for her bridesmaids' dresses.
    a. chose   **c.** choose
    b. choosed   **d.** chosen

___B___   **10.** The story was about a man who foolishly ____*hid*____ some money in an old trash barrel.
    a. hide   **c.** hided
    b. hid   **d.** hidded

3 Subject-Verb Agreement

Basics about Subject-Verb Agreement

In a correctly written sentence, the subject and verb **agree** (match) in number. Singular subjects have singular verbs, and plural subjects have plural verbs.

In simple sentences of a few words, it's not difficult to make the subject and verb agree:

- Our *baby* **sleeps** more than ten hours a day. Some *babies* **sleep** even longer.

However, not all sentences are as straightforward as the above examples. Here are two situations that can cause problems with subject-verb agreement.

1 WORDS BETWEEN THE SUBJECT AND VERB

A verb often comes right after its subject, as in this example:

- The sealed *boxes* **belong** to my brother.

   NOTE In the following examples, the *subject* is shown in *italic type,* and the **verb** is shown in **boldface type.**

However, at times the subject and verb are separated by a prepositional phrase. A **prepositional phrase** is a group of words that begins with a preposition and ends with a noun or pronoun. *By, for, from, in, of, on,* and *to* are common prepositions. (A longer list of prepositions is on page 144.) Look at the following sentences:

- A small *bag* of potato chips **contains** 440 calories.

   In this sentence, the subject and verb are separated by the prepositional phrase *of potato chips*. The verb must agree with the singular subject *bag*—not with a word in the prepositional phrase.

- The *tomatoes* in this salad **are** brown and mushy.

   Because the subject, *tomatoes*, is plural, the verb must also be plural. The prepositional phrase *in this salad* has no effect on subject and verb agreement.

- *Books* about baseball **fill** my brother's room.

   The plural subject *books* takes the plural verb *fill. About baseball* is a prepositional phrase.

2 COMPOUND SUBJECTS

A **compound subject** is made up of two nouns connected by a joining word. Subjects joined by *and* generally take a plural verb.

- *Running* and *lifting* weights **are** good ways to keep in shape.

- *Fear* and *ignorance* **have** a lot to do with hatred.

Subject-Verb Agreement: PRACTICE

For each sentence below, choose the correct form of the verb from the words in the margin, and write it in the space provided.

taste, tastes   1. Bananas and peanut butter _____taste_____ good together.

wait, waits   2. A basket of dirty clothes _____waits_____ at the top of the basement steps.

has, have   3. My counselor and my English teacher _____have_____ agreed to write recommendations for me.

look, looks   4. The old house at the corner of State and Creek Roads _____looks_____ as if it's ready to fall down.

see, sees   5. Shantell and Justin both _____see_____ better with contact lenses than they did with glasses.

eat, eats   6. Hawks and eagles _____eat_____ meat instead of seeds.

is, are   7. The jokes in that movie _____are_____ not at all funny.

sleep, sleeps   8. The cat and the dog _____sleep_____ curled up together.

live, lives   9. Kara and her children _____live_____ in a shelter.

do, does   10. What _____does_____ it mean when the computer screen turns blue?

Name _____ Section _____ Date _____

Score: (Number right) _____ x 10 = _____ %

Subject-Verb Agreement: TEST 1

For each sentence, fill in the correct form of the missing verb.

NOTE To help you review subject-verb agreement, explanations are given for the first two sentences.

belong, belongs 1. The bones in the backyard _____belong_____ to our neighbor's dog.
Bones, the subject, is a plural noun and so needs a plural verb. *In the backyard* is a prepositional phrase. The subject is never in—or affected by—a prepositional phrase.

is, are 2. Sunflower seeds and peanuts _____are_____ the main ingredients in this bird-food mix.
Seeds and peanuts is a compound subject requiring a plural verb.

draw, draws 3. Students in the art class _____draw_____ with a charcoal stick.

look, looks 4. The men sitting in the corner booth _____look_____ unhappy with their food.

bake, bakes 5. Darcy and her mother _____bake_____ cakes and cookies for a local restaurant.

play, plays 6. The teenager in the apartment upstairs _____plays_____ a guitar late at night.

echo, echoes 7. The singing of the caged canaries _____echoes_____ through the tiny pet shop.

seem, seems 8. The questions on this test _____seem_____ unfair to me.

is, are 9. E-mail and text messaging _____are_____ the main ways that some people communicate with each other.

attract, attracts 10. A colorful assortment of toys _____attracts_____ shoppers to the mall store's display window.

Name _____ Section _____ Date _____

Score: (Number right) _____ x 10 = _____ %

Subject-Verb Agreement: TEST 2

For each sentence, fill in the correct form of the missing verb.

have, has   1. The ice cubes in the punch bowl _____*have*_____ melted.

is, are   2. The old telephones in my grandparents' home _____*are*_____ still in working order.

appear, appears 3. Garlic and onions _____*appear*_____ in almost everything my grandmother cooks.

wail, wails   4. The tired, cranky baby _____*wails*_____ while his mother tries to comfort him.

belong, belongs 5. The leather cap and jacket on the desk _____*belong*_____ to our teacher.

forget, forgets 6. Members of the audience sometimes _____*forget*_____ to turn off their cell phones during a performance.

is, are   7. Goat and rabbit _____*are*_____ two of the more unusual items on the restaurant's menu.

greet, greets   8. Moans and groans _____*greet*_____ the teacher whenever she announces a pop quiz.

show, shows   9. Dirt and grease _____*show*_____ clearly on the windows when the sun shines through them.

do, does   10. Contrary to public opinion, cats and dogs _____*do*_____ not really hate each other.

Name _____   Section _____   Date _____

Score: (Number right) _____ x 10 = _____ %

Subject-Verb Agreement: **TEST 3**

Read each sentence below. Then choose the correct verb, fill in the blank, and write the letter of your choice in the space provided in the margin.

___A___   **1.** Our friends in the country _____*get*_____ rid of the insects in their yard without using poisonous sprays—they keep chickens.
a. get   **b.** gets

___A___   **2.** The chickens _____*eat*_____ most of the insects. In addition, our friends get to enjoy fresh eggs.
a. eat   **b.** eats

___B___   **3.** The children and their mother _____*are*_____ disappointed in the frozen dinners. The peas look wrinkled and dry.
a. is   **b.** are

___A___   **4.** Also, mounds of soggy stuffing in the frozen dinners _____*cover*_____ a small piece of meat.
a. cover   **b.** covers

___A___   **5.** Our kitchen is anything but quiet. The microwave and the dishwasher _____*produce*_____ all kinds of noise.
a. produce   **b.** produces

___B___   **6.** Furthermore, the refrigerator in the kitchen hums, and the clock hanging over the cabinets _____*chimes*_____ every hour.
a. chime   **b.** chimes

___A___   **7.** The coins in the jar on my dresser _____*weigh*_____ almost three pounds. I wonder how much money is actually there.
a. weigh   **b.** weighs

___A___   **8.** Unfortunately, pennies and nickels _____*make*_____ up most of the total in the jar.
a. make   **b.** makes

___A___   **9.** The Bradleys have made their property much more attractive. Flowers and an evergreen hedge now _____*line*_____ the sidewalk.
a. line   **b.** lines

___B___   **10.** Also, a birdbath near the front steps _____*attracts*_____ robins, blue jays, and other colorful birds.
a. attract   **b.** attracts

Name _____ Section _____ Date _____

Score: (Number right) _____ x 10 = _____ %

Subject-Verb Agreement: TEST 4

Read each sentence below. Then choose the correct verb, fill in the blank, and write the letter of your choice in the space provided in the margin.

___B___ **1.** Few people ever _____recall_____ seeing baby pigeons. The reason is simple.
    a. recalls   **b.** recall

___A___ **2.** Baby pigeons in the nest _____eat_____ a huge amount of food each day. Upon leaving the nest, they are nearly as large as their parents.
    a. eat   **b.** eats

___A___ **3.** The books in your book bag _____weigh_____ a ton. How can you carry them around all day?
    a. weigh   **b.** weighs

___B___ **4.** I'm afraid that book bag will hurt your back. The strain on your muscles _____is_____ enormous.
    a. are   **b.** is

___B___ **5.** Ricardo picks up his bowling ball. The pins at the end of the lane _____look_____ so defenseless. He almost feels sorry for them.
    a. looks   **b.** look

___A___ **6.** But then Ricardo releases the ball. He and his friends _____watch_____ the pins come crashing down.
    a. watch   **b.** watches

___A___ **7.** The presents under the Christmas tree _____tempt_____ the children. They want to squeeze, shake, and investigate every one.
    a. tempt   **b.** tempts

___B___ **8.** The adults _____tell_____ the children that they have to be patient.
    a. tells   **b.** tell

___A___ **9.** My friends and I _____enjoy_____ going to the movies.
    a. enjoy   **b.** enjoys

___A___ **10.** But some people in the theater really _____irritate_____ us. They talk as loudly as if they were in their own living rooms.
    a. irritate   **b.** irritates

4 Sentence Types

Basics about Sentence Types

There are three basic kinds of sentences in English:

SIMPLE SENTENCES

A **simple sentence** has only one subject-verb combination and expresses one complete thought.

- My brother cooked dinner tonight.
  Brother is the subject, and *cooked* is the verb.

A simple sentence may have more than one subject or more than one verb:

- Shorts and T-shirts sway on the clothesline.
  Shorts and *T-shirts* are the two subjects; *sway* is the verb.

- The children splashed and squealed in the swimming pool.
  Children is the subject; *splashed* and *squealed* are the two verbs.

COMPOUND SENTENCES

A **compound sentence** is made up of two or more complete thoughts. Following are two complete thoughts, joined to form a compound sentence:

- Rose wants chili for dinner, but she forgot to buy beans.

By using a comma and a joining word such as *but*, we can combine what would otherwise be two simple sentences (*Rose wants chili for dinner* and *She forgot to buy beans*) into one compound sentence. In addition to *but*, the words *and* and *so* are the joining words most often used to connect two complete thoughts. Here are examples of *and* and *so* as joining words:

- The driver failed to signal, and he went through a stop sign.

- The meal was not hot, so we sent it back to the kitchen.

COMPLEX SENTENCES

A **complex sentence** is made up of one complete thought and another thought that begins with a dependent word like *after, although, as, because, before, if, since, unless, until, when, where,* and *while.*

NOTE A comma is placed after a dependent statement when it starts a sentence.

- Although I had a free ticket to the game, I was too tired to go.

- I set my alarm for 5 a.m. because I wanted to finish a paper.

- After the test was over, we got something to eat.

When you write, try to make your sentences varied and interesting. Using all three kinds of sentences will both help you express more complex thoughts and give your writing a lively style.

Sentence Types: PRACTICE

A. Use a comma and a logical joining word to combine the following pairs of simple sentences into compound sentences. Choose from **and, but,** or **so**. Place a comma before the joining word.

> **HINT** Be sure to choose the logical joining word in each case. Keep in mind that
> **and** means *in addition*
> **but** means *however*
> **so** means *as a result*

Some answers may vary.

1. Kwan is quite attractive. She sees herself as ugly.

   Kwan is quite attractive, but she sees herself as ugly.

2. Jared is good at math. He writes well, too.

   Jared is good at math, and he writes well, too.

3. I lost my watch. I don't know what time it is.

   I lost my watch, so I don't know what time it is.

4. My sister doesn't usually eat candy. She ate a box of chocolates yesterday.

   My sister doesn't usually eat candy, but she ate a box of chocolates yesterday.

5. The night air was chilly. I put on a sweater.

   The night air was chilly, so I put on a sweater.

B. Use a suitable dependent word to combine the following pairs of simple sentences into complex sentences. Choose from **although, because, since,** and **when**. Place a comma after a dependent statement when it starts a sentence.

6. Strawberries are expensive. I don't often buy them.

   Because strawberries are expensive, I don't often buy them.

7. An elephant's skin is very thick. It is also very sensitive.

   Although an elephant's skin is very thick, it is also very sensitive.

8. The city pools have been crowded. The weather turned hot.

   The city pools have been crowded since the weather turned hot.

9. I quickly called the police. I heard a scream outside.

   I quickly called the police when I heard a scream outside.

10. Jessica seems unfriendly. She is really just shy.

    Although Jessica seems unfriendly, she is really just shy.

Name _____   Section _____   Date _____

Sentence Types: TEST 1

A. Use a comma and a suitable joining word to combine the following pairs of simple sentences into compound sentences. Choose from **and** (which means *in addition*), **but** (which means *however*), or **so** (which means *as a result*).

NOTE To help you master sentence combining, hints are given for the first two sentences.

Some answers may vary.

1. The coffee is cold. It is also too strong.
   Hint: Use the word that means "in addition."
   The coffee is cold, and it is also too strong.

2. Our car runs well. Its body is dented and rusty.
   Hint: Use the word that means "however."
   Our car runs well, but its body is dented and rusty.

3. The book was very expensive. I didn't buy it.
   The book was very expensive, so I didn't buy it.

4. Gene laughed throughout the movie. His date didn't laugh once.
   Gene laughed throughout the movie, but his date didn't laugh once.

5. The electricity was out. We had no candles.
   The electricity was out, and we had no candles.

B. Use a suitable dependent word to combine the following pairs of simple sentences into complex sentences. Choose from **although, because, since**, and **when**. Place a comma after a dependent statement when it starts a sentence.

6. The ball game was postponed. It began to rain heavily.
   The ball game was postponed because it began to rain heavily.

7. Sam practices his saxophone. The dog howls.
   When Sam practices his saxophone, the dog howls.

8. The house looks beautiful. It seems cold and unfriendly to me.
   Although the house looks beautiful, it seems cold and unfriendly to me.

9. She doesn't drive. Mia must walk or take the bus to work.
   Since she doesn't drive, Mia must walk or take the bus to work.

10. The beautiful fireworks exploded. The audience gasped and applauded.
    When the beautiful fireworks exploded, the audience gasped and applauded.

Name _____   Section _____   Date _____

Score: (Number right) _____ × 10 = _____ %

Sentence Types: TEST 2

A. Use a comma and a suitable joining word to combine the following pairs of simple sentences into compound sentences. Choose from **and, but,** or **so.**   Some answers may vary.

1. Eddie was tired of his appearance. He shaved all the hair off his head.

Eddie was tired of his appearance, so he shaved all the hair off his head.

2. Eddie bought new clothing in bright colors. He added an earring as well.

Eddie bought new clothing in bright colors, and he added an earring as well.

3. Twenty students were enrolled in the class. Only eight were present that stormy day.

Twenty students were enrolled in the class, but only eight were present that stormy day.

4. Thirty percent of M&M's are brown. Twenty percent of them are red.

Thirty percent of M&M's are brown, and twenty percent of them are red.

5. The stain did not wash out of my white pants. I dyed the pants tan.

The stain did not wash out of my white pants, so I dyed the pants tan.

B. Use a suitable dependent word to combine the following pairs of simple sentences into complex sentences. Choose from **although, because, since,** and **when**. Place a comma after a dependent statement when it starts a sentence.

6. I need to improve my grades. I will start taking more notes in class.

Because I need to improve my grades, I will start taking more notes in class.

7. There used to be many small stores downtown. They are gone now.

Although there used to be many small stores downtown, they are gone now.

8. The bus came into sight. Connie shouted "Goodbye!" and rushed out the door.

When the bus came into sight, Connie shouted "Goodbye!" and rushed out the door.

9. Mental illness is so little understood. It has always frightened people.

Since mental illness is so little understood, it has always frightened people.

10. I'm allergic to most animals. Siamese cats don't bother me.

Although I'm allergic to most animals, Siamese cats don't bother me.

Name _____   Section _____   Date _____

Score: (Number right) _____ x 10 = _____ %

Sentence Types: TEST 3

In the space provided, write the letter of the combined sentence that reads most smoothly, clearly, and logically.

__C__ **1.** **a.** Because my parents are both quite short, we kids are all on the tall side.
   b. My parents are both quite short, so we kids are all on the tall side.
   c. Although my parents are both quite short, we kids are all on the tall side.

__B__ **2.** **a.** My cousin was falling behind in algebra class, but he decided to work with a tutor.
   b. Because my cousin was falling behind in algebra class, he decided to work with a tutor.
   c. My cousin was falling behind in algebra class because he decided to work with a tutor.

__C__ **3.** **a.** The thunderstorm rattled the windows, but the dog hid in the closet.
   b. Although the thunderstorm rattled the windows, the dog hid in the closet.
   c. While the thunderstorm rattled the windows, the dog hid in the closet.

__A__ **4.** **a.** The movie turned out to be too scary, so they took their children home.
   b. The movie turned out to be too scary, but they took their children home.
   c. Although the movie turned out to be too scary, they took their children home.

__A__ **5.** **a.** Although the baby goat was cute and fluffy, it had a vicious temper.
   b. The baby goat was cute and fluffy, and it had a vicious temper.
   c. Because the baby goat was cute and fluffy, it had a vicious temper.

__B__ **6.** **a.** Nobody was very hungry Thanksgiving night, but we ate cereal for dinner.
   b. Nobody was very hungry Thanksgiving night, so we ate cereal for dinner.
   c. Nobody was very hungry Thanksgiving night because we ate cereal for dinner.

__B__ **7.** **a.** The mechanic called about our car, so he didn't have good news.
   b. When the mechanic called about our car, he didn't have good news.
   c. Before the mechanic called about our car, he didn't have good news.

__A__ **8.** **a.** Alan is limping badly because he twisted his ankle playing basketball.
   b. Because Alan is limping badly, he twisted his ankle playing basketball.
   c. Alan is limping badly, and he twisted his ankle playing basketball.

__A__ **9.** **a.** Before I met my new neighbor, I had never been friends with a blind person.
   b. I met my new neighbor, but I had never been friends with a blind person.
   c. I met my new neighbor, so I had never been friends with a blind person.

__C__ **10.** **a.** You put masking tape around the windows and doors, but I'll get the paint and brushes.
   b. Although you put masking tape around the windows and doors, I'll get the paint and brushes.
   c. While you put masking tape around the windows and doors, I'll get the paint and brushes.

Name _____   Section _____   Date _____

Score: (Number right) _____ x 10 = _____ %

Sentence Types: TEST 4

In the space provided, write the letter of the combined sentence that reads most smoothly, clearly, and logically.

___C___ **1. a.** After I have a test in the morning, I'd better get to bed early.
　　　　　b. Although I have a test in the morning, I'd better get to bed early.
　　　　　c. I have a test in the morning, so I'd better get to bed early.

___C___ **2. a.** Because these shoes are comfortable, their price is reasonable.
　　　　　b. These shoes are comfortable, but their price is reasonable.
　　　　　c. These shoes are comfortable, and their price is reasonable.

___B___ **3. a.** Although the clothes were being washed, we sat in the laundromat reading magazines.
　　　　　b. While the clothes were being washed, we sat in the laundromat reading magazines.
　　　　　c. The clothes were being washed, but we sat in the laundromat reading magazines.

___B___ **4. a.** I am afraid of heights, and flying in an airplane doesn't bother me.
　　　　　b. Although I am afraid of heights, flying in an airplane doesn't bother me.
　　　　　c. Because I am afraid of heights, flying in an airplane doesn't bother me.

___A___ **5. a.** After rain began falling heavily, the umpires cancelled the game.
　　　　　b. Although rain began falling heavily, the umpires cancelled the game.
　　　　　c. Rain began falling heavily while the umpires cancelled the game.

___C___ **6. a.** When I always hang up on telemarketers, they keep calling.
　　　　　b. Because I always hang up on telemarketers, they keep calling.
　　　　　c. Although I always hang up on telemarketers, they keep calling.

___A___ **7. a.** When my mother was a young girl, she quit school to help support her family.
　　　　　b. Because my mother was a young girl, she quit school to help support her family.
　　　　　c. My mother was a young girl, so she quit school to help support her family.

___C___ **8. a.** The towels look soft and fluffy, so they feel scratchy.
　　　　　b. When the towels look soft and fluffy, they feel scratchy.
　　　　　c. Although the towels look soft and fluffy, they feel scratchy.

___B___ **9. a.** We studied in the library all evening when we went out for pizza.
　　　　　b. After we studied in the library all evening, we went out for pizza.
　　　　　c. We studied in the library all evening, but we went out for pizza.

___A___ **10. a.** The newlyweds are trying to save money, so they clip coupons and buy items on sale.
　　　　　b. Although the newlyweds are trying to save money, they clip coupons and buy items on sale.
　　　　　c. The newlyweds are trying to save money, but they clip coupons and buy items on sale.

5 Fragments I

Basics about Fragments

To be a complete sentence, a group of words must contain a subject and a verb. It must also express a complete thought. If it lacks a subject, a verb, or a complete thought, it is a **fragment**.

The most common kind of fragment is the **dependent-word fragment**, which has a subject and verb but does not express a complete thought. Here is an example:

- Because Laura was tired.

Although this word group contains a subject (*Laura*) and a verb (*was*), it is an incomplete thought. The reader wants to know **what happened** because Laura was tired. A word group that begins with *because* or another dependent word cannot stand alone; another idea is needed to complete the thought. For example, we could correct the above fragment like this:

- Because Laura was tired, **she took a nap**.

  The words *she took a nap* complete the thought.

Here are two more dependent-word fragments.

- When I saw the big spider on my leg.

- After I turned off the television set.

Each of these word groups begins with a dependent word (*when, after*) and expresses an incomplete idea. See if you can add words to each fragment that would complete the thought.   Answers will vary.

- When I saw the big spider on my leg, _____ I jumped out of my chair _____.

- _____ I picked up a book _____ after I turned off the television set.

Here are some ways to complete the above fragments:

- When I saw the big spider on my leg, **I jumped out of my chair**.

- **I picked up a book** after I turned off the television set.

  Punctuation note When a dependent-word group starts a sentence, follow it with a comma.

When you use a dependent word, take care that you complete the thought in the same sentence. Otherwise, a fragment may result. Here is a list of common dependent words:

after	even though	unless	wherever
although	even when	until	whether
as	if	what	which
because	since	when	while
before	that	whenever	who
even if	though	where	

Note that very often the way to correct a dependent-word fragment will be to connect it to the sentence that comes before or after it.

Fragments I: PRACTICE

Underline the dependent-word fragment in each of the following items. Then correct it in the space provided. Add a comma after a dependent-word group that begins a sentence.

1. Because the movie was so violent. Some people left the theater.

    Because the movie was so violent, some people left the theater.

2. Everything was peaceful. Before Martha stormed into the room.

    Everything was peaceful before Martha stormed into the room.

3. Even though I've never seen a ghost. I still believe ghosts exist.

    Even though I've never seen a ghost, I still believe ghosts exist.

4. The batter argued with the umpire. While the crowd booed.

    The batter argued with the umpire while the crowd booed.

5. When two guests began to argue. The hostess moved the party outside.

    When two guests began to argue, the hostess moved the party outside.

6. There's always a big party in the park. After the last day of school.

    There's always a big party in the park after the last day of school.

7. We jumped up from the sofa. When we heard the crash in the kitchen.

    We jumped up from the sofa when we heard the crash in the kitchen.

8. Although the car was totaled. The passengers were unharmed.

    Although the car was totaled, the passengers were unharmed.

9. Emily takes a quick walk at lunchtime. Because it keeps her from getting sleepy at work.

    Emily takes a quick walk at lunchtime because it keeps her from getting sleepy at work.

10. Our neighbor is a quiet man. Who works as a nurse on the night shift.

    Our neighbor is a quiet man who works as a nurse on a night shift.

Name _____ Section _____ Date _____

Score: (Number right) _____ x 10 = _____ %

Fragments I: TEST 1

Underline the dependent-word fragment in each of the following items. Then correct it in the space provided. Add a comma after a dependent-word group that begins a sentence.

NOTE To help you correct fragments, directions are given for the first two sentences.

1. Because we have smoke detectors. We survived the fire.
   The first word group begins with the dependent word *because*.
   Correct the fragment by adding it to the second word group.

   Because we have smoke detectors, we survived the fire.

2. The kitchen looked like new. After we painted it.
   The second word group begins with the dependent word *after*.
   Correct the fragment by adding it to the first word group.

   The kitchen looked like new after we painted it.

3. My sister is always out of money. Although she has a good job.

   My sister is always out of money although she has a good job.

4. Before the game even started. I could tell team morale was low.

   Before the game even started, I could tell team morale was low.

5. I wouldn't date him again. If he begged me on his knees.

   I wouldn't date him again if he begged me on his knees.

6. Our car is making a chugging noise. Which sounds ominous.

   Our car is making a chugging noise which sounds ominous.

7. Young elephants stay with their mothers. Until they are about sixteen years old.

   Young elephants stay with their mothers until they are about sixteen years old.

8. After this rain stops. The children can play outside.

   After this rain stops, the children can play outside.

9. A crowd showed up to meet the author. Who had written a best-selling novel at the age of nineteen.

   A crowd showed up to meet the author who had written a best-selling novel at the age of nineteen.

10. Until the tornado warning ended. Everyone stayed in the basement.

    Until the tornado warning ended, everyone stayed in the basement.

Name _____ Section _____ Date _____

Score: (Number right) _____ x 10 = _____ %

Fragments I: TEST 2

Underline the dependent-word fragment in each of the following items. Then correct it in the space provided. Add a comma after a dependent-word group that begins a sentence.

1. Although the sign said "No Parking." A rude driver parked there.

   Although the sign said "No Parking," a rude driver parked there.

2. I'll never be ready for the test tomorrow. Even if I study all night.

   I'll never be ready for the test tomorrow even if I study all night.

3. Because pearls are quite soft. They are easily scratched.

   Because pearls are quite soft, they are easily scratched.

4. I wasn't able to sleep. Until I found out how the book ended.

   I wasn't able to sleep until I found out how the book ended.

5. People at the pancake house gasped. When the movie star walked in.

   People at the pancake house gasped when the movie star walked in.

6. After running a block to catch his bus. Mack missed it by seconds.

   After running a block to catch his bus, Mack missed it by seconds.

7. My pet peeve is people laughing at my jokes. Before I get to the punch line.

   My pet peeve is people laughing at my jokes before I get to the punch line.

8. You won't enjoy dinner. Unless you like burned chicken and soggy beans.

   You won't enjoy dinner unless you like burned chicken and soggy beans.

9. If the weather is bad tomorrow. We'll have to reschedule the reunion.

   If the weather is bad tomorrow, we'll have to reschedule the reunion.

10. When the huge dog rushed up to him. Troy almost stopped breathing.

    When the huge dog rushed up to him, Troy almost stopped breathing.

Name _____   Section _____   Date _____

Score: (Number right) _____ x 20 = _____ %

Fragments I: TEST 3

Read each group below. Then write the letter of the item that contains a fragment.

___C___ **1. a.** Leon was very nervous. He had not studied for the exam. A failing grade could result in his failing the course.

  b. Leon was very nervous because he had not studied for the exam. A failing grade could result in his failing the course.

  c. Because Leon had not studied for the exam. He was very nervous. A failing grade could result in his failing the course.

___A___ **2. a.** In 1969, the Oscar for Best Actor went to John Wayne. Who had appeared in nearly 250 movies by then.

  b. In 1969, the Oscar for Best Actor went to John Wayne. He had appeared in nearly 250 movies by then.

  c. In 1969, the Oscar for Best Actor went to John Wayne, who had appeared in nearly 250 movies by then.

___B___ **3. a.** Before Tamika went to the party, she tried on six different outfits. She finally chose the one she'd tried on first.

  b. Before Tamika went to the party. She tried on six different outfits. She finally chose the one she'd tried on first.

  c. Tamika tried on six different outfits before she went to the party. She finally chose the one she'd tried on first.

___A___ **4. a.** On our drive into the city, we came across an accident. Which had closed three of the four lanes of traffic. It added an extra hour to our trip.

  b. On our drive into the city, we came across an accident which had closed three of the four lanes of traffic. It added an extra hour to our trip.

  c. On our drive into the city, we came across an accident. It had closed three of the four lanes of traffic, and it added an extra hour to our trip.

___A___ **5. a.** Unless you are ready to work hard. Don't even think of enrolling in Mr. Reynold's class. He is a very demanding teacher.

  b. Don't even think of enrolling in Mr. Reynold's class unless you are ready to work hard. He is a very demanding teacher.

  c. Unless you are ready to work hard, don't even think of enrolling in Mr. Reynold's class. He is a very demanding teacher.

Name _____   Section _____   Date _____

Score: (Number right) _____ x 20 = _____ %

Fragments I: TEST 4

Read each group below. Then write the letter of the item that contains a fragment.

__A__ **1. a.** When a flock of birds is resting in the trees. One seems to act as the lookout. If it sees danger, it will alert the others to fly away.
  b. When a flock of birds is resting in the trees, one seems to act as the lookout. If it sees danger, it will alert the others to fly away.
  c. A flock of birds is resting in the trees, with one acting as the lookout. If it sees danger, it will alert the others to fly away.

__B__ **2. a.** Karen hung a big mirror at the end of her living room because it made the room look larger. She painted the dark walls a light color for the same reason.
  b. Karen hung a big mirror at the end of her living room. Because it made the room look larger. She painted the dark walls a light color for the same reason.
  c. Because it made the room look larger, Karen hung a big mirror at the end of her living room. She painted the dark walls a light color for the same reason.

__A__ **3. a.** Our dog loves to retrieve sticks. He will beg you to throw them for hours. Even if it's clear that he is exhausted.
  b. Our dog loves to retrieve sticks. He will beg you to throw them for hours even if it's clear that he is exhausted.
  c. Our dog loves to retrieve sticks. Even if it's clear that he is exhausted, he will beg you to throw them for hours.

__C__ **4. a.** Unless Nate apologizes, I am not going to speak to him again. What he said was unforgivable.
  b. I am not going to speak to Nate again unless he apologizes. What he said was unforgivable.
  c. Unless Nate apologizes. I am not going to speak to him again because what he said was unforgivable.

__C__ **5. a.** The police believed the witness until she picked the wrong person out of a lineup. Then they began to have their doubts about her story.
  b. Until the witness picked the wrong person out of a lineup, the police believed her. Then they began to have their doubts about her story.
  c. The police believed the witness. Until she picked the wrong person out of a lineup. Then they began to have their doubts about her story.

More about Fragments

In addition to dependent-word fragments, there are three other common types of fragments:

FRAGMENTS WITHOUT A SUBJECT

Some fragments do have a verb, but lack a subject.

Fragment   Joe Davis lowered himself from the van into his wheelchair. And then rolled up the sidewalk ramp.
The second word group lacks a subject, so it is a fragment.

You can often fix such a fragment by adding it to the sentence that comes before it.

Sentence   Joe Davis lowered himself from the van into his **wheelchair and** then rolled up the sidewalk ramp.

–*ING* AND *TO* FRAGMENTS

When *-ing* appears at or near the beginning of a word group, a fragment may result.

Fragment   Hoping to furnish their new home cheaply. The newlyweds go to garage sales.
The first word group lacks both a subject and a verb, so it is a fragment.

A fragment may also result when a word group begins with *to* followed by a verb.

Fragment   Leo jogged through the park. To clear his mind before the midterm.
The second word group is a fragment that lacks both a subject and a complete verb. (A word that follows *to* cannot be the verb of a sentence.)

You can often fix such fragments by attaching them to the sentence that comes before or after.

Sentence   Hoping to furnish their new home **cheaply, the** newlyweds go to garage sales.
Sentence   Leo jogged through the **park to** clear his mind before the midterm.

Punctuation note   When an *-ing* or *to* word group starts a sentence, follow it with a comma.

EXAMPLE FRAGMENTS

Word groups that begin with words like *including, such as, especially,* and *for example* are sometimes fragments.

Fragment   For class, we had to read several books. Including *The Diary of Anne Frank.*

Fragment   My grandfather has many interests. For example, playing poker and watching old cowboy movies.

You can often fix such fragments by attaching them to the sentence that comes before, or by adding a subject and a verb.

Sentence   For class we had to read several **books, including** *The Diary of Anne Frank.*

Sentence   My grandfather has many interests. For example, **he plays** poker and **watches** old cowboy movies.

Fragments II: PRACTICE

Underline the fragment in each item that follows. Then rewrite and correct the fragment in the space provided.   *Methods of correction may vary.*

1. Jan is talking out loud in her bedroom. Practicing a speech for her English class.

    Jan is talking out loud in her bedroom. She is practicing a speech for her English class.

2. Puffing on a bad-smelling cigar. Mr. Bloom said, "You ought to take better care of your health."

    Puffing on a bad-smelling cigar, Mr. Bloom said, "You ought to take better care of your health."

3. I enjoy reading scary books. Especially ones about vampires.

    I enjoy reading scary books, especially ones about vampires.

4. Ticking loudly. The clock reminded me how little time I had to get ready.

    Ticking loudly, the clock reminded me how little time I had to get ready.

5. We get 112 channels on our TV. But don't have anything we want to watch.

    We get 112 channels on our TV but don't have anything we want to watch.

6. Hank runs four miles every day after school. To get ready for track season.

    Hank runs four miles every day after school to get ready for track season.

7. Staring at me with an icy look on her face. The clerk refused to answer my question.

    Staring at me with an icy look on her face, the clerk refused to answer my question.

8. I eat only healthy snacks. Such as ice cream made with natural ingredients.

    I eat only healthy snacks, such as ice cream made with natural ingredients.

9. John refused to help clean the garage. After finding several huge spider webs and a dead snake there.

    John refused to help clean the garage after finding several huge spider webs and a dead snake there.

10. Some nursery rhymes tell unpleasant stories. One example, "Three Blind Mice."

    Some nursery rhymes tell unpleasant stories. One example is "Three Blind Mice."

Name _____   Section _____   Date _____

Fragments II: TEST 1

Underline the fragment in each item that follows. Then correct the fragment in the space provided.

NOTE To help you correct fragments, directions are given for the first three sentences.

Methods of correction may vary.

1. Glancing at his watch frequently. The man seemed anxious to leave.

The first word group lacks a subject and verb. Connect it to the complete statement that follows it.

Glancing at his watch frequently, the man seemed anxious to leave.

2. There are many healthful desserts. Including sherbet and fruit salad.

The second word group lacks a subject and verb. Connect it to the complete statement that comes before it.

There are many healthful desserts, including sherbet and fruit salad.

3. Our teacher sometimes loses her temper. However, always apologizes afterward.

Add a subject to the second word group to make it a complete thought.

However, she always apologizes afterward.

4. To keep his bike from being stolen. Gilbert bought a padlock.

To keep his bike from being stolen, Gilbert bought a padlock.

5. The small town is a beautiful place to visit. Especially in the spring.

The small town is a beautiful place to visit, especially in the spring.

6. Tarik lost the key to the front door. As a result, had to call a locksmith.

As a result, he had to call a locksmith.

7. Certain dogs are well suited to be guide dogs. Including German shepherds and golden retrievers.

Certain dogs are well suited to be guide dogs, including German shepherds and golden retrievers.

8. To get to school on time. I keep the clock in my room set ten minutes ahead.

To get to school on time, I keep the clock in my room set ten minutes ahead.

9. Relaxing on the beach. Anna said, "I want to be a lifeguard."

Relaxing on the beach, Anna said, "I want to be a lifeguard."

10. Many towns in the United States have amusing names. Such as Boring, Oregon; Peculiar, Missouri; and Okay, Oklahoma.

Many towns in the United States have amusing names, such as Boring, Oregon; Peculiar, Missouri; and Okay, Oklahoma.

Name _____ Section _____ Date _____

Score: (Number right) _____ x 10 = _____ %

Fragments II: TEST 2

Underline the fragment in each item that follows. Then correct the fragment in the space provided.

Methods of correction may vary.

1. Walking is excellent exercise. <u>Especially when you walk at a brisk pace.</u>

   Walking is excellent exercise, especially when you walk at a brisk pace.

2. Diane sat down with her boyfriend. <u>Then gently said, "I can't marry you."</u>

   Then she gently said, "I can't marry you."

3. <u>To get her brother's attention.</u> Lydia stood up on the stands and waved.

   To get her brother's attention, Lydia stood up on the stands and waved.

4. <u>Sweating from the workout.</u> Kyle grabbed his water bottle and drank deeply.

   Sweating from the workout, Kyle grabbed his water bottle and drank deeply.

5. Mother elephants devote much of their time to childcare. <u>Nursing their babies up to eight years.</u>

   They nurse their babies up to eight years.

6. Hamburgers come with your choice of cheese. <u>Including Swiss, cheddar, American, provolone, or mozzarella.</u>

   Hamburgers come with your choice of cheese, including Swiss, cheddar, American, provolone, or mozzarella.

7. A mouse popped out from under our sofa. <u>Then scurried back quickly.</u>

   Then it scurried back quickly.

8. Sam was helpful to his mother all afternoon. <u>Hoping to borrow her car that night.</u>

   He hoped to borrow her car that night.

9. I look terrible in certain colors. <u>Such as baby blue and pale yellow.</u>

   I look terrible in certain colors, such as baby blue and pale yellow.

10. We do what we can to save money. <u>For example, renting a DVD instead of going to the movie theater.</u>

    For example, we rent a DVD instead of going to the movie theater.

Name _____   Section _____   Date _____

Fragments II: TEST 3

Read each group below. Then write the letter of the item in each group that contains a fragment.

__A__ **1. a.** Rolling slowly backward. The car had no driver. People nearby began to jump out of the way.
　　b. Rolling slowly backward, the car had no driver. People nearby began to jump out of the way.
　　c. The car that was rolling slowly backward had no driver. People nearby began to jump out of the way.

__B__ **2. a.** To keep squirrels off their birdfeeders, people have tried all kinds of things. They have even smeared Vaseline on the pole on which the feeder is mounted.
　　b. To keep squirrels off their birdfeeders. People have tried all kinds of things. They have even smeared Vaseline on the pole on which the feeder is mounted.
　　c. People have tried all kinds of things to keep squirrels off their birdfeeders. They have even smeared Vaseline on the pole on which the feeder is mounted.

__C__ **3. a.** Cynthia has developed wrist pain from spending so many hours using her computer. She is going to see her doctor about it.
　　b. Cynthia is going to see her doctor about her wrist pain. She developed it from spending so many hours at her computer.
　　c. Spending so many hours using her computer. Cynthia has developed wrist pain. She is going to see her doctor about it.

__A__ **4. a.** Our speech teacher does not have a good fashion sense. He puts together odd clothing combinations. Such as a red flowered shirt with purple striped pants.
　　b. Our speech teacher does not have a good fashion sense. He puts together odd clothing combinations, such as a red flowered shirt with purple striped pants.
　　c. Our speech teacher puts together odd clothing combinations, such as a red flowered shirt with purple striped pants. He does not have a good fashion sense.

__C__ **5. a.** To try to hear the conversation going on in the room, Irina put her ear to the keyhole. She was embarrassed when the door opened suddenly.
　　b. Irina put her ear to the keyhole to try to hear the conversation going on in the room. She was embarrassed when the door opened suddenly.
　　c. Irina put her ear to the keyhole. To try to hear the conversation going on in the room. She was embarrassed when the door opened suddenly.

Name _____ Section _____ Date _____

Score: (Number right) _____ x 20 = _____ %

Fragments II: TEST 4

Read each group below. Then write the letter of the item in each group that contains a fragment.

_____B_____ **1. a.** Staring at the people standing outside, the tiger paced from one end of its cage to the other. It looked hungry.

b. The tiger paced from one end of its cage to the other. Staring at the people standing outside. It looked hungry.

c. The tiger paced from one end of its cage to the other, staring at the people standing outside. It looked hungry.

_____C_____ **2. a.** Calling every half hour, the man seemed extremely anxious to reach my father. "I have to talk to him," he kept saying.

b. The man who called every half hour seemed extremely anxious to reach my father. "I have to talk to him," he kept saying.

c. Calling every half hour. The man seemed extremely anxious to reach my father. "I have to talk to him," he kept saying.

_____A_____ **3. a.** Two outfielders raced toward the center-field wall. To try to catch the long fly ball. It dropped between them and bounced into the stands.

b. Two outfielders raced toward the center-field wall to try to catch the long fly ball. It dropped between them and bounced into the stands.

c. Trying to catch the long fly ball, two outfielders raced toward the center-field wall. The ball dropped between them and bounced into the stands.

_____A_____ **4. a.** There's an item on the dessert menu that contains most of my favorite ingredients. Such as chocolate, caramel, coconut, and nuts. I wonder if it's low in calories.

b. There's an item on the dessert menu that contains most of my favorite ingredients, such as chocolate, caramel, coconut, and nuts. I wonder if it's low in calories.

c. There's an item on the dessert menu that contains chocolate, caramel, coconut, and nuts, which are my favorite ingredients. I wonder if it's low in calories.

_____B_____ **5. a.** People who can't read well run into constant problems. For example, they may have problems filling out a job application. They are often too embarrassed to admit they can't read it.

b. People who can't read well run into constant problems. For example, filling out a job application. They are often too embarrassed to admit they can't read it.

c. People who can't read well run into constant problems. Filling out a job application, for example, they are often too embarrassed to admit they can't read it.

Run-ons and Comma Splices I

Basics about Run-Ons and Comma Splices

A **run-on** is made up of two complete thoughts that are incorrectly run together without a connection between them. Here is an example of a run-on:

- Dolphins have killed sharks they never attack humans.

  The complete thoughts are *dolphins have killed sharks* and *they never attack humans.*

A **comma splice** is made up of two complete thoughts that are incorrectly joined (or spliced) together with only a comma. A comma alone is not enough to connect two complete thoughts. Here's an example of a comma splice:

- Dolphins have killed sharks, they never attack humans.

How to Correct Run-Ons and Comma Splices

There are two common ways to correct run-ons and comma splices.

METHOD 1 Use a Period and a Capital Letter

Put each complete thought into its own sentence.

Run-on	The computer hummed loudly the sound was annoying.
Comma splice	The computer hummed loudly, the sound was annoying.
Correct version	The computer hummed **loudly. The** sound was annoying.

METHOD 2 Use a Comma and a Joining Word

Connect two complete thoughts into one sentence with a comma and a joining word. Perhaps the most common joining words are *and*, *but*, and *so*.

Run-on	Dolphins have killed sharks they never attack humans.
Comma splice	Dolphins have killed sharks, they never attack humans.
Correct version	Dolphins have killed **sharks, but they** never attack humans.

Run-on	The garden is overgrown the fence is falling down.
Comma splice	The garden is overgrown, the fence is falling down.
Correct version	The garden is **overgrown, and the** fence is falling down.

Run-on	The little boy appeared to be lost several women stopped to help him.
Comma splice	The little boy appeared to be lost, several women stopped to help him.
Correct version	The little boy appeared to be **lost, so** several women stopped to help him.

Run-ons and Comma Splices I: PRACTICE

Draw a line (|) between the two complete thoughts in each of the run-ons and comma splices that follow. Then rewrite each sentence. Correct it in one of two ways:

1 Use a period and a capital letter to create two sentences.

2 Use a comma and a logical joining word to connect the two complete thoughts. Choose from the following joining words:

   and (which means *in addition*)   **but** (which means *however*)   **so** (which means *as a result*)

Do not use the same correction technique for all the sentences.   *Methods of correction may vary.*

1. Some people are morning people|I'm not one of them.

   Some people are morning people, but I'm not one of them.

2. I was out of jelly and butter|I spread yogurt on my toast.

   I was out of jelly and butter, so I spread yogurt on my toast.

3. The dog walks on three legs|its ear is chewed up.

   The dog walks on three legs, and its ear is chewed up.

4. My little sister won't eat broccoli,|she says it looks too much like a little tree.

   My little sister won't eat broccoli. She says it looks too much like a little tree.

5. Someone unplugged the freezer|all the ice cream has melted.

   Someone unplugged the freezer, and all the ice cream has melted.

6. I backed away from the growling dog,|I also looked for its owner.

   I backed away from the growling dog, but I also looked for its owner.

7. One side of the moon faces the sun,|the other side is always dark.

   One side of the moon faces the sun, so the other side is always dark.

8. My brother runs like the wind at track meets|he moves like a turtle at home.

   My brother runs like the wind at track meets, but he moves like a turtle at home.

9. Fast-food restaurants are changing|they now offer healthier food choices.

   Fast-food restaurants are changing. They now offer healthier food choices.

10. The button fell off the waist of my pants|I fastened them with a safety pin.

   The button fell off the waist of my pants. I fastened them with a safety pin.

Name _____   Section _____   Date _____

Score: (Number right) _____ × 10 = _____ %

Run-Ons and Comma Splices I: TEST 1

Draw a line (|) between the two complete thoughts in each of the following run-ons or comma splices. Then rewrite the sentences, using either **1)** a period and a capital letter or **2)** a comma and a joining word (*and*, *but*, or *so*).

NOTE To help you correct run-ons, directions are given for the first two sentences.

Methods of correction may vary.

1. The sun was going down | the air was growing chilly.

   Use a logical joining word (*and, but,* or *so*) to connect the two complete thoughts.

   The sun was going down, and the air was growing chilly.

2. Rick is not a good babysitter | he treats his little brother like an insect.

   Put each complete thought into its own sentence.

   Rick is not a good babysitter. He treats his little brother like an insect.

3. My throat is very sore | a gallon of ice cream will relieve it.

   My throat is very sore, but a gallon of ice cream will relieve it.

4. The plumber repaired the water heater, | now the family can shower again.

   The plumber repaired the water heater. Now the family can shower again.

5. Saturday is the worst day of the week to shop, | people fill up many of the stores.

   Saturday is the worst day of the week to shop. People fill up many of the stores.

6. The phone rang | someone knocked on the door at the same time.

   The phone rang, and someone knocked on the door at the same time.

7. The TV commercial was much too loud | I pressed the mute button on the remote.

   The TV commercial was much too loud, so I pressed the mute button on the remote.

8. A burglar alarm went off | three men raced away from the store.

   A burglar alarm went off, and three men raced away from the store.

9. The bear looked at me hungrily, | I decided not to photograph him.

   The bear looked at me hungrily, so I decided not to photograph him.

10. We decided to leave the restaurant, | we were tired of waiting in line.

    We decided to leave the restaurant. We were tired of waiting in line.

Name _____ Section _____ Date _____

Score: (Number right) _____ × 10 = _____ %

Run-Ons and Comma Splices I: TEST 2

Draw a line (|) between the two complete thoughts in each of the following run-ons or comma splices. Then rewrite the sentences, using either **1)** a period and a capital letter or **2)** a comma and a joining word (*and*, *but*, or *so*). Methods of correction may vary.

1. Omar started writing the paper at 9 p.m.|he finished it at 4 a.m.
   Omar started writing the paper at 9 p.m. He finished it at 4 a.m.

2. This coffee is several hours old|it probably tastes like mud.
   This coffee is several hours old, so it probably tastes like mud.

3. I called Kendra three times last night,|she never answered.
   I called Kendra three times last night, but she never answered.

4. We lost our electricity last night|all the food in our freezer thawed.
   We lost our electricity last night, and all the food in our freezer thawed.

5. Mia looked tired and miserable|I asked her what was wrong.
   Mia looked tired and miserable, so I asked her what was wrong.

6. Thousands of actors go to Hollywood,|few ever become stars.
   Thousands of actors go to Hollywood, but few ever become stars.

7. Coupons help shoppers save money,|they also help stores sell products.
   Coupons help shoppers save money. They also help stores sell products.

8. The fortuneteller offered to read my palm|I said, "No, thanks."
   The fortuneteller offered to read my palm, but I said, "No, thanks."

9. I never eat the hamburgers in the cafeteria|they taste like rubber tires.
   I never eat the hamburgers in the cafeteria. They taste like rubber tires.

10. There was an accident on the bridge today,|traffic was stopped for an hour.
    There was an accident on the bridge today, and traffic was stopped for an hour.

Name _____   Section _____   Date _____

Run-Ons and Comma Splices I: TEST 3

In each group below, **one** sentence is punctuated correctly. Write the letter of that sentence in the space provided.

___C___ **1.** **a.** The cat slept on the windowsill she was wrapped in warm sunlight.
        b. The cat slept on the windowsill, she was wrapped in warm sunlight.
        c. The cat slept on the windowsill. She was wrapped in warm sunlight.

___A___ **2.** **a.** The motorcycle wouldn't start, so the man called a taxi.
        b. The motorcycle wouldn't start, the man called a taxi.
        c. The motorcycle wouldn't start the man called a taxi.

___C___ **3.** **a.** Mom is grumpy early in the morning, she is cheerful after drinking her coffee.
        b. Mom is grumpy early in the morning she is cheerful after drinking her coffee.
        c. Mom is grumpy early in the morning, but she is cheerful after drinking her coffee.

___A___ **4.** **a.** One remedy always works for my hiccups. I swallow a teaspoon of white sugar.
        b. One remedy always works for my hiccups, I swallow a teaspoon of white sugar.
        c. One remedy always works for my hiccups I swallow a teaspoon of white sugar.

___C___ **5.** **a.** The alarm clock fell on the floor, then it started to ring.
        b. The alarm clock fell on the floor then it started to ring.
        c. The alarm clock fell on the floor. Then it started to ring.

___B___ **6.** **a.** Gina is allergic to animals she can't have a pet.
        b. Gina is allergic to animals, so she can't have a pet.
        c. Gina is allergic to animals, she can't have a pet.

___A___ **7.** **a.** The flowers in that yard look wonderful, but the grass needs cutting.
        b. The flowers in that yard look wonderful, the grass needs cutting.
        c. The flowers in that yard look wonderful the grass needs cutting.

___B___ **8.** **a.** Mr. Dobbs is friendly with his customers, he is rude to his workers.
        b. Mr. Dobbs is friendly with his customers, but he is rude to his workers.
        c. Mr. Dobbs is friendly with his customers he is rude to his workers.

___B___ **9.** **a.** My back itched in a hard-to-reach place I scratched it on the doorpost.
        b. My back itched in a hard-to-reach place, so I scratched it on the doorpost.
        c. My back itched in a hard-to-reach place, I scratched it on the doorpost.

___C___ **10.** **a.** June is a month of nice weather it is also the most popular month for weddings.
        b. June is a month of nice weather, it is also the most popular month for weddings.
        c. June is a month of nice weather. It is also the most popular month for weddings.

Name _____   Section _____   Date _____

Score: (Number right) _____ x 10 = _____ %

Run-Ons and Comma Splices I: TEST 4

In each group below, **one** sentence is punctuated correctly. Write the letter of that sentence in the space provided.

___A___   1.   **a.** Raoul is colorblind, so his wife lays out his clothes every morning.
               b. Raoul is colorblind his wife lays out his clothes every morning.
               c. Raoul is colorblind, his wife lays out his clothes every morning.

___C___   2.   **a.** The weatherman predicted a sunny day, it is cold and cloudy.
               b. The weatherman predicted a sunny day it is cold and cloudy.
               c. The weatherman predicted a sunny day, but it is cold and cloudy.

___B___   3.   **a.** The hammer and saw began to rust they had been left out in the rain.
               b. The hammer and saw began to rust. They had been left out in the rain.
               c. The hammer and saw began to rust, they had been left out in the rain.

___B___   4.   **a.** My final exams are next week, I am very worried about passing.
               b. My final exams are next week, and I am very worried about passing.
               c. My final exams are next week I am very worried about passing.

___C___   5.   **a.** I was sick a lot at the start of the semester, I was not able to keep up with the work.
               b. I was sick a lot at the start of the semester I was not able to keep up with the work.
               c. I was sick a lot at the start of the semester, so I was not able to keep up with the work.

___C___   6.   **a.** I do not enjoy feeling stress I never intend to get so far behind in class again.
               b. I do not enjoy feeling stress, I never intend to get so far behind in class again.
               c. I do not enjoy feeling stress. I never intend to get so far behind in class again.

___A___   7.   **a.** The children have been eating chocolate. It is smeared all over their faces.
               b. The children have been eating chocolate it is smeared all over their faces.
               c. The children have been eating chocolate, it is smeared all over their faces.

___A___   8.   **a.** The air is very stale in the library, and the lighting is poor.
               b. The air is very stale in the library the lighting is poor.
               c. The air is very stale in the library, the lighting is poor.

___C___   9.   **a.** My ancestors came from Greece, they arrived in this country in 1912.
               b. My ancestors came from Greece they arrived in this country in 1912.
               c. My ancestors came from Greece. They arrived in this country in 1912.

___C___   10. **a.** The magician locked his assistant in a box then he cut her in half with a chainsaw.
               b. The magician locked his assistant in a box, then he cut her in half with a chainsaw.
               c. The magician locked his assistant in a box. Then he cut her in half with a chainsaw.

Another Way to Correct Run-Ons and Comma Splices

The previous chapter described two ways to correct run-ons and comma splices:

● Use a period and a capital letter, dividing the thoughts into two sentences.

● Use a joining word (*and, but,* or *so*) to logically connect the two complete thoughts.

A third way is to add a **dependent word** to one of the complete thoughts. The sentence will then include one thought that depends upon the remaining complete thought for its full meaning. Here are some common dependent words:

after	because	since	when
although	before	unless	where
as	if, even if	until	while

For example, look at a run-on and comma splice considered in the previous chapter.

Run-on	Dolphins have killed sharks they never attack humans.
Comma splice	Dolphins have killed sharks, they never attack humans.

Using the dependent word *although,* the sentence can be corrected as follows:

Although dolphins have killed sharks, they never attack humans.

Below are other run-ons or comma splices that have been corrected by adding dependent words. In each case, a dependent word that logically connects the two thoughts has been chosen.

Punctuation note When a dependent thought begins a sentence, it is followed by a comma.

Run-on	The roads are covered with ice school has been canceled.
Corrected	**Because** the roads are covered with ice**,** school has been canceled.

Comma splice	The water began to boil**,** I added ears of corn.
Corrected	**After** the water began to boil**,** I added ears of corn.

Run-on	The fish was served with its head on Carlo quickly lost his appetite.
Corrected	**When** the fish was served with its head on**,** Carlo quickly lost his appetite.

Comma splice	You'd better not store cereal in the basement, there are mice there.
Corrected	You'd better not store cereal in the basement **since** there are mice there.

Run-Ons and Comma Splices II: PRACTICE

Correct each run-on or comma splice by adding the dependent word shown to one of the complete thoughts. Include a comma if the dependent thought starts the sentence.

Corrections may vary slightly.

1. **(although)** These boots are supposed to be waterproof my feet are soaked.

   Although these boots are supposed to be waterproof, my feet are soaked.

2. **(when)** The driver jumped out quickly the car burst into flames.

   The driver jumped out quickly when the car burst into flames.

3. **(before)** My family left for the restaurant I called to reserve a table.

   Before my family left for the restaurant, I called to reserve a table.

4. **(if)** You need to make a call you can borrow my cell phone.

   If you need to make a call, you can borrow my cell phone.

5. **(since)** Ricardo was late to school, he had briefly lost his contact lens.

   Ricardo was late to school since he had briefly lost his contact lens.

6. **(while)** It was still raining, a beautiful rainbow appeared in the west.

   While it was still raining, a beautiful rainbow appeared in the west.

7. **(until)** The wet paint on the woodwork dries, you should not touch it.

   Until the wet paint on the woodwork dries, you should not touch it.

8. **(after)** The players looked depressed the team lost the game.

   The players looked depressed after the team lost the game.

9. **(as)** The sky darkened bats began to appear in the air.

   As the sky darkened, bats began to appear in the air.

10. **(because)** That painkiller has serious side effects you should take it only when needed.

    Because that painkiller has serious side effects, you should take it only when needed.

Name _____   Section _____   Date _____

Score: (Number right) _____ x 10 = _____ %

Run-Ons and Comma Splices II: TEST 1

Draw a line (|) between the two complete thoughts in each of the following run-ons or comma splices. Then rewrite the sentences, correcting each one by adding a logical dependent word to one of the thoughts. Include a comma if the dependent thought starts the sentence. Choose from these words: **because, after, although, if, when**.   *Corrections in items 4–10 may vary.*

NOTE To help you correct run-ons, directions are given for the first three sentences.

1. Nuts are high in protein | they are a healthier snack than chips.
    Because nuts are high in protein, they are a healthier snack than chips.

    Use *because* to begin the first complete thought.

2. Many people are afraid of spiders, | most spiders are quite harmless.
    Many people are afraid of spiders although most spiders are quite harmless.

    Use *although* to begin the second complete thought.

3. It starts to rain, | bring in the clothes hanging on the line.
    If it starts to rain, bring in the clothes hanging on the line.

    Use *if* to begin the first complete thought.

4. The dishes were done | we relaxed by watching some TV.
    When the dishes were done, we relaxed by watching some TV.

5. Elaine laid down the sleeping baby, | she tiptoed out of the room.
    After Elaine laid down the sleeping baby, she tiptoed out of the room.

6. You will be late to the party, | let the host know ahead of time.
    If you will be late to the party, let the host know ahead of time.

7. I haven't spent much time outdoors, | it has been very cold.
    I haven't spent much time outdoors because it has been very cold.

8. Geneva apologized for yelling at Evan, | she felt better.
    After Geneva apologized for yelling at Evan, she felt better.

9. You win the contest, | what will you do with the prize money?
    If you win the contest, what will you do with the prize money?

10. I could not open the childproof bottle, | I was following the directions carefully.
    I could not open the childproof bottle although I was following the directions carefully.

Name _____   Section _____   Date _____

Score: (Number right) _____ x 10 = _____ %

Run-Ons and Comma Splices II: TEST 2

Correct each run-on or comma splice by adding the dependent word shown to one of the complete thoughts. Include a comma if the dependent thought starts the sentence. *Corrections may vary slightly.*

1. *(because)* Nobody answered the phone the whole family had gone to bed early.

Nobody answered the phone because the whole family had gone to bed early.

2. *(after)* Debbie took a self-defense course, she felt more strong and confident.

After Debbie took a self-defense course, she felt more strong and confident.

3. *(before)* You start answering a multiple-choice question, read every one of the possible answers.

Before you start answering a multiple-choice question, read every one of the possible answers.

4. *(because)* My brother was tired of worrying how his hair looked, he shaved his head.

Because my brother was tired of worrying how his hair looked, he shaved his head.

5. *(although)* Garlic may smell bad it tastes delicious.

Although garlic may smell bad, it tastes delicious.

6. *(after)* I finished watching the sad movie my eyes were red for hours.

After I finished watching the sad movie, my eyes were red for hours.

7. *(although)* Mrs. Hernandez is not an easy teacher her students love her.

Although Mrs. Hernandez is not an easy teacher, her students love her.

8. *(because)* I am more alert in the morning, early classes are better for me.

Because I am more alert in the morning, early classes are better for me.

9. *(after)* We had three hours of cleaning up to do, the party ended at 1 a.m.

We had three hours of cleaning up to do after the party ended at 1 a.m.

10. *(if)* You want to be a famous rapper, you'd better have a second career plan just in case.

If you want to be a famous rapper, you'd better have a second career plan just in case.

Name _____   Section _____   Date _____

Score: (Number right) _____ x 10 = _____ %

Run-Ons and Comma Splices II: TEST 3

In each group below, **one** sentence is punctuated correctly. Write the letter of that sentence in the space provided.

___B___ **1.** **a.** I locked all the doors and windows I still felt too nervous to sleep.
  b. Although I locked all the doors and windows, I still felt too nervous to sleep.
  c. Although I locked all the doors and windows. I still felt too nervous to sleep.

___A___ **2.** **a.** Our local elementary school closed for three days because many students had the flu.
  b. Our local elementary school closed for three days. Because many students had the flu.
  c. Our local elementary school closed for three days, many students had the flu.

___C___ **3.** **a.** The engine has started to cool you can add more water to the radiator.
  b. When the engine has started to cool. You can add more water to the radiator.
  c. When the engine has started to cool, you can add more water to the radiator.

___A___ **4.** **a.** Nita played with every puppy before she picked out the one she liked best.
  b. Nita played with every puppy. Before she picked out the one she liked best.
  c. Nita played with every puppy she picked out the one she liked best.

___B___ **5.** **a.** Mr. Bradley starts class promptly. After he takes attendance.
  b. Mr. Bradley starts class promptly after he takes attendance.
  c. Mr. Bradley starts class promptly, he takes attendance.

___B___ **6.** **a.** Because Marisol wants to help her community. She works as a volunteer translator.
  b. Because Marisol wants to help her community, she works as a volunteer translator.
  c. Marisol wants to help her community she works as a volunteer translator.

___C___ **7.** **a.** You should talk to a counselor. Before you decide on what courses to take.
  b. You should talk to a counselor, decide on what courses to take.
  c. You should talk to a counselor before you decide on what courses to take.

___A___ **8.** **a.** Emma is a Democrat although both her parents are Republicans.
  b. Emma is a Democrat. Although both her parents are Republicans.
  c. Emma is a Democrat both her parents are Republicans.

___A___ **9.** **a.** Because the movie was scary, I turned on all the lights in the house.
  b. Because the movie was scary. I turned on all the lights in the house.
  c. The movie was scary, I turned on all the lights in the house.

___C___ **10.** **a.** Follow the instructions carefully the computer will be set up and working in no time.
  b. If you follow the instructions carefully. The computer will be set up and working in no time.
  c. If you follow the instructions carefully, the computer will be set up and working in no time.

Name _____   Section _____   Date _____

Score: (Number right) _____ x 10 = _____ %

Run-Ons and Comma Splices II: TEST 4

In each group below, **one** sentence is punctuated correctly. Write the letter of that sentence in the space provided.

____A____   **1.**   **a.** Although friends had told us the restaurant was very good, we had a dreadful meal.
  b. Friends had told us the restaurant was very good we had a dreadful meal.
  c. Although friends had told us the restaurant was very good. We had a dreadful meal.

____B____   **2.**   **a.** You don't enjoy the party, we can leave early.
  b. If you don't enjoy the party, we can leave early.
  c. If you don't enjoy the party. We can leave early.

____C____   **3.**   **a.** I nearly had a heart attack. When the smoke alarm started shrieking at 2 a.m.
  b. I nearly had a heart attack the smoke alarm started shrieking at 2 a.m.
  c. I nearly had a heart attack when the smoke alarm started shrieking at 2 a.m.

____C____   **4.**   **a.** I let myself eat that chocolate cake, I will finish my homework.
  b. Before I let myself eat that chocolate cake. I will finish my homework.
  c. Before I let myself eat that chocolate cake, I will finish my homework.

____B____   **5.**   **a.** Kristen came back from her blind date, she said, "Never, ever, ever again."
  b. After Kristen came back from her blind date, she said, "Never, ever, ever again."
  c. After Kristen came back from her blind date. She said, "Never, ever, ever again."

____B____   **6.**   **a.** Although I love spicy Mexican food. I do not love the heartburn it gives me.
  b. Although I love spicy Mexican food, I do not love the heartburn it gives me.
  c. I love spicy Mexican food I do not love the heartburn it gives me.

____A____   **7.**   **a.** The two brothers seldom speak because they had an argument ten years ago.
  b. The two brothers seldom speak they had an argument ten years ago.
  c. Because they had an argument ten years ago. The two brothers seldom speak.

____C____   **8.**   **a.** You are afraid of snakes, you might not want to go on the hike with us.
  b. You might not want to go on the hike with us. If you are afraid of snakes.
  c. If you are afraid of snakes, you might not want to go on the hike with us.

____C____   **9.**   **a.** The soup was too hot to eat, I dropped in two ice cubes to cool it.
  b. Because the soup was too hot to eat. I dropped in two ice cubes to cool it.
  c. Because the soup was too hot to eat, I dropped in two ice cubes to cool it.

____B____   **10.**   **a.** The neighbors saw a police car pull up outside they turned off their lights and watched through the window.
  b. When the neighbors saw a police car pull up outside, they turned off their lights and watched through the window.
  c. When the neighbors saw a police car pull up outside. They turned off their lights and watched through the window.

9 Commas ,

Basics about the Comma

Here are three main uses of the comma:

1 The comma is used to separate three or more items in a series.

- The school cafeteria has learned not to serve broccoli, spinach, or Brussels sprouts.
- The letters *k*, *j*, *x*, *z*, and *q* are the least frequently used letters of the alphabet.
- Our tasks for the party are blowing up balloons, setting the table, and planning the music.

2 The comma is used to separate introductory material from the rest of the sentence.

- After taking a hot shower, Vince fell asleep on the sofa.
- When covered with chocolate syrup, frozen yogurt is not a diet food.
- As the movie credits rolled, we stretched and headed toward the exits.

3 The comma is used between two complete thoughts connected by *and, but,* or *so.*

- Lee broke her leg in the accident, and her car was badly damaged.
- The forecast called for rain, but it's a beautiful sunny day.
- My glasses broke, so I mended them with duct tape.

NOTES

- A comma often marks a slight pause, or break, in a sentence. When you read a sentence aloud, you can often hear the points where slight pauses occur.

- In general, use a comma only when a comma rule applies or when a comma is otherwise needed to help a sentence read clearly.

- Regarding Rule 3 above, do not use a comma just because a sentence contains *and, but,* or *so.* Use a comma only when the *and, but,* or *so* comes between two complete thoughts. Each of the two thoughts must have its own subject and verb.

Comma Lee broke her leg in the accident, and her car was badly damaged.
Each complete thought has a subject and a verb: *Lee broke* and *car was damaged.*

No comma Lee broke her leg in the accident and badly damaged her car.
This sentence expresses only one complete thought. The subject *Lee* has two verbs: *broke* and *damaged.*

For additional information about commas, see pages 183–186.

Commas: PRACTICE

On the lines provided, write the word or words in each sentence that need to be followed by a comma. Include each missing comma as well.

1. Although she is seventy-five my grandmother can do thirty pushups.

   seventy-five,

2. The zookeeper fed raw meat to the lions gave fresh fish to the polar bears and conducted a guided tour.

   lions, . . . bears,

3. Our apartment walls are very thin so we hear most of our neighbors' conversations.

   thin,

4. False names that students have used when substitute teachers were in class include Sandy Beech Frank Furter and Ben Dover.

   Beech, . . . Furter,

5. In typical horror movies characters often do incredibly stupid things.

   movies,

6. The bookcase was filled with magazines paperbacks basketball trophies and DVDs.

   magazines, paperbacks, basketball trophies,

7. The sign said, "No Smoking" but many people were ignoring it.

   Smoking,"

8. I like everything about housework except vacuuming dusting making beds and washing dishes.

   vacuuming, dusting, making beds,

9. I let the dog go outside after her bath and she immediately rolled in a mud puddle.

   bath,

10. Before home computers became popular people had to go to the library to look up information.

    popular,

Name _____ Section _____ Date _____

Score: (Number right) _____ x 10 = _____ %

Commas: TEST 1

Add commas where needed in each sentence. Then refer to the box below and, in the space provided, write the letter of the comma rule that applies.

> **a** Between items in a series
> **b** After introductory material
> **c** Between complete thoughts

NOTE To help you master the comma, explanations are given for the first three sentences.

___C___ **1.** My neighbor's dog dislikes children, and it hates the mail carrier.
A comma is needed before the word that joins two complete thoughts.

___B___ **2.** Before the movie started, there were twenty minutes of "coming attractions."
Use a comma after introductory material.

___A___ **3.** This recipe calls for a can of tuna, a bag of frozen peas, a box of noodles, and a can of mushroom soup.
A comma is needed after each item in a series.

___C___ **4.** Our apartment was too small after the twins were born, so we started looking for a house.

___B___ **5.** Because of the bad weather, school was delayed by two hours today.

___A___ **6.** The travel brochure showed lots of sunny skies, blue water, gorgeous beaches, and tropical sunsets.

___B___ **7.** If you have a fever, you should not go out today.

___A___ **8.** Evan came to the door stretching, yawning, and rubbing his eyes.

___B___ **9.** Carrying sodas and popcorn, the couple looked for a seat in the theater.

___C___ **10.** The movie was in Spanish, so I had to read the subtitles.

Name _____   Section _____   Date _____

Score: (Number right) _____ x 10 = _____ %

Commas: TEST 2

Add commas where needed in each sentence. Then refer to the box below and, in the space provided, write the letter of the comma rule that applies.

> **a** Between items in a series
> **b** After introductory material
> **c** Between complete thoughts

___C___   **1.** These shoes are my usual size, but they are still too small for me.
                                              ^

___B___   **2.** If you ask me, that milk has gone bad.
                          ^

___C___   **3.** The car is badly rusted, and the rear window is cracked.
                                   ^

___A___   **4.** Lainie's chills, fever, and headache warned her she was coming down with something.
                          ^   ^

___B___   **5.** While I enjoy reading books, I hate having to write a book report.
                                        ^

___A___   **6.** The dog bared its teeth, flattened its ears, and snarled when it saw me.
                                  ^   ^

___B___   **7.** Unused to the silence of the forest, the campers found it hard to sleep.
                                            ^

___A___   **8.** Every day starts with bringing in the newspaper, turning on a morning news show, and
                  feeding the cat.   ^   ^

___B___   **9.** Because it increases unrest among inmates, prison overcrowding is dangerous.
                                              ^

___C___   **10.** I wasn't wearing my glasses, so I couldn't read the small print on the bottle of pills.
                               ^

Name _____ Section _____ Date _____

Score: (Number right) _____ × 10 = _____ %

Commas: TEST 3

In each group below, **one** sentence uses the comma correctly. Write the letter of that sentence in the space provided.

___B___ **1. a.** The smoke detector was buzzing and we, could smell something burning.
    b. The smoke detector was buzzing, and we could smell something burning.
    c. The smoke detector was, buzzing, and we could smell something burning.

___C___ **2. a.** When my sister was little she thought lima beans, were stuffed with mashed potatoes.
    b. When my sister was little she thought lima beans were stuffed, with mashed potatoes.
    c. When my sister was little, she thought lima beans were stuffed with mashed potatoes.

___A___ **3. a.** The driving instructor asked me to turn on my headlights, windshield wipers, and emergency flashers.
    b. The driving instructor, asked me to turn on my headlights windshield wipers and emergency flashers.
    c. The driving instructor asked, me to turn on my headlights windshield wipers, and emergency flashers.

___A___ **4. a.** I woke up feeling tired and groggy, so I drank three cups of coffee.
    b. I woke up, feeling tired and groggy so I drank three cups of coffee.
    c. I woke up feeling tired and groggy so, I drank three cups of coffee.

___A___ **5. a.** Many people are afraid of spiders, and I can certainly understand why.
    b. Many people are afraid of spiders and I, can certainly understand why.
    c. Many people, are afraid of spiders and I can certainly understand why.

___C___ **6. a.** Looking embarrassed the man asked, if he could borrow bus fare.
    b. Looking embarrassed the man asked if he could, borrow bus fare.
    c. Looking embarrassed, the man asked if he could borrow bus fare.

___C___ **7. a.** You'll need to have some onions, garlic carrots tomatoes, and parsley.
    b. You'll need to have some, onions garlic carrots tomatoes and parsley.
    c. You'll need to have some onions, garlic, carrots, tomatoes, and parsley.

___B___ **8. a.** If you are approached, by a vicious dog you should stand still.
    b. If you are approached by a vicious dog, you should stand still.
    c. If you are approached by a vicious dog you should, stand still.

___C___ **9. a.** The little boy said that, his favorite subjects were lunch gym and recess.
    b. The little boy said that his favorite subjects were lunch gym, and recess.
    c. The little boy said that his favorite subjects were lunch, gym, and recess.

___A___ **10. a.** Without a sound, the thief quickly emptied the cash register.
    b. Without a sound the thief, quickly emptied the cash register.
    c. Without a sound the thief quickly, emptied the cash register.

Name _____ Section _____ Date _____

Score: (Number right) _____ x 10 = _____ %

Commas: TEST 4

In each group below, **one** sentence uses the comma correctly. Write the letter of that sentence in the space provided.

___A___ **1. a.** No one volunteered to read his or her paper out loud, so the teacher called on Amber.
    b. No one volunteered, to read his or her paper out loud so the teacher called on Amber.
    c. No one volunteered to read his or her paper out loud so, the teacher called on Amber.

___B___ **2. a.** On most television shows people live in beautiful homes.
    b. On most television shows, people live in beautiful homes.
    c. On most television shows people live, in beautiful homes.

___C___ **3. a.** Politics money, and religion are topics that people often argue about.
    b. Politics, money and religion are topics, that people often argue about.
    c. Politics, money, and religion are topics that people often argue about.

___A___ **4. a.** During a thunderstorm, it's best not to use the telephone.
    b. During a thunderstorm it's best, not to use the telephone.
    c. During a thunderstorm, it's best not to use, the telephone.

___C___ **5. a.** A customer was waiting but, the clerk kept chatting with her friend.
    b. A customer was waiting but the clerk, kept chatting with her friend.
    c. A customer was waiting, but the clerk kept chatting with her friend.

___B___ **6. a.** The Seven Dwarfs had silly names, like Sneezy Grumpy Bashful and Dopey.
    b. The Seven Dwarfs had silly names like Sneezy, Grumpy, Bashful, and Dopey.
    c. The Seven Dwarfs had silly names like Sneezy, Grumpy, Bashful, and, Dopey.

___C___ **7. a.** Her courtesy compassion and patience, help make Sarah very good at her job.
    b. Her courtesy compassion and patience help make Sarah, very good, at her job.
    c. Her courtesy, compassion, and patience help make Sarah very good at her job.

___B___ **8. a.** Greg has to work, the night of his birthday so we will celebrate the night before.
    b. Greg has to work the night of his birthday, so we will celebrate the night before.
    c. Greg has to work the night of his birthday so, we will celebrate the night before.

___A___ **9. a.** By the end of the day, we had painted the entire apartment.
    b. By the end of the day we had painted, the entire apartment.
    c. By the end, of the day, we had painted the entire apartment.

___B___ **10. a.** The drinks on the menu include, coffee, tea soda lemonade, orange juice and milk.
    b. The drinks on the menu include coffee, tea, soda, lemonade, orange juice, and milk.
    c. The drinks on the menu, include coffee tea soda, lemonade orange juice and milk.

Basics about the Apostrophe

There are two main uses of the apostrophe:

1 The apostrophe takes the place of one or more missing letters in a contraction. (A **contraction** is a word formed by combining two or more words, leaving some of the letters out.)

- I am sleepy. —> **I'm** sleepy.
  The letter *a* in *am* has been left out.

- Hank did not know the answer. —> Hank **didn't** know the answer.
  The letter *o* in *not* has been left out.

- They would keep the secret. —> **They'd** keep the secret.
  The letters *woul* in *would* have been left out.

Here are a few more common contractions:

it + is = **it's** (the *i* in *is* has been left out)

does + not = **doesn't** (the *o* in *not* has been left out)

do + not = **don't** (the *o* in *not* has been left out)

she + will = **she'll** (the *wi* in *will* has been left out)

he + is = **he's** (the *i* in *is* has been left out)

we + have = **we've** (the *ha* in *have* has been left out)

could + not = **couldn't** (the *o* in *not* has been left out)

will + not = **won't** (the *o* replaces *ill*; the *o* in *not* has been left out)

2 The apostrophe shows that something belongs to someone or something. (This is called **possession**.)

- the fin of the shark —> the **shark's** fin
  The apostrophe goes after the last letter of the name of the owner, *shark*. The *'s* added to *shark* tells us that the fin belongs to the shark.

- the grades of Nina —> **Nina's** grades
  The apostrophe goes after the last letter of the name of the owner, *Nina*. The *'s* added to *Nina* tells us that the grades belong to Nina.

  NOTE No apostrophe is used with simple plurals such as *grades,* which just means "more than one grade."

- the cheering of the crowd —> the **crowd's** cheering
  The apostrophe goes after the last letter of the name of the owner, *crowd*. The *'s* added to *crowd* tells us that the cheering belongs to the crowd.

For additional information about apostrophes, including their use with words that already end in *s*, see "More about Apostrophes," pages 189–194.

Apostrophes: PRACTICE

Each of the sentences below contains **one** word that needs an apostrophe. Write each word, with its apostrophe, in the space provided.

1. A lobsters claws are used to crush prey and then tear it into pieces.

_____lobster's_____

2. We havent seen our waitress since she gave us menus twenty minutes ago.

_____haven't_____

3. My cousins know the stores owner, a man named Mr. Sherwin.

_____store's_____

4. The mystery books final ten pages were missing.

_____book's_____

5. School wont be opening until noon because of the power failure.

_____won't_____

6. A dogs collar should not be too tight.

_____dog's_____

7. My friends and I watched a TV movie about an adult who couldnt read.

_____couldn't_____

8. For Halloween, Barry dressed up in a cheerleaders outfit, complete with pompoms.

_____cheerleader's_____

9. There was a rumor that some employees would be laid off, but it wasnt true.

_____wasn't_____

10. The models teeth were so white that they did not look real.

_____model's_____

Name _____   Section _____   Date _____

Score: (Number right) _____ x 10 = _____ %

Apostrophes: **TEST 1**

Each of the sentences below contains **one** word that needs an apostrophe. Underline the word. Then write the word, with its apostrophe, in the space provided.

NOTE To help you master the apostrophe, explanations are given for the first three sentences.

1. My <u>fathers</u> thunderous snores can be heard all over the house.
    The snores belong to the father. *Snores* is a simple plural; no apostrophe is used.
    _____father's_____

2. The movie star wore a hat and dark glasses, but she <u>couldnt</u> fool her waiting fans.
    An apostrophe should take the place of the missing *o* in the contraction.
    _____couldn't_____

3. The <u>tigers</u> pacing never stopped as the big cat watched the crowd of zoo visitors.
    The pacing belongs to the tiger. *Visitors* is a simple plural; no apostrophe is used.
    _____tiger's_____

4. Some students are unhappy about the <u>schools</u> decision to remove soft-drink machines.
    _____school's_____

5. Even though they <u>didnt</u> finish elementary school, my grandparents want me to get a college degree.
    _____didn't_____

6. The <u>grasshoppers</u> powerful hind legs allow the insect to jump many times its own height.
    _____grasshopper's_____

7. Sheer white curtains and fresh lilacs added to the <u>rooms</u> simple charm.
    _____room's_____

8. The <u>hypnotists</u> only tools are a soothing voice and a watch that ticks very loudly.
    _____hypnotist's_____

9. If you keep eating the cheese dip, there <u>wont</u> be enough to serve our guests.
    _____won't_____

10. "Since lemons are so cheap right now," Grandma said, "<u>Im</u> going to buy enough to make lemonade, lemon cake, and lemon chicken."
    _____I'm_____

Name _____   Section _____   Date _____

Score: (Number right) _____ x 10 = _____ %

Apostrophes: TEST 2

Each of the sentences below contains **one** word that needs an apostrophe. Underline the word. Then write the word, with its apostrophe, in the space provided.

1. In American culture, it <u>isnt</u> considered polite to point at someone.

    _____isn't_____

2. The doodles in <u>Andys</u> notebook show just how much he pays attention in his history class.

    _____Andy's_____

3. Yolanda and Marco <u>werent</u> speaking six months ago, but now they are getting married.

    _____weren't_____

4. Smudges on the <u>CDs</u> surface made it skip while it was playing.

    _____CD's_____

5. The sun <u>hasnt</u> shone for eight days in a row.

    _____hasn't_____

6. The chocolates in the silver box were a gift from my <u>mothers</u> best friend.

    _____mother's_____

7. The <u>coachs</u> daughter is one of the best runners on the track team.

    _____coach's_____

8. The suspects <u>couldnt</u> explain what they were doing inside the fast-food restaurant at 2 a.m.

    _____couldn't_____

9. Gina plucked the <u>daisys</u> petals, saying, "He loves me, he loves me not."

    _____daisy's_____

10. <u>Hakims</u> alarm clock can buzz, play music, or make sounds like a babbling brook.

    _____Hakim's_____

Name _____   Section _____   Date _____

Score: (Number right) _____ × 10 = _____ %

Apostrophes: TEST 3

In each group below, **one** sentence uses apostrophes correctly. Write the letter of that sentence in the space provided.

___B___ **1. a.** It shouldn't take more than ten minute's to reach Phil's house.
　　　　b. It shouldn't take more than ten minutes to reach Phil's house.
　　　　c. It shouldn't take more than ten minutes to reach Phils house.

___C___ **2. a.** The patients eye's havent opened since the surgery.
　　　　b. The patients eyes haven't opened since the surgery.
　　　　c. The patient's eyes haven't opened since the surgery.

___C___ **3. a.** The kitchens warmth and the coffee's aroma were very welcoming.
　　　　b. The kitchen's warmth and the coffees aroma were very welcoming.
　　　　c. The kitchen's warmth and the coffee's aroma were very welcoming.

___C___ **4. a.** I dont have half of this recipe's ingredient's.
　　　　b. I dont have half of this recipe's ingredients.
　　　　c. I don't have half of this recipe's ingredients.

___A___ **5. a.** You'll either love or hate the movie's surprise ending.
　　　　b. You'll either love or hate the movies surprise ending.
　　　　c. Youll either love or hate the movie's surprise ending.

___B___ **6. a.** My sisters taste in music and my brother's taste in friend's drive me crazy.
　　　　b. My sister's taste in music and my brother's taste in friends drive me crazy.
　　　　c. My sister's taste in music and my brothers taste in friend's drive me crazy.

___C___ **7. a.** Emily won't wear anything made from an animals fur.
　　　　b. Emily wont wear anything made from an animal's fur.
　　　　c. Emily won't wear anything made from an animal's fur.

___A___ **8. a.** My jacket's zipper is broken, so I can't take the jacket off.
　　　　b. My jacket's zipper is broken, so I cant take the jacket off.
　　　　c. My jackets zipper is broken, so I can't take the jacket off.

___B___ **9. a.** The houses window's are shattered, and the lawn hasn't been mowed for years.
　　　　b. The house's windows are shattered, and the lawn hasn't been mowed for years.
　　　　c. The house's windows are shattered, and the lawn hasnt been mowed for year's.

___A___ **10. a.** Our parrot's loud shrieks haven't made him popular with our neighbors.
　　　　b. Our parrot's loud shrieks havent made him popular with our neighbor's.
　　　　c. Our parrots loud shrieks haven't made him popular with our neighbor's.

Name _____   Section _____   Date _____

Score: (Number right) _____ x 10 = _____ %

Apostrophes: TEST 4

In each group below, **one** sentence uses apostrophes correctly. Write the letter of that sentence in the space provided.

____C____   **1.**   **a.** My aunts hairstyle hasnt changed in twenty years.
              b. My aunt's hairstyle hasnt changed in twenty year's.
              c. My aunt's hairstyle hasn't changed in twenty years.

____A____   **2.**   **a.** The veterinarian's assistant quickly examined our puppy's hurt paws.
              b. The veterinarian's assistant quickly examined our puppys hurt paw's.
              c. The veterinarians assistant quickly examined our puppy's hurt paws.

____A____   **3.**   **a.** The romance novel's cover showed a woman fainting in a man's arms.
              b. The romance novel's cover showed a woman fainting in a man's arm's.
              c. The romance novels cover showed a woman fainting in a man's arm's.

____C____   **4.**   **a.** Sheila's boyfriend work's part-time in his fathers barbershop.
              b. Sheilas boyfriend work's part-time in his father's barbershop.
              c. Sheila's boyfriend works part-time in his father's barbershop.

____B____   **5.**   **a.** The police didn't show up until four hour's after wed called them.
              b. The police didn't show up until four hours after we'd called them.
              c. The police didnt show up until four hour's after we'd called them.

____B____   **6.**   **a.** I can't believe youve never eaten in a Chinese restaurant.
              b. I can't believe you've never eaten in a Chinese restaurant.
              c. I cant believe you've never eaten in a Chinese restaurant.

____A____   **7.**   **a.** The witch's gingerbread house wasn't visible to grownups.
              b. The witch's gingerbread house wasnt visible to grownups.
              c. The witchs gingerbread house wasn't visible to grownup's.

____C____   **8.**   **a.** The oceans floor isn't flat; it contains mountain's, plains, and ridges.
              b. The ocean's floor isnt flat; it contains mountain's, plains, and ridges.
              c. The ocean's floor isn't flat; it contains mountains, plains, and ridges.

____B____   **9.**   **a.** An ostrich eggs shell is as thick as a nickel and can't be easily broken.
              b. An ostrich egg's shell is as thick as a nickel and can't be easily broken.
              c. An ostrich egg's shell is as thick as a nickel and cant be easily broken.

____C____   **10.**   **a.** The homeless man's feet were wrapped in page's of yesterdays newspaper.
              b. The homeless mans feet were wrapped in page's of yesterday's newspaper.
              c. The homeless man's feet were wrapped in pages of yesterday's newspaper.

Basics about Quotation Marks

Use quotation marks to set off all exact words of a speaker or writer.

- The little girl's mother said, **"**It wasn't nice to fill up the sugar bowl with salt.**"**
  The mother's exact words are enclosed within quotation marks.

- **"**I'm afraid,**"** the mechanic muttered to Fred, **"**that your car is in big trouble.**"**
  The mechanic's exact words are enclosed within quotation marks.

- **"**Our math teacher is unfair,**"** complained Wanda. **"**He assigns two hours of homework for each class. Does he think we have nothing else to do?**"**
  Wanda's exact words are enclosed within quotation marks. Note that even though Wanda's second set of exact words is more than one sentence, only one pair of quotation marks is used. Do not use quotation marks for each new sentence as long as the quotation is not interrupted.

- **"**We cannot solve a problem by hoping that someone else will solve it for us,**"** wrote psychiatrist M. Scott Peck.
  The exact words that Dr. Peck wrote are enclosed in quotation marks.

PUNCTUATION NOTES

- Quoted material is usually set off from the rest of the sentence by a comma. When the comma comes at the end of quoted material, it is included inside the quotation marks. The same is true for a period, exclamation point, or question mark that ends quoted material:

Incorrect	"Watching golf", complained Rosie, "is like watching grass grow".
Correct	"Watching golf**,**" complained Rosie, "is like watching grass grow**.**"

Incorrect	"Aren't you ready yet"? Dad yelled. "Hurry up, or we're leaving without you"!
Correct	"Aren't you ready yet**?**" Dad yelled. "Hurry up, or we're leaving without you**!**"

- Notice, too, that a quoted sentence begins with a capital letter, even when it is preceded by other words:

Incorrect	The diner asked suspiciously, "is this fish fresh?"
Correct	The diner asked suspiciously, "**I**s this fish fresh?"

For additional information about quotation marks, see pages 195–199.

Quotation Marks: PRACTICE

Insert quotation marks where needed in the following sentences. Look at the example below.

Example The game announcer called out, "Looks like we have a winner!"

1. "I won't take any more criticism," Kylie said to her boyfriend. "Our relationship is over."

2. The flight attendant announced, "The captain has turned on the seat belt sign. Please stay in your seat with the belt securely fastened."

3. When Gwen opened the door, everyone in the room jumped up and yelled, "Surprise!"

4. The label on the chlorine bleach says, "Do not mix this product with other cleansers."

5. "This is a movie that will scare everyone in the family," the reviewer said.

6. The boat captain said sternly, "Please keep your arms and legs inside the boat. Failure to do so will make the alligators very happy."

7. It was the late Robert Kennedy who said, "The purpose of life is to contribute in some way to making things better."

8. "Cut the onions into thin slices," the cooking instructor explained. "Then place them in the hot skillet."

9. "Could you turn the radio down just a little?" the passenger shouted to the taxi driver.

10. Anne Frank wrote the following in her diary: "It's a wonder I haven't abandoned all my ideals, which seem so absurd and impractical. Yet I cling to them because I still believe, in spite of everything, that people are truly good at heart."

Name _____   Section _____   Date _____

Score: (Number right) _____ x 10 = _____ %

Quotation Marks: TEST 1

On the lines provided, rewrite the following sentences, adding quotation marks as needed.

NOTE To help you master quotation marks, explanations are given for the first three sentences.

1. My mother said, Take some vitamin C for your cold.
   The mother's words and the period at the end of the sentence should be included within quotation marks.

   My mother said, "Take some vitamin C for your cold." _____

2. Do not discuss the trial during your break, the judge reminded the jury.
   The judge's words and the comma at the end of his words should be enclosed within quotation marks.

   "Do not discuss the trial during your break," the judge reminded the jury. _____

3. That movie, my friend complained, is full of nonstop violence.
   Each of the two parts of the friend's words requires a set of quotation marks. The words *my friend complained* do not get quotation marks because the friend did not speak them aloud.

   "That movie," my friend complained, "is full of nonstop violence." _____

4. The children's voices sang, Row, row, row your boat, gently down the stream.

   The children's voices sang, "Row, row, row your boat, gently down the stream." _____

5. My computer screen is frozen, I said to the instructor.

   "My computer screen is frozen," I said to the instructor. _____

6. Let's eat, Rochelle said, before we go to the movie.

   "Let's eat," Rochelle said, "before we go to the movie." _____

7. A sign on my father's desk reads, In the rat race, only the rats win.

   A sign on my father's desk reads, "In the rat race, only the rats win." _____

8. Who would like another slice of turkey? Mr. Brandon asked the dinner guests.

   "Who would like another slice of turkey?" Mr. Brandon asked the dinner guests. _____

9. Keep your voice down! the little boy shouted loudly to the woman using a cell phone.

   "Keep your voice down!" the little boy shouted loudly to the woman using a cell phone. _____

10. Take a lot of notes, Lamont warned, if you want to do well on tests.

    "Take a lot of notes," Lamont warned, "if you want to do well on tests." _____

Name _____   Section _____   Date _____

Score: (Number right) _____ x 10 = _____ %

Quotation Marks: TEST 2

On the lines provided, rewrite the following sentences, adding quotation marks as needed.

1. It can't be time to get up yet, Isaac groaned as his alarm clock rang.

   "It can't be time to get up yet," Isaac groaned as his alarm clock rang.

2. The waitress said, What'll it be, folks?

   The waitress said, "What'll it be, folks?"

3. Get away from that hot stove! Maria ordered her daughter.

   "Get away from that hot stove!" Maria ordered her daughter.

4. The tag on the hair dryer said, Do not use this product while taking a bath.

   The tag on the hair dryer said, "Do not use this product while taking a bath."

5. Where did you buy that great bag? a woman on the bus asked me.

   "Where did you buy that great bag?" a woman on the bus asked me.

6. The crowd chanted loudly, Defense! Defense! Defense!

   The crowd chanted loudly, "Defense! Defense! Defense!"

7. On the front page of the *New York Times* are these words: All the news that's fit to print.

   On the front page of the *New York Times* are these words: "All the news that's fit to print."

8. To get an A in this class, the teacher said, you must laugh at all my jokes.

   "To get an A in this class," the instructor said, "you must laugh at all my jokes."

9. My grandfather used to say, Sometimes you eat the bear. Sometimes the bear eats you.

   My grandfather used to say, "Sometimes you eat the bear. Sometimes the bear eats you."

10. Jan's voice-mail message says, I'm not home, or else I'm pretending not to be home.

   Jan's voice-mail message says, "I'm not home, or else I'm pretending not to be home."

Name _____   Section _____   Date _____

Score: (Number right) _____ x 10 = _____ %

Quotation Marks: TEST 3

In each group below, **one** sentence uses quotation marks correctly. Write the letter of that sentence in the space provided.

___C___   **1. a.** "My grades are going downhill, Laura whispered.
　　　　b. My grades are going downhill," Laura whispered.
　　　　c. "My grades are going downhill," Laura whispered.

___C___   **2. a.** The movie star said, "I only ride in limousines.
　　　　b. "The movie star said, I only ride in limousines."
　　　　c. The movie star said, "I only ride in limousines."

___B___   **3. a.** "Why are your eyes closed? the instructor asked Simon."
　　　　b. "Why are your eyes closed?" the instructor asked Simon.
　　　　c. "Why are your eyes closed? the instructor asked Simon.

___A___   **4. a.** The instructions say, "Open the battery compartment. Insert 4 AA batteries."
　　　　b. The instructions say, "Open the battery compartment." Insert 4 AA batteries.
　　　　c. "The instructions say, Open the battery compartment. Insert 4 AA batteries."

___C___   **5. a.** "It says right here in our lease," "The landlord is responsible for taking care of the yard."
　　　　b. "It says right here in our lease," The landlord is responsible for taking care of the yard.
　　　　c. It says right here in our lease, "The landlord is responsible for taking care of the yard."

___B___   **6. a.** "I hate that music, said my brother, "and you know it.
　　　　b. "I hate that music," said my brother, "and you know it."
　　　　c. "I hate that music, said my brother, and you know it."

___A___   **7. a.** The sign in the restaurant window reads, "Breakfast served anytime."
　　　　b. "The sign in the restaurant window reads, "Breakfast served anytime."
　　　　c. The sign in the restaurant window reads, "Breakfast served anytime.

___A___   **8. a.** As I sat at the baseball game, I heard someone call, "Get your fresh hot peanuts."
　　　　b. As I sat at the baseball game, "I heard someone call, Get your fresh hot peanuts."
　　　　c. "As I sat at the baseball game, I heard someone call," Get your fresh hot peanuts.

___B___   **9. a.** Dale said, "If that salesman were covered in gravy and dropped into a pit of lions, he could talk them into becoming vegetarians.
　　　　b. Dale said, "If that salesman were covered in gravy and dropped into a pit of lions, he could talk them into becoming vegetarians."
　　　　c. "Dale said, If that salesman were covered in gravy and dropped into a pit of lions, he could talk them into becoming vegetarians."

___B___   **10. a.** "The first line in the novel *1984* reads," It was a bright cold day in April, and the clocks were striking thirteen.
　　　　b. The first line in the novel *1984* reads, "It was a bright cold day in April, and the clocks were striking thirteen."
　　　　c. "The first line in the novel *1984* reads," "It was a bright cold day in April, and the clocks were striking thirteen."

Name _____   Section _____ Date _____

Score: (Number right) _____ x 10 = _____ %

Quotation Marks: TEST 4

In each group below, **one** sentence uses quotation marks correctly. Write the letter of that sentence in the space provided.

____B____ **1. a.** I don't like your lollipops, "the little girl said to the dentist."
     b. "I don't like your lollipops," the little girl said to the dentist.
     c. "I don't like your lollipops, the little girl said to the dentist."

____C____ **2. a.** Rachel announced, "I can open the locked door with a bent coat hanger.
     b. "Rachel announced, I can open the locked door with a bent coat hanger."
     c. Rachel announced, "I can open the locked door with a bent coat hanger."

____A____ **3. a.** The boss advised, "Don't be late again. If you are, I'll fire you."
     b. The boss advised, Don't be late again. If you are, I'll fire you."
     c. The boss advised, "Don't be late again. If you are, I'll fire you.

____B____ **4. a.** "Albert Einstein wrote, Will it matter that I was?"
     b. Albert Einstein wrote, "Will it matter that I was?"
     c. Albert Einstein wrote, "Will it matter that I was?

____B____ **5. a.** How do you like it? "Cindy asked, showing off her new purple fake-fur jacket."
     b. "How do you like it?" Cindy asked, showing off her new purple fake-fur jacket.
     c. "How do you like it? Cindy asked, showing off her new purple fake-fur jacket."

____A____ **6. a.** Her mother paused and then said, "Well, it certainly is a cheerful color."
     b. Her mother paused and then said, "Well, it certainly is a cheerful color.
     c. Her mother paused and then said, Well, it certainly is a cheerful color."

____C____ **7. a.** Her brother was less tactful. You look like a giant purple marshmallow, he said.
     b. Her brother was less tactful. "You look like a giant purple marshmallow, he said."
     c. Her brother was less tactful. "You look like a giant purple marshmallow," he said.

____C____ **8. a.** Most people don't plan to fail, "the counselor said," but they fail to plan.
     b. "Most people don't plan to fail," the counselor said, but they fail to plan.
     c. "Most people don't plan to fail," the counselor said, "but they fail to plan."

____A____ **9. a.** "Reading is to the mind what exercise is to the body," wrote Richard Steele.
     b. "Reading is to the mind what exercise is to the body, wrote Richard Steele."
     c. Reading is to the mind what exercise is to the body, "wrote Richard Steele."

____A____ **10. a.** Mother Teresa said, "Kind words can be easy to speak, but their echoes are truly endless."
     b. Mother Teresa said, "Kind words can be easy to speak, but their echoes are truly endless.
     c. "Mother Teresa said, "Kind words can be easy to speak, but their echoes are truly endless."

12 Homonyms

Basics about Homonyms

Homonyms are two or more words that have the same sound but different spellings and meanings. The following four groups of homonyms cause writers the most trouble.

> *its*   belonging to it
> *it's*   contraction of *it is*

- **It's** a shame that the shiny car lost **its** muffler and now roars like an old truck.

  It is a shame that the shiny car lost *the muffler belonging to it* and now roars like an old truck.

  Spelling hint   In *it's*, the apostrophe takes the place of the *i* in the word *is*.

> *their*   belonging to them
> *there*   (1) in or to that place; (2) used with *is, are, was, were,* and other forms of the verb *to be*
> *they're* contraction of *they are*

- Our neighbors are health-food addicts. When we attend parties at **their** home, they serve pizza with broccoli florets on top. **They're** also fond of serving carrot juice. I hope they won't be offended if we don't go **there** very often.

  Our neighbors are health-food addicts. When we attend parties at the home *belonging to them*, they serve pizza with broccoli florets on top. *They are* also fond of serving carrot juice. I hope they won't be offended when we don't go *to that place* very often.

  Spelling hints   *There, where,* and *here,* which all end in *-ere,* all refer to places.
          In *they're*, the apostrophe takes the place of the *a* in *are*.

> *to*   (1) used before a verb, as in "to serve"; (2) so as to reach
> *too*   (1) overly or extremely; (2) also
> *two* the number 2

- I'll take these **two** letters **to** the post office for you, but you'll need **to** put more postage on one of them. It is **too** heavy for only one stamp.

  I'll take these *2* letters *so as to reach* the post office for you, but you'll need *to put* more postage on one of them. It is *overly* heavy for only one stamp.

  Spelling hint   *Too* has one *o*, and it **also** has another one.

> *your*   belonging to you
> *you're* contraction of *you are*

- **You're** going to need a first-aid kit and high boots for **your** camping trip.

  You are going to need a first-aid kit and high boots for the camping trip *belonging to you*.

  Spelling hint   In *you're*, the apostrophe takes the place of the *a* in *are*.

Other Common Homonyms

brake	— slow or stop		*plain*	— not fancy; obvious
break	— to cause to come apart		*plane*	— airplane
hear	— take in by ear		*right*	— correct
here	— in this place		*write*	— to form letters and words
hole	— an empty spot		*threw*	— past tense of *throw*
whole	— complete		*through*	— into and out of; finished
knew	— past tense of *know*		*wear*	— to have on (clothing)
new	— opposite of old		*where*	— in what place
know	— to understand		*weather*	— outside conditions
no	— the opposite of *yes*		*whether*	— if
peace	— absence of war; quiet		*whose*	— belonging to whom
piece	— a part of something		*who's*	— contraction of *who is* or *who has*

 Homonyms: **PRACTICE**

For each sentence, underline the correct word in parentheses.

1. There is only one *(write / <u>right</u>)* answer to a math problem.

2. No child will be able to *(<u>break</u> / brake)* this toy.

3. We drove *(<u>through</u> / threw)* the entire state in only three hours.

4. Everyone wants *(piece / <u>peace</u>)* on Earth.

5. My best friend always tells me I'm cute, but I think my face is too *(<u>plain</u> / plane)*.

6. Witnesses in trials have to swear to tell the truth, the *(hole / <u>whole</u>)* truth, and nothing but the truth.

7. The *(<u>weather</u> / whether)* in England is rainy much of the time.

8. Ray and Coral, who just got married, want all *(<u>new</u> / knew)* furniture in their house.

9. People who cannot *(<u>hear</u> / here)* often communicate by American Sign Language.

10. The sign in the bus said, "*(<u>There</u> / They're, / Their)* is no excuse for domestic violence."

Name _____ Section _____ Date _____

Score: (Number right) _____ x 5 = _____ %

Homonyms: TEST 1

Cross out the **two** homonym mistakes in each sentence. Then write the correct words in the spaces provided.

NOTE To help you review some of the homonyms in the chapter, definitions are given in the first four of the sentences.

_It's_   _your_
1. ~~Its~~ not too late to change ~~you're~~ mind.
_It is_ not too late to change the mind *that belongs to you.*

brakes   _whether_
2. Russ ~~breaks~~ at every intersection, ~~weather~~ there is a stop sign or not.
Russ *stops* at every intersection, *if* there is a stop sign or not.

write   _whole_
3. Chen showed me how to ~~right~~ my ~~hole~~ name in Chinese characters.
Chen showed me how to *form the letters of* my *complete* name.

know   _there_
4. Before we visited friends in Montreal, I didn't ~~no~~ that French and English are both spoken ~~their~~.
I didn't *understand* that French and English are both spoken *in that place.*

peace   _right_
5. My uncle is the kind of person who gives you no ~~piece~~ and quiet until you agree that he is ~~write~~.

whose   _their_
6. Farm turkeys, ~~who's~~ bodies are big and fat, have lost ~~there~~ ability to fly.

too   _plane_
7. Because ~~to~~ many flights were scheduled to leave at the same time, our ~~plain~~ had to sit waiting on the runway for over an hour.

break   _who's_
8. If you ~~brake~~ your promises, ~~whose~~ going to accept your word in the future?

hear   _no_
9. I ~~here~~ you brought canned soup on your camping trip, but ~~know~~ spoons.

knew   _threw_
10. No one ~~new~~ who ~~through~~ the soda can onto the basketball court while the game was in progress.

Name _____ Section _____ Date _____

Score: (Number right) _____ x 5 = _____ %

Homonyms: TEST 2

Cross out the **two** homonym mistakes in each sentence. Then write the correct words in the spaces provided.

_____where_____   **1.** The words on the tombstone read, "I'd rather be ~~wear~~ ~~your~~ standing."

_____you're_____

_____whole_____   **2.** In the ~~hole~~ world, there are only a few hundred Siberian tigers. In fact, ~~their~~ almost extinct.

_____they're_____

_____There_____   **3.** ~~Their~~ is a custom at a Jewish wedding for the groom to step on a glass and ~~brake~~ it.

_____break_____

_____weather_____   **4.** In really cold ~~whether~~, Jeremy always wears ~~to~~ pairs of socks.

_____two_____

_____it's_____   **5.** The doctor says ~~its~~ going to take at least six weeks for Jenna's sprained foot ~~too~~ heal.

_____to_____

_____new_____   **6.** Please place each of these ~~knew~~ books in ~~it's~~ proper place on the shelves.

_____its_____

_____know_____   **7.** Many young people don't ~~no~~ where ~~there~~ ancestors came from.

_____their_____

_____to_____   **8.** The test was full of silly questions I didn't know how ~~two~~ answer, such as "~~Whose~~ buried in Grant's Tomb?"

_____Who's_____

_____threw_____   **9.** My wasteful sister ~~through~~ out a pepperoni pizza because she prefers ~~plane~~ pizza.

_____plain_____

_____know_____   **10.** If fortunetellers really ~~no~~ the future, why aren't they all lottery winners? They should be able to choose the ~~write~~ numbers.

_____right_____

Name _____   Section _____   Date _____

Score: (Number right) _____ x 10 = _____ %

Homonyms: TEST 3

In each group below, **one** sentence uses homonyms correctly. Write the letter of that sentence in the space provided.

_A___ 1. **a.** It's easy to see from your face that you're very tired.
　　　　b. Its easy to see from your face that you're very tired.
　　　　c. It's easy to see from your face that your very tired.

_B___ 2. **a.** It isn't right to brake your promise.
　　　　b. It isn't right to break your promise.
　　　　c. It isn't write to break your promise.

_C___ 3. **a.** Does anyone no why this empty box is sitting hear?
　　　　b. Does anyone know why this empty box is sitting hear?
　　　　c. Does anyone know why this empty box is sitting here?

_C___ 4. **a.** Surely your not going to eat that whole cake all by yourself.
　　　　b. Surely your not going to eat that hole cake all by yourself.
　　　　c. Surely you're not going to eat that whole cake all by yourself.

_A___ 5. **a.** Maura and Julie are so different that it's difficult to believe that they're sisters.
　　　　b. Maura and Julie are so different that its difficult to believe that their sisters.
　　　　c. Maura and Julie are so different that it's difficult to believe that there sisters.

_C___ 6. **a.** Since beginning his karate class, Brian claims he can brake a stack of two bricks with his bare hand.
　　　　b. Since beginning his karate class, Brian claims he can break a stack of too bricks with his bare hand.
　　　　c. Since beginning his karate class, Brian claims he can break a stack of two bricks with his bare hand.

_B___ 7. **a.** Its impossible to cancel the party—the guests are already on they're way.
　　　　b. It's impossible to cancel the party—the guests are already on their way.
　　　　c. Its impossible to cancel the party—the guests are already on their way.

_C___ 8. **a.** You're cat is going to break its leg if it jumps down from that tall tree.
　　　　b. Your cat is going to break it's leg if it jumps down from that tall tree.
　　　　c. Your cat is going to break its leg if it jumps down from that tall tree.

_B___ 9. **a.** The water is so cold that it's hard to breathe when your in it.
　　　　b. The water is so cold that it's hard to breathe when you're in it.
　　　　c. The water is so cold that its hard to breathe when you're in it.

_C___ 10. **a.** If they're is life on other planets, it's probably very different from life on Earth.
　　　　b. If there is life on other planets, its probably very different from life on Earth.
　　　　c. If there is life on other planets, it's probably very different from life on Earth.

Name _____   Section _____   Date _____

Score: (Number right) _____ x 10 = _____ %

Homonyms: TEST 4

In each group below, **one** sentence uses homonyms correctly. Write the letter of that sentence in the space provided.

___C___   **1. a.** Now that Mrs. Ringwald is in the hospital, no one nos whose going to teach her class.
        b. Now that Mrs. Ringwald is in the hospital, no one knows whose going to teach her class.
        c. Now that Mrs. Ringwald is in the hospital, no one knows who's going to teach her class.

___A___   **2. a.** Here in Nashville, many people earn their living in the music business.
        b. Hear in Nashville, many people earn their living in the music business.
        c. Hear in Nashville, many people earn they're living in the music business.

___C___   **3. a.** It's rude to keep talking on you're cell phone when you are with other people.
        b. Its rude to keep talking on your cell phone when you are with other people.
        c. It's rude to keep talking on your cell phone when you are with other people.

___A___   **4. a.** Too many people write unsigned letters to the newspaper.
        b. To many people right unsigned letters to the newspaper.
        c. Two many people write unsigned letters to the newspaper.

___C___   **5. a.** To brake the habit of smoking takes a whole lot of willpower.
        b. To break the habit of smoking takes a hole lot of willpower.
        c. To break the habit of smoking takes a whole lot of willpower.

___C___   **6. a.** You're wasting to much time worrying about things you can't control.
        b. Your wasting to much time worrying about things you can't control.
        c. You're wasting too much time worrying about things you can't control.

___A___   **7. a.** After two weeks, the lost cat returned, thin and dirty and without its collar.
        b. After too weeks, the lost cat returned, thin and dirty and without it's collar.
        c. After to weeks, the lost cat returned, thin and dirty and without its collar.

___B___   **8. a.** Unfortunately, it's easy to take you're family and friends for granted.
        b. Unfortunately, it's easy to take your family and friends for granted.
        c. Unfortunately, its easy to take your family and friends for granted.

___B___   **9. a.** Their are too many empty storefronts in the downtown area.
        b. There are too many empty storefronts in the downtown area.
        c. They're are two many empty storefronts in the downtown area.

___A___   **10. a.** Where will the party be held if the weather turns bad?
        b. Wear will the party be held if the whether turns bad?
        c. Where will the party be held if the whether turns bad?

13 Capital Letters

Basics about Capital Letters

Here are six main uses of capital letters:

1 THE FIRST WORD IN A SENTENCE OR DIRECT QUOTATION

- The ice-cream man said, "Try a frozen banana bar. They're delicious."

2 THE WORD "I" AND PEOPLE'S NAMES

- Because I was the first caller in the radio contest, I won two backstage passes to the Jennifer Lopez concert. My friend Maria Santana went with me.

3 NAMES OF SPECIFIC PLACES, INSTITUTIONS, AND LANGUAGES

- Janice, who lives in Boston and works as a lab technician at Newton Hospital, grew up on a farm in Kokomo, Indiana.

- The signs in the airport terminal were written in Spanish, English, and Japanese.

4 PRODUCT NAMES

Capitalize the brand name of a product, but not the kind of product it is.

- Every morning Ben has Tropicana orange juice and Total cereal with milk.

5 CALENDAR ITEMS

Capitalize the names of days of the week, months, and holidays.

- At first, Thanksgiving was celebrated on the last Thursday in November, but it was changed to the fourth Thursday of the month.

6 TITLES

Capitalize the titles of books, TV or stage shows, songs, magazines, movies, articles, poems, stories, papers, and so on.

- Sitting in the waiting room, Dennis nervously paged through issues of *National Geographic* and *People* magazines.

- Gwen wrote a paper titled "Portrayal of Women in Rap Music Videos" that was based on videos shown on MTV.

NOTE The words *the, of, a, an, and*, and other little, unstressed words are not capitalized when they appear in the middle of a title. That is why *of* and *in* are not capitalized in "Portrayal of Women in Rap Music Videos."

Capital Letters: PRACTICE

Underline the **two** words that need capitalizing in each sentence. Then write these words correctly in the spaces provided.

1. Our brother's usual breakfast of <u>pepsi</u> and <u>doritos</u> makes me shake my head.

   _____Pepsi_____   _____Doritos_____

2. The first thing we did after arriving in <u>california</u> was to visit <u>disneyland</u>.

   _____California_____   _____Disneyland_____

3. <u>my</u> parents asked, "<u>why</u> did you get in so late last night?"

   _____My_____   _____Why_____

4. This <u>june</u>, <u>i</u> will graduate from community college and start looking for a job as a medical technician.

   _____June_____   _____I_____

5. Few people recognize the name of Chester <u>arthur</u>, who was the twenty-first president of the United <u>states</u>.

   _____Arthur_____   _____States_____

6. Before <u>thanksgiving</u>, our church always delivers turkeys and cases of <u>progresso</u> soup to poor families.

   _____Thanksgiving_____   _____Progresso_____

7. Norm's "dream car" for some day is a <u>lexus</u>, but meanwhile he drives an old <u>chevrolet</u> station wagon.

   _____Lexus_____   _____Chevrolet_____

8. Every <u>january</u>, our grandparents travel to <u>florida</u> for a winter vacation.

   _____January_____   _____Florida_____

9. When you get to <u>penn</u> <u>avenue</u>, you will find a lot of fast-food restaurants.

   _____Penn_____   _____Avenue_____

10. *The Night of the <u>living</u> <u>dead</u>,* George Romero's 1968 horror film about zombies, has become a classic.

    _____Living_____   _____Dead_____

Name _____ Section _____ Date _____

Score: (Number right) _____ x 5 = _____ %

Capital Letters: **TEST 1**

Underline the **two** words that need to be capitalized in each sentence. Then write the words correctly in the spaces provided.

NOTE To help you master capitalization, explanations are given for the first four sentences.

1. Last summer, my mother and i visited my aunt in New orleans.
   Capitalize the word *I* and the names of specific places.
   _____I_____   _____Orleans_____

2. The car salesman said, "here's a used buick you folks might be interested in."
   Capitalize the first word of a direct quotation and the brand name of a car.
   _____Here's_____   _____Buick_____

3. Every wednesday after school, Cara goes to chinese-language school.
   Capitalize the days of the week and the names of foreign languages.
   _____Wednesday_____   _____Chinese_____

4. The november issue of *prevention* magazine had an article you could use for your report.
   Capitalize the months of the year and the titles of magazines, but not the word *magazine*.
   _____November_____   _____Prevention_____

5. My grandfather's real name is henrik, but when he left norway, he started calling himself Hank.
   _____Henrik_____   _____Norway_____

6. When i was a little girl, I thought that cheerios grew on a cereal bush.
   _____I_____   _____Cheerios_____

7. Being located right on Lake michigan makes chicago a very windy city.
   _____Michigan_____   _____Chicago_____

8. Every other july, the members of the baker family get together for a big reunion.
   _____July_____   _____Baker_____

9. To celebrate my birthday next thursday, my family is taking me out to my favorite vietnamese restaurant.
   _____Thursday_____   _____Vietnamese_____

10. At least once a year, my cousin james and I make popcorn, sit down, and watch the movie *The Wizard of oz*.
    _____James_____   _____Oz_____

Name _____   Section _____   Date _____

Score: (Number right) _____ x 5 = _____ %

Capital Letters: TEST 2

Underline the **two** words that need to be capitalized in each sentence. Then write the words correctly in the spaces provided.

1. The friends argued over whether to get pizza from <u>domino's</u> or Pizza <u>hut</u>.

    _____Domino's_____   _____Hut_____

2. Every day in <u>may</u>, our local <u>kroger</u> supermarket is giving away a $100 gift certificate.

    _____May_____   _____Kroger_____

3. The disc jockey said, "<u>be</u> the ninth caller and win a trip to beautiful <u>bermuda</u>!"

    _____Be_____   _____Bermuda_____

4. Next term in <u>english</u> class, we'll be reading *The great Gatsby*.

    _____English_____   _____Great_____

5. Members of the high-school marching band are selling giant <u>hershey</u> bars to raise funds for their trip to <u>hawaii</u>.

    _____Hershey_____   _____Hawaii_____

6. This issue of *glamour* magazine has an article called "Look Like a <u>million</u> Dollars for Ten Bucks."

    _____Glamour_____   _____Million_____

7. This year, the month of <u>february</u> will contain a <u>friday</u> the thirteenth.

    _____February_____   _____Friday_____

8. Our favorite roller coaster is in an amusement park called Cedar <u>point</u> in <u>sandusky</u>, Ohio.

    _____Point_____   _____Sandusky_____

9. <u>everybody</u> in my mother's family speaks <u>greek</u> as well as English.

    _____Everybody_____   _____Greek_____

10. At the computer store on <u>washington</u> Boulevard, there are great prices on <u>macintosh</u> computers.

    _____Washington_____   _____Macintosh_____

Name _____   Section _____   Date _____

Score: (Number right) _____ x 10 = _____ %

Capital Letters: TEST 3

In each group below, **one** sentence uses capital letters correctly. Write the letter of that sentence in the space provided.

___C___ **1. a.** Before moving into the house, lynn scrubbed the floors with lysol.
        b. Before moving into the house, Lynn scrubbed the floors with lysol.
        c. Before moving into the house, Lynn scrubbed the floors with Lysol.

___B___ **2. a.** Ellen's dinner was a Roast Beef Sandwich from Arby's and a Salad from Wendy's.
        b. Ellen's dinner was a roast beef sandwich from Arby's and a salad from Wendy's.
        c. Ellen's dinner was a roast beef Sandwich from Arby's and a Salad from Wendy's.

___A___ **3. a.** Our hostess asked, "Have you ever visited Nashville before?"
        b. Our hostess asked, "have you ever visited Nashville before?"
        c. Our hostess asked, "have You ever visited Nashville before?"

___C___ **4. a.** My little niece often watches her DVD of *Beauty and the beast.*
        b. My little niece often watches her DVD of *Beauty and The Beast.*
        c. My little niece often watches her DVD of *Beauty and the Beast.*

___B___ **5. a.** Brian foolishly complained to the police officer, "But sir, i never stop at that Stop Sign."
        b. Brian foolishly complained to the police officer, "But sir, I never stop at that stop sign."
        c. Brian foolishly complained to the police officer, "but sir, I never stop at that stop sign."

___A___ **6. a.** On the last Friday in May, Ross Hospital stopped admitting emergency patients.
        b. On the last friday in may, Ross hospital stopped admitting emergency patients.
        c. On the last Friday in May, ross hospital stopped admitting emergency patients.

___C___ **7. a.** On Memorial day and the Fourth of july, our dog howls when she hears the fireworks.
        b. On Memorial day and the fourth of July, our dog howls when she hears the fireworks.
        c. On Memorial Day and the Fourth of July, our dog howls when she hears the fireworks.

___A___ **8. a.** Grandpa heated up some Log Cabin syrup to pour over his Eggo waffles.
        b. Grandpa heated up some Log Cabin Syrup to pour over his Eggo Waffles.
        c. Grandpa heated up some Log cabin syrup to pour over his Eggo waffles.

___B___ **9. a.** When I visited Mexico, I had a chance to practice my spanish.
        b. When I visited Mexico, I had a chance to practice my Spanish.
        c. When I visited mexico, I had a chance to practice my Spanish.

___C___ **10. a.** On Monday, I must have a paper titled "Hate Crimes" ready for my english class.
        b. On Monday, I must have a paper titled "Hate crimes" ready for my english class.
        c. On Monday, I must have a paper titled "Hate Crimes" ready for my English class.

Name _____   Section _____   Date _____

Score: (Number right) _____ x 10 = _____ %

Capital Letters: TEST 4

In each group below, **one** sentence uses capital letters correctly. Write the letter of that sentence in the space provided.

___C___ **1. a.** The man at the door said, "Can I interest you in a subscription to *time* magazine?"
        b. The man at the door said, "can I interest you in a subscription to *Time* magazine?"
        c. The man at the door said, "Can I interest you in a subscription to *Time* magazine?"

___A___ **2. a.** The teacher asked us to write a paper titled "The Dangers of Television."
        b. The teacher asked us to write a paper titled "The Dangers Of Television."
        c. The teacher asked us to write a paper titled "The dangers of television."

___A___ **3. a.** A tractor-trailer loaded with chemicals flipped over at the corner of Oak and Cherry.
        b. A Tractor-Trailer loaded with chemicals flipped over at the corner of Oak and Cherry.
        c. A tractor-trailer loaded with chemicals flipped over at the corner of oak and cherry.

___C___ **4. a.** On sunday, Trina cut her visa card in half to try to stop her impulse buying.
        b. On Sunday, trina cut her visa card in half to try to stop her impulse buying.
        c. On Sunday, Trina cut her Visa card in half to try to stop her impulse buying.

___C___ **5. a.** For years, the slogan for Timex Watches was "It takes a licking and keeps on ticking."
        b. For years, the slogan for Timex watches was "it takes a licking and keeps on ticking."
        c. For years, the slogan for Timex watches was "It takes a licking and keeps on ticking."

___B___ **6. a.** My friend Pedro is taking two classes at blackstone Community College.
        b. My friend Pedro is taking two classes at Blackstone Community College.
        c. My friend pedro is taking two classes at Blackstone community college.

___B___ **7. a.** A woman rushed into the restaurant asking, "has anyone found a Canon camera?"
        b. A woman rushed into the restaurant asking, "Has anyone found a Canon camera?"
        c. A woman rushed into the restaurant asking, "Has anyone found a Canon Camera?"

___A___ **8. a.** I'm looking forward to the Thursday night marathon of old *I Love Lucy* episodes.
        b. I'm looking forward to the Thursday night marathon of old *I love lucy* episodes.
        c. I'm looking forward to the thursday night marathon of old *I love Lucy* episodes.

___C___ **9. a.** Kendra is taking language courses at Rider college. She plans to become a high-school Spanish Teacher.
        b. Kendra is taking language courses at Rider college. She plans to become a high-school spanish teacher.
        c. Kendra is taking language courses at Rider College. She plans to become a high-school Spanish teacher.

___C___ **10. a.** My brother, a physical therapist, has worked at grandview hospital since september.
        b. My brother, a physical therapist, has worked at grandview Hospital since september.
        c. My brother, a physical therapist, has worked at Grandview Hospital since September.

14 Parallelism

Basics about Parallelism

Two or more equal ideas should be expressed in **parallel**, or matching, form. Parallelism will help your words flow smoothly and clearly. The absence of parallelism is jarring and awkward to read. Here's an example:

Not parallel   The new restaurant has fresh food, reasonable prices, and service that is fast.

The first two features of the restaurant—*fresh food* and *reasonable prices*—are described in parallel form. In each case, we get a descriptive word followed by the word being described:

fresh food, reasonable prices

But with the last feature, we get the word being described first and then a descriptive word:

service that is fast

To achieve parallelism, the nonparallel item must have the same form as the first two:

Parallel   The new restaurant has fresh food, reasonable prices, and **fast service**.

Here are some additional examples of problems with parallelism and explanations of how to correct them:

Not parallel   The children were arguing in the lobby, talked during the movie, and complained on the ride home.

Talked and *complained* are similar in form. But *were arguing* is not. It must be changed so that it has the same form as the other two.

Parallel   The children **argued** in the lobby, talked during the movie, and complained on the ride home.

Not parallel   Our neighbors spend a lot of time shopping, visiting friends, and they go to the movies.

The sentence lists a series of activities. *Shopping* and *visiting* both end in *-ing*. To be parallel, *they go to the movies* must be revised to include an *-ing* word.

Parallel   Our neighbors spend a lot of time shopping, visiting friends, and **going to the movies**.

Not parallel   My aunt is selfish, impatient, and she is not a kind person.

To be parallel, *she is not a kind person* should have a form that matches *selfish* and *impatient*.

Parallel   My aunt is selfish, impatient, and **unkind.**

Not parallel   Every morning I have to feed the dog and bringing in the mail.

Feed the dog and *bringing in the mail* are not parallel. For parallelism, both must be in the same form.

Parallel   Every morning I have to feed the dog and **bring in the mail.**

Parallelism: PRACTICE

The part of each sentence that needs revising is *italicized*. On the line, rewrite this part to make it match the other item(s) listed.

1. My little brother would play video games night and day if it weren't for eating and *to have to sleep.*

   having to sleep [OR sleeping]

2. Amos chose a bouquet of white roses, red carnations, and *tulips that were yellow.*

   yellow tulips

3. Smoking and *to spit* are both prohibited on the subway.

   spitting

4. These apples are not only small but also *have a sour taste.*

   sour

5. It is harder to get in shape than *staying* in shape.

   [to] stay

6. In a foreign country, a visitor is overwhelmed with strange sounds, *smells that surprise*, and unusual sights.

   surprising smells

7. Laura's older brother spends half his time flirting with me and the other half *he ignores me.*

   ignoring me

8. Detective stories, popular music, and *sports that are on television* are the things that my grandparents enjoy most.

   television sports [OR televised sports]

9. For lunch we were given limp bologna sandwiches, *peanut-butter crackers that were stale*, and warm sugary punch.

   stale peanut-butter crackers

10. Many runaways are lured to the city by the bright lights, *activity going on constantly*, and empty promises.

    constant activity

Name _____   Section _____   Date _____

Score: (Number right) _____ x 10 = _____ %

Parallelism: TEST 1

The part of each sentence that needs revising is *italicized*. On the line, rewrite this part to make it match the other item(s) listed.

NOTE   To help you master parallelism, explanations are given for the first three sentences.

1. Nina has a high fever and *a throat that is sore*.
   A throat that is sore must be changed to the same form as *a high fever*.

   a sore throat _____

2. On a busy highway, traveling too slow is almost as bad as *to drive* too fast.
   To drive must be changed to the same form as *traveling*.

   driving _____

3. Humming computers, beeping fax machines, and *the ring of telephones* are part of almost every modern office.
   The ring of telephones must have the same form as *humming computers* and *beeping fax machines*.

   ringing telephones _____

4. These grapes are big, sweet, and *full of juice*.

   juicy _____

5. To love your family, your work, and *giving love to your friends*—this is happiness.

   your friends _____

6. Tonight's menu includes *chicken that is roasted*, baked potatoes, and steamed broccoli.

   roast [OR roasted] chicken _____

7. I never thought I'd miss my sister's shrill laughter and *jokes that are stupid*, but I do.

   stupid jokes _____

8. All dumbbell Donald asks of a girlfriend is that she adore him, *the lending of money,* and center her entire life around him.

   lend him money _____

9. My New Year's resolutions were to stop talking so much, *losing weight*, and to do more reading.

   to lose weight _____

10. The diner at the table next to me made choking noises, *was turning red*, and pointed to his throat.

    turned red _____

Name _____   Section _____   Date _____

Score: (Number right) _____ x 10 = _____ %

Parallelism: TEST 2

The part of each sentence that needs revising is *italicized*. On the line, rewrite this part to make it match the other item(s) listed.

1. Golden retriever puppies are adorable, with big eyes, soft fur, and *expressions of sweetness.*
   sweet expressions
   _____

2. Long hours, *pay that was low*, and unpleasant coworkers are the reasons Kevin left his job.
   low pay
   _____

3. Our hostess told us to help ourselves to the buffet and *we could get drinks* in the kitchen.
   [to] get drinks
   _____

4. The sick boy's mother gave her son some vitamin C, tucked him in bed, and *was pouring* him a cup of tea.
   poured
   _____

5. The house we wanted to buy had a big backyard, sunny rooms, and *a kitchen that was modern.*
   a modern kitchen
   _____

6. My uncle usually wears loud ties, *shoes that are scuffed*, and wrinkled shirts.
   scuffed shoes
   _____

7. The speaker had sweaty hands, an upset stomach, and *a voice that was nervous.*
   a nervous voice
   _____

8. For exercise, I either play basketball at the gym or *the riding of a bike* in the park.
   ride a bike
   _____

9. Our neighbors include a dress designer, *a person who teaches second grade*, and a car salesperson.
   a second-grade teacher
   _____

10. Without warning, the sky got dark, a wind sprang up, and *there was a drop in the temperature.*
    the temperature dropped
    _____

Name _____   Section _____   Date _____

Score: (Number right) _____ x 10 = _____ %

Parallelism: TEST 3

In each group below, **one** sentence uses parallelism correctly. Write the letter of that sentence in the space provided.

___B___ **1. a.** My older brother and the only sister I have are coming to my graduation.
  b. My older brother and my only sister are coming to my graduation.
  c. My older brother and the only sister of mine are coming to my graduation.

___A___ **2. a.** On hot days I open the windows, turn on the fans, and complain a lot.
  b. On hot days I open the windows, turn on the fans, and am complaining a lot.
  c. On hot days I open the windows, turning on the fans, and complain a lot.

___B___ **3. a.** Our manager requires us to smile constantly, to speak in a cheerful way, and to move quickly.
  b. Our manager requires us to smile constantly, to speak cheerfully, and to move quickly.
  c. Our manager requires us to smile constantly, to speak in a cheerful way, and to be moving quickly.

___A___ **4. a.** Grass like velvet and flowers like jewels make the park a beautiful place to visit.
  b. Grass like velvet and jewel-like flowers make the park a beautiful place to visit.
  c. Grass like velvet and flowers that look like jewels make the park a beautiful place to visit.

___C___ **5. a.** By the end of the hike, many of us complained of blistered feet, backs that ached, or skinned knees.
  b. By the end of the hike, many of us complained of feet that were blistered, aching backs, or skinned knees.
  c. By the end of the hike, many of us complained of blistered feet, aching backs, or skinned knees.

___C___ **6. a.** Writing a research paper and science test studying are my tasks for the weekend.
  b. Writing a research paper and to study for a science test are my tasks for the weekend.
  c. Writing a research paper and studying for a science test are my tasks for the weekend.

___A___ **7. a.** Which do you appreciate more: something given or something earned?
  b. Which do you appreciate more: something that is given to you or something earned?
  c. Which do you appreciate more: something given or something that you earn?

___A___ **8. a.** Students who make sacrifices to be in school are often the most focused, serious, and motivated.
  b. Students who make sacrifices to be in school are often the most focused, serious, and having motivation.
  c. Students who make sacrifices to be in school are often the most focused, they are serious, and motivated.

___A___ **9. a.** Watching movies, eating pizza, and playing country music are Lenny's ideas of a good time.
  b. Watching movies, to eat pizza, and playing country music are Lenny's ideas of a good time.
  c. Watching movies, eating pizza, and the playing of country music are Lenny's ideas of a good time.

___C___ **10. a.** When Marco returned home from the dance, he was frustrated, angry, and feeling depression.
  b. When Marco returned home from the dance, he was frustrated, there was anger, and he felt depressed.
  c. When Marco returned home from the dance, he was frustrated, angry, and depressed.

Name _____ Section _____ Date _____

Score: (Number right) _____ x 10 = _____ %

Parallelism: TEST 4

In each group below, one sentence uses parallelism correctly. Write the letter of that sentence in the space provided.

__C__ **1. a.** Peeling paint and windows that were broken made the old house look sad.
 b. Peeling paint and the breaking of windows made the old house look sad.
 c. Peeling paint and broken windows made the old house look sad.

__B__ **2. a.** The loud voices, air that has smoke in it, and stale smells in the room all made me want to leave quickly.
 b. The loud voices, smoky air, and stale smells in the room all made me want to leave quickly.
 c. Voices that were loud, smoky air, and stale smells in the room all made me want to leave quickly.

__C__ **3. a.** Fran sucked in her stomach, held her breath, and was trying to pull the zipper up.
 b. Fran sucked in her stomach, she stopped breathing, and tried to pull the zipper up.
 c. Fran sucked in her stomach, held her breath, and tried to pull the zipper up.

__C__ **4. a.** The book, with its tattered pages and cover that was missing, had been read many times.
 b. The book, with its tattered pages and that had a cover missing, had been read many times.
 c. The book, with its tattered pages and missing cover, had been read many times.

__A__ **5. a.** College students from lower-income families often have to hold jobs, go to school, and take care of children all at the same time.
 b. College students from lower-income families often have to hold jobs, go to school, and caring for children all at the same time.
 c. College students from lower-income families often have to hold jobs, going to school, and take care of children all at the same time.

__B__ **6. a.** The movie featured terrible acting, excessive violence, and plot twists that were ridiculous.
 b. The movie featured terrible acting, excessive violence, and ridiculous plot twists.
 c. The movie featured terrible acting, violence to excess, and ridiculous plot twists.

__A__ **7. a.** Attending class regularly and taking notes carefully are real keys to success in school.
 b. Attending class regularly and to take notes carefully are real keys to success in school.
 c. To attend class regularly and taking notes carefully are real keys to success in school.

__B__ **8. a.** The babysitter's nails, long and red, heavy eye makeup, and jangling jewelry all frightened the twins.
 b. The babysitter's long red nails, heavy eye makeup, and jangling jewelry all frightened the twins.
 c. The babysitter's long red nails, eye makeup that was heavy, and jangling jewelry all frightened the twins.

__B__ **9. a.** The driving rain turned the park into a swamp and the highway was a river.
 b. The driving rain turned the park into a swamp and the highway into a river.
 c. The driving rain turned the park into a swamp and made a river of the highway.

__A__ **10. a.** I know not how others may feel, but as for me, give me liberty or give me death.
 b. I know not how others may feel, but as for me, give me liberty or else I would prefer to die.
 c. I know not how others may feel, but as for me, liberty or give me death.

15   Preparing a Paper

Basics about Preparing a Paper

Here are important guidelines for preparing a paper.

THE TITLE

Most of your school papers will begin with a title. The title of a paper prepared on a computer should be about an inch and a half from the top of the page. The title of a handwritten paper should be on the top line of the first page. For example, here are the title and the opening part of a paper about the author's brother.

	A Shy Brother
	My older brother is the shyest person I know. Whenever there
	are more than two people in a group, he will stop talking. He has
	never raised his hand to answer a question in class. . . .

Use the above correctly written example to identify each of the following statements as either true (**T**) or false (**F**).

___F___   **1.** The title should be set off in quotation marks.

___F___   **2.** The title should have a period after it.

___T___   **3.** The title should be capitalized.

___T___   **4.** The title should be centered on the page.

___T___   **5.** A line should be skipped between the title and the first sentence.

You should have answered "False" for the first two items and "True" for the last three. Here is a checklist for how to handle a title:

● Type the title about an inch and a half below the top of the first page. For handwritten papers, put the title on the top line of the first page.

● Center the title.

● Do not use quotation marks around the title or put a period after the title.

● Capitalize each word in the title. (The only exceptions are small words such as *a, the, and, of, in,* and *for* in the middle of a title.)

● Skip a line between the title and the first sentence of the paper.

INDENTING THE FIRST LINE

The first line of a paragraph should be **indented**—that is, set in—about one-half inch from the left-hand margin. (Note the indentation of the first line of the paper about the shy brother.) Do not indent the other sentences in a paragraph.

MARGINS

Leave enough margin on all four sides of a paper to avoid a crowded look. The standard margins on a typed paper are an inch to an inch and a half on all four sides.

OTHER GUIDELINES

1 Use full-sized paper (8 ½ by 11 inches).

2 Write or type on only one side of the paper.

3 Ideally, double-space your paper. If you are writing by hand, do the following:
   ● Use blue or black ink—never pencil.
   ● Use wide-lined paper, or write on every other line of narrow-lined paper.
   ● Write letters and punctuation marks as clearly as you can, taking care to distinguish between small and capital letters.

4 If your teacher so requests, include a cover page on which you put your name, the date, the title, and the section number of your course.

Practice

What **five** corrections are needed in the student paper shown below? Explain the corrections needed in the five numbered spaces below.

	Family meetings
	My family has found various ways to get along well. One way is having
	family meetings. We meet twice a month to discuss and handle our
	problems before they get out of hand. This has saved the members of
	my family a great deal of aggravation. For instance, when my brother . . .

1. The title should be centered.

2. The second word of the title needs to be capitalized.

3. A line should be skipped after the title.

4. The paragraph's first line should be indented.

5. A margin is needed on the right side.

Eight Types of Punctuation Marks

This chapter first describes three marks of punctuation that are used to end a sentence: the period (.), the question mark (?), and the exclamation point (!). The chapter then describes five additional marks of punctuation: the colon (:), semicolon (;), hyphen (-), dash (—), and parentheses ( ).

THE PERIOD (.)

Use a **period** at the end of a statement, a mild command, or an indirect question.

- The children jumped over all the rain puddles.
  (A statement)
- Hand me the red pen.
  (A mild command)
- I wonder if there will be a surprise quiz today.
  (An indirect question)

THE QUESTION MARK (?)

Use a **question mark** after a sentence that asks a question.

- Are you ready for the test?
- How did the car get scratched?
- "Can I have your phone number?" Susanne asked Phil.

Indirect questions tell the reader about questions, rather than asking them directly. They end with periods, not question marks.

- The teacher asked if we were ready for the test.
- I wonder how the car got scratched.
- Susanne asked Phil if she could have his phone number.

THE EXCLAMATION POINT (!)

Use an **exclamation point** after a word or statement that expresses extreme emotion or that gives a strong command.

- Help!
- Wow!
- I got an A on my report!
- Cut that out!

NOTE Exclamation points lose their power if they are used too frequently. Use them only when you wish to emphasize strong emotion.

Practice 1

Place a period, question mark, or exclamation point at the end of each of the following sentences.

Example   Will we see each other again ?

1. Our family car has trouble starting on cold or wet mornings.
2. Why is your cell phone making weird noises?
3. Watch out for that barbed wire!
4. Please fill out an application, and then take a seat.
5. May I use your computer?
6. Iced tea was first served at the 1904 World's Fair.
7. That speeding car is going to hit us!
8. My brother asked if he could use my computer.
9. Do you think it's going to rain?
10. Bicycles, which don't pollute, may be the world's best method of transportation.

THE COLON (:)

The **colon** directs attention to what follows. It has three main uses:

1 Use a colon to introduce a list.

● On her first day of vacation, Carrie did three things: she watched a funny movie, took a long nap, and ate at her favorite restaurant.

2 Use a colon to introduce a long or a formal quotation.

● The autobiography of Arthur Ashe begins with the following Biblical quotation: "Since we are surrounded by so great a cloud of witnesses, let us lay aside every weight, and the sin which so easily ensnares us, and let us run with endurance the race that is set before us."

3 Use a colon to introduce an explanation.

● Bert suddenly canceled his evening plans for a simple reason: his car was out of gas.

The use of a colon in the opening of a letter is explained in "More about Commas" on page 185.

Practice 2

Add **one** colon to each sentence.

1. The sign in the no-smoking area reads:"If we see smoke, we will assume you are on fire and will take appropriate action."
2. The book *Anna Karenina* begins with this famous observation:"Happy families are all alike; every unhappy family is unhappy in its own way."
3. By the end of her first date with Bill, Julie was positive of one thing:there would never be a second.
4. James left the carnival loaded down with treats:cotton candy, stuffed toys, balloons, and three live goldfish.
5. Instead of the anger he expected, Darryl felt only one emotion when his son was brought home by the police:great relief.

THE SEMICOLON (;)

A **semicolon** indicates that the reader should pause. It has three main uses:

1 Use a semicolon to join two complete thoughts that are closely related, but are not connected by a joining word (such as *and*, *but*, or *so*).

● Our cat knocked over a can of Coca-Cola; the soda foamed over the white carpet.

2 Use a semicolon to join two closely related complete thoughts with a transitional word or word group (such as *afterward, however, instead, therefore,* and *on the other hand*). Follow the transitional word or word group with a comma.

● LeQuita began school without knowing any English; nevertheless, she will graduate at the top of her class.

The use of a semicolon to join two complete thoughts is explained in "More about Run-Ons and Comma Splices" on pages 179–180.

3 Use semicolons to separate items in a series when the items themselves contain commas.

● Driving down Sunset Strip, we passed La Boutique, which sells women's clothing; The Friendly Cafe, which serves twenty different kinds of coffee; and Pet Palace, which sells snakes, parrots, and spiders.

Practice 3

Add one or more semicolons to each sentence.

1. Many hopeful actors move to Hollywood;most leave disappointed.

2. We went to the airport to pick up my cousin;however, her flight had been canceled.

3. Winners in the dog show were Lady Luck, a German shepherd;Skipper's Delight, a golden retriever;and Nana, a miniature poodle.

4. The emergency room was crowded;everyone looked worried.

5. Hank thought the glass contained lemonade;instead, he drank pure lemon juice.

THE HYPHEN (-)

Hyphens are used within a word or between two words. Following are three main uses of hyphens:

1 Use a hyphen to divide a word at the end of a line of writing.

● The lawyer stood up, put on her jacket, shoved a bundle of papers into her brief-case, and hurried to court.

NOTE Here are rules for dividing a word at the end of a line:

    a Never divide a word which has only one syllable.

    b Divide words only between syllables.

    c Never divide a word in a way that leaves only one or two letters alone on a line.

    d When dividing a word that already contains a hyphen, divide where the hyphen is.

2 Use a hyphen in a **compound adjective**: to join two or more words that act together to describe a noun that follows them.

● The sports car swerved around the slow-moving truck.

3 Put a hyphen in any number from twenty-one to ninety-nine and in a fraction that is written out, such as *one-fourth* or *two-thirds*.

NOTE Words made up of two or more words are sometimes hyphenated (for example, *baby-sit* and *fine-tune*). There is no clear rule to cover such cases, so when you're unsure about whether or not to hyphenate such words, check your dictionary.

 Practice 4

Add a hyphen to each sentence.

   1. Polls show that two-thirds of the voters would support higher taxes.

   2. You've handed in a very well-written story.

   3. That angry-looking boss actually has a sweet personality.

   4. Although Trudy turned thirty last month, she tells everyone she's twenty-eight.

   5. José was telling me about a beautiful green-eyed girl he saw on the subway.

THE DASH (—)

While the hyphen is used within or between individual words, the **dash** is used between parts of a sentence. Following are three common uses of the dash:

1 Dashes may be used to set off and emphasize interrupting material. Use them when you wish to give special attention to words that interrupt the flow of the sentence.

● Everyone in that family—including the teenagers—has a weight problem.

2 Use a dash to signal the end of a list of items.

● Family support, prayer, and hope—these are what got Grady through all those months in recovery.

3 A dash may be used to introduce a final element—a list of items, an explanation, or a dramatic point.

● Anne's refrigerator was packed with food for the party—trays of cold cuts, bottles of pickles, loaves of bread, and several pitchers of lemonade.

● Ravi hurriedly left work in the middle of the day—his wife was having labor pains.

● My wallet was found in a trash can—minus its cash.

NOTE As mentioned above, the colon can also be used to introduce a list or an explanation. A colon tends to add more formality and less drama to a sentence than a dash.

When typing, form a dash with two hyphens, leaving no space between them, or use your computer's dash character. Do not leave spaces before or after the dash.

Practice 5

Add **one** or **two** dashes, as needed, to each sentence.

1. Several papers very important papers are missing from my desk.

2. A year after their divorce, Oscar and Ruby did something surprising they got married again.

3. Delicious food, wonderful service, and low prices that's all I ask in a restaurant.

4. The maple tree in our front yard it had been standing there for sixty years blew down last night.

5. Harold walked into the room wearing an odd outfit an elegant tuxedo, a rose in his buttonhole, and cheap rubber sandals.

PARENTHESES ( )

Here are two common uses of **parentheses**:

1 Use parentheses to set off material that interrupts the flow of a sentence. While dashes are used to emphasize interrupting material, parentheses are generally used for material you do not wish to emphasize.

- Aunt Fern **(**who arrived two hours late**)** brought the biggest gift.

2 Place parentheses around numbers that introduce items in a list within a sentence.

- Ron's work for the evening is as follows: **(1)** finish a history paper, **(2)** read a chapter in the science text, and **(3)** wash a load of laundry.

Practice 6

Add **one** set of parentheses to each sentence.

1. The tree by our front door(a weeping willow)is home to a family of robins.

2. My mother(whose maiden name is Wojcik)was born in a small town in Poland.

3. The Twice Around Resale Shop(it's at Fifth and Maple)has wonderful clothing bargains.

4. To perform this magic trick, you need (1) a styrofoam cup,(2)a rubber band, and (3) two feet of thread.

5. Harvey Whitman and Erica Whitman(they're not related)will conduct a seminar on leadership for company managers.

Name _____   Section _____   Date _____

Score: (Number right) _____ x 10 = _____ %

Punctuation Marks: TEST 1

Place a period (**.**), question mark (**?**), or exclamation point (**!**) at the end of each of the following sentences.

1. The moon is about 239,000 miles from Earth.

2. Are you ready for the test?

3. That's a great white shark heading toward the swimmers!

4. I wonder if this water is safe to drink.

5. I'm so happy right now I could fly!

6. I can't figure out how to turn on this computer.

7. Would you like some help with that suitcase?

8. Your choices for breakfast are scrambled eggs, pancakes, or cereal.

9. That man must be having a heart attack!

10. Did you take any notes in the class?

Name _____   Section _____   Date _____

Score: (Number right) _____ x 10 = _____ %

Punctuation Marks: **TEST 2**

Each of the following sentences needs one of the kinds of punctuation marks in the box. In the space provided, write the letter of the mark needed. Then add that mark to the sentence.

a Colon **:**	**d** Dash or dashes ——
b Semicolon **;**	**e** Parentheses **( )**
c Hyphen **-**	

____D____ **1.** Horrible acting, laughable dialogue, and a ridiculous plot‾if you like these things, you'll love this movie.

____B____ **2.** The soup simmered all morning;its delicious aroma filled the house.

____C____ **3.** The story of Ferdinand is about a fierce-looking bull who loves flowers.

____A____ **4.** Groucho Marx had this to say about people, dogs, and reading:"Outside of a dog, a book is man's best friend. Inside of a dog it's too dark to read."

____B____ **5.** The beach was clean and inviting;the water was cool and blue.

____A____ **6.** There will be auditions tomorrow for three parts in the play:the father, the mother, and the twelve-year-old daughter.

____C____ **7.** My usually soft-spoken brother began to shout angrily.

____D____ **8.** Before I waded into the pond, I noticed someone else was already there‾a baby alligator.

____E____ **9.** My grandfather(actually, he's my great-grandfather)will be visiting us over the holidays.

____A____ **10.** Eleanor Roosevelt wrote this about courage:"You gain strength, courage and confidence by every experience in which you really stop to look fear in the face. You are able to say to yourself, 'I lived through this horror. I can take the next thing that comes along.'"

17 Pronoun Forms

Basics about Pronouns

A **pronoun** is a word that can be used in place of a noun.

- Mel scrubbed the potatoes. Then **he** peeled some carrots.

  In the second sentence above, the word *he* is a pronoun that is used in place of the noun *Mel*.

For more information on pronouns, see "Parts of Speech," pages 212–214.

This chapter explains how to choose the correct pronoun to use in a sentence. It covers the following four areas:

1 Personal pronouns as subjects, objects, and possessives

2 Pronouns with *and* or *or*

3 Pronouns in comparisons

4 *Who* and *whom*

PERSONAL PRONOUNS AS SUBJECTS, OBJECTS, AND POSSESSIVES

Pronouns have different forms, or **cases**, depending on their use in a sentence. As explained below, they may serve as **subjects**, **objects**, or **possessives**.

Subject Pronouns

Subject pronouns act as the subjects of verbs. Here are the subject forms of personal pronouns:

	First Person	Second Person	Third Person
Singular	I	you	he, she, it
Plural	we	you	they

- **I** have an itch.

  I is the subject of the verb *have*.

- **She** always remembers her nieces' birthdays.

  She is the subject of the verb *remembers*.

- **They** agreed to the deal and shook hands.

  They is the subject of the verbs *agreed* and *shook*.

Object Pronouns

Object pronouns act as the objects of verbs or of prepositions. Here is a list of the object forms of personal pronouns:

	First Person	**Second Person**	**Third Person**
Singular	me	you	him, her, it
Plural	us	you	them

When a pronoun receives the action of a verb, an object pronoun should be used.

- Clara pinched **him**.
  Him receives the action of the verb *pinched*. *Him* tells who was pinched.

- Jeff is addicted to Coca-Cola. He drinks **it** for breakfast.
  It receives the action of the verb *drinks*. *It* tells what Jeff drinks for breakfast.

When a pronoun is the object of a preposition, an object pronoun should be used. Prepositions are words such as *to, for, with*, and *from*. (A longer list of prepositions is on page 4.)

- My sister tossed the car keys to **me**.
  Me is the object of the preposition *to*.

- Because it was her husband's birthday, Flo knitted a tie for **him**.
  Him is the object of the preposition *for*.

When the preposition *to* or *for* is understood, an object pronoun must still be used.

- My sister tossed **me** the car keys.
  The preposition *to* is implied before the pronoun *me*.

- Flo knitted **him** a tie.
  The preposition *for* is implied before the pronoun *him*.

Possessive Pronouns

Possessive pronouns show that something is owned, or possessed. Here are possessive forms of personal pronouns:

	First Person	**Second Person**	**Third Person**
Singular	my, mine	your, yours	his, her, hers, its
Plural	our, ours	your, yours	their, theirs

● If Lucille needs a sweater, she can borrow **mine**.
  Mine means *the sweater belonging to me.*

● The house lost most of **its** roof during the tornado.
  Its roof means *the roof belonging to the house.*

● Roger and Emily saw many of **their** friends at the party.
  Their friends means *the friends belonging to Roger and Emily.*

NOTE Possessive pronouns never contain an apostrophe.

● During the last storm, our apple tree lost all of **its** blossoms (not "it's blossoms").

Practice 1

Each sentence contains one pronoun. Underline each pronoun. Then, in the space provided, identify the pronoun by writing **S** for a subject pronoun, **O** for an object pronoun, and **P** for a possessive pronoun. The first item is done for you as an example.

__O__   **1.** The concert gave <u>me</u> a headache.

__P__   **2.** <u>Your</u> father is very friendly.

__S__   **3.** <u>They</u> once lived in Texas.

__O__   **4.** Read the letter out loud to <u>us</u>.

__S__   **5.** Apparently <u>she</u> is somebody famous.

__P__   **6.** The door on <u>my</u> closet has a broken hinge.

__O__   **7.** A stone almost hit <u>me</u> in the eye.

__O__   **8.** Stu gave <u>them</u> nothing but trouble.

__S__   **9.** <u>I</u> often forget to bring a calculator to math class.

__P__   **10.** Next Friday, <u>our</u> brother will be twenty-eight.

Practice 2

Fill in each blank with the appropriate pronoun in the margin. Before making your choice, decide if you need a subject, an object, or a possessive pronoun.

her, she   1. Over the summer, Melba changed ____her____ hair color, job, and boyfriend.

Me, I   2. ____I____ will treat you to lunch today.

our, us   3. Over the last ten years, twenty-three foster children have lived with ____us____.

your, you   4. You should iron ____your____ shirt before going to the job interview.

we, us   5. Would you bring ____us____ a bag of ice and some soda?

They, Them   6. ____They____ cannot find an apartment they like in this neighborhood.

I, me   7. Richard must give ____me____ a ride to school tomorrow.

him, his   8. When he died at the age of ninety-six, my great-grandfather still had all of ____his____ teeth.

he, him   9. Jill spotted her son on the playground and brought ____him____ a sandwich.

We, Us   10. ____We____ held a family meeting to decide how to split up household chores.

PRONOUNS WITH *AND* AND *OR*

Deciding which pronoun to use may become confusing when there are two subjects or two objects joined by *and* or *or*. However, the rules remain the same: Use a subject pronoun for the subject of a verb; use an object pronoun for the object of a verb or preposition.

- My brother and **I** loved *The Wizard of Oz* books.
  I is a subject of the verb *loved*. *Brother* is also a subject of *loved*.

- Our parents often read to my brother and **me**.
  Me is an object of the preposition *to*. *Brother* is also an object of *to*.

You can figure out which pronoun to use by mentally leaving out the other word that goes with *and* or *or*. For instance, in the first example above, omitting the words *my brother and* makes it clear that **I** is the correct pronoun to use: . . . **I** loved *The Wizard of Oz* books. (You would never say "**Me** loved *The Wizard of Oz* books.")

Try mentally omitting words in the following sentences. Then fill in each blank with the correct pronoun in parentheses.

- The prom was so long ago, I can't remember all of the details. Either Gene or *(I, me)* ____I____ drove. Furthermore, I can't remember whether Katie Davis went with him or *(I, me)* ____me____.

The correct choice for the first blank becomes clear when the words "Either Gene or" are omitted: *I drove. I* is a subject of the verb *drove*.

The correct choice for the second blank becomes clear when the words "him or" are omitted: *I can't remember whether Katie Davis went with . . . me. Me* is an object of the preposition *with*.

Practice 3

In each sentence, a choice of a subject or an object pronoun is given in parentheses. In the blank space, write the correct pronoun.

1. Is that package addressed to my brother or *(I, me)* __me__ ?

2. According to Jess, either *(he, him)* __he__ or his roommate will fix the broken window.

3. The piano is too heavy for Kate and *(she, her)* __her__ to move on their own.

4. Robbie and *(he, him)* __he__ first met when they were in the fourth grade.

5. That strong coffee kept Dad and *(we, us)* __us__ awake for hours.

6. My mother heard that the new position of floor manager will go to either her coworker Ken or *(she, her)* __her__.

7. For many years, *(we, us)* __we__ and Dale have sat next to each other at football games.

8. In the books about the Hardy boys, *(they, them)* __they__ and their detective father work together to solve mysteries.

9. Mark and *(I, me)* __I__ had been arguing loudly when our teacher walked into the room.

10. She simply frowned at Mark and *(I, me)* __me__ and left.

PRONOUNS IN COMPARISONS

When pronouns are used in comparisons, they often follow the word *than* or *as*.

● My best friend, Matt, is a better athlete than **I**.

● Rhonda's behavior puzzled you as much as **me**.

Words are often omitted in comparisons to avoid repetition. To see whether you should use a subject or an object pronoun, mentally fill in the missing words. In the first sentence above, *I* is the subject of the understood verb *am*:

● My best friend, Matt, is a better athlete than **I** [am].

In the second sentence, *me* is the object of the verb *puzzled*. That verb is understood, but not stated, in the second part of the comparison:

● Rhonda's behavior puzzled you as much as [it puzzled] me.

Now try to fill in the correct pronouns in the following comparisons:

● Brad was my first crush. I never adored anyone as much as *(he, him)* __him__.

● I had never met anyone as playful and kind as *(he, him)* __he__.

In the first blank above, you should have written the object form of the pronoun, *him*: *I never adored anyone as much as [I adored] him*. *Him* is the object of the verb *adored*, which is missing but understood in the sentence.

In the second blank above, you should have written the subject form of the pronoun, *he*: *I had never met anyone as playful and kind as he [was]*. *He* is the subject of the understood verb *was*.

Practice 4

In each sentence, a choice of a subject or an object pronoun is given in parentheses. In the blank space, write the correct pronoun.

1. Della has been in the choir longer than *(we, us)* _____we_____.

2. Our argument bothers you as much as *(I, me)* _____me_____.

3. Omar told his teammates he runs faster than *(they, them)* _____they_____.

4. My little brother is five inches taller than *(I, me)* _____I_____.

5. The math final worries me more than *(she, her)* _____her_____; she is hardly studying for it.

6. Our neighbors have a bigger house, but they don't give parties as often as *(we, us)* _____we_____.

7. As a child, I had a pet collie; there was no relative I loved as much as *(he, him)* _____him_____.

8. My family and our friends all caught the flu, but we weren't as sick as *(they, them)* _____they_____.

9. Julius hits the ball farther than his sister, but she runs the bases faster than *(he, him)* _____he_____.

10. That buzzing noise in the lamp annoys Dad more than *(we, us)* _____us_____; he has to leave the room.

WHO AND WHOM

Who is a subject pronoun; *whom* is an object pronoun.

● The person **who** owns the expensive car won't let anybody else park it.
Who owns the expensive car is a dependent word group. *Who* is the subject of the verb *owns.*

● The babysitter **whom** they trust cannot work tonight.
Whom they trust is a dependent word group. *Whom* is the object of the verb *trust.* The subject of *trust* is *they.*

As a general rule, to know whether to use *who* or *whom*, find the first verb after *who* or *whom*. Decide whether that verb already has a subject. If it doesn't have a subject, use the subject pronoun *who*. If it does have a subject, use the object pronoun *whom*.

See if you can fill in the right pronoun in the following sentences.

● The arrested person is a man *(who, whom)* _____whom_____ my sister once dated.

● The man and woman *(who, whom)* _____who_____ live next door argue constantly.

In the first sentence above, look at the verb *dated*. Does it have a subject? Yes, the subject is *sister*. Therefore the object pronoun *whom* is the correct choice: *The arrested person is a man whom my sister once dated. Whom* is the object of the verb *dated*.

In the second sentence above, look at the verb *live*. Does it have a subject? No. Therefore the subject pronoun *who* is the correct choice: *The man and woman who live next door argue constantly. Who* is the subject of the verb *live*.

NOTE In informal speech and writing, *who* is often substituted for *whom*:

● The babysitter who they trust cannot work tonight.

In formal writing, however, *whom* is generally used. In the practices and tests in this chapter, use the formal approach.

Practice 5

In each blank space, write the correct choice of pronoun.

1. The company hired a secretary *(who, whom)* _____who_____ can speak Spanish.

2. Ron's first boss was a man *(who, whom)* _____whom_____ he could not please.

3. I admire a man *(who, whom)* _____who_____ cries at movies.

4. Millard Fillmore is a President *(who, whom)* _____whom_____ few Americans remember.

5. Students *(who, whom)* _____who_____ cheated on the test were suspended.

WHO AND WHOM IN QUESTIONS

In questions, *who* is a subject pronoun, and *whom* is an object pronoun. You can often decide whether to use *who* or *whom* in a question in the same way you decide whether to use *who* or *whom* in a statement.

● **Who** should go?

   The verb after *who* is *should go*, which does not have another subject. Therefore use the subject form of the pronoun, *who*.

● **Whom** should I send?

   I is the subject of the verb *should send*, so use the object form of the pronoun, *whom*.

Practice 6

Fill in each blank with either *who* or *whom*.

1. *(Who, Whom)* _____Who_____ will do the dishes tonight?

2. *(Who, Whom)* _____Whom_____ were you expecting?

3. *(Who, Whom)* _____Who_____ woke up in the middle of the night?

4. *(Who, Whom)* _____Who_____ is making all that racket?

5. *(Who, Whom)* _____Whom_____ did you just call on the phone?

Name _____   Section _____   Date _____

Score: (Number right) _____ x 10 = _____ %

Pronoun Forms: TEST 1

Fill in each blank with the appropriate pronoun from the margin.

She, Her   1. _____She_____ got the highest grade on the mid-term test.

they, their   2. The twins had braces on _____their_____ teeth for three years.

we, us   3. "We are sure," Len said, "that getting married is the right thing for ____us____."

they, them   4. Since my aunt and uncle enjoy basketball more than I do, I gave the tickets to _____them_____.

I, me   5. She and _____I_____ have been friends since we were little children.

he, him   6. I don't know whether to believe you or _____him_____.

she, her   7. Hector and his sister both speak some Spanish, but Hector is more fluent than _____she_____.

he, him   8. We enjoyed no teacher as much as _____him_____; he was always interesting.

who, whom   9. Our mayor is a former nun _____who_____ decided to enter politics.

who, whom   10. The principal is a young man _____whom_____ both students and teachers respect.

Name _____   Section _____   Date _____

Score: (Number right) _____ x 10 = _____ %

Pronoun Forms: TEST 2

Fill in each blank with the appropriate pronoun from the margin.

we, us   1. You are welcome to drive to the meeting with _____us_____.

they, their   2. All of my blue jeans have holes in _____their_____ knees.

I, me   3. My mother changes her mind more frequently than _____I_____.

who, whom   4. The man _____whom_____ the car hit is my uncle.

we, us   5. Next weekend, you and _____we_____ should go to a movie together.

I, me   6. My dog and _____I_____ often hike in the woods for hours at a time.

she, her   7. Sarah's boss said there was no employee he valued as much as _____her_____.

he, him   8. Does that red sports car belong to his parents or _____him_____?

who, whom   9. The mechanic _____who_____ usually works on our car is on vacation.

he, him   10. When the cruise ship's captain sailed too close to shore and his ship capsized,

_____he_____ and his passengers had a dangerous adventure.

18 Pronoun Problems

Three Common Pronoun Problems

This chapter explains three common problems with pronouns:

1 Pronoun shifts in number   A pronoun must agree in number with the noun it refers to.

Incorrect	Each of my sisters has **their** own room.
Correct	Each of my sisters has **her** own room.

2 Pronoun shifts in person   Pronouns must be consistent in person. Unnecessary shifts in person (for example, from *I* to *one*) confuse readers.

Incorrect	**One's** patience runs thin when I am faced with a slow-moving line at the bank.
Correct	**My** patience runs thin when I am faced with a slow-moving line at the bank.

3 Unclear pronoun reference   A pronoun must clearly refer to the noun it stands for.

Incorrect	Michael gave Arnie **his** car keys. (Does *his* refer to Michael or Arnie?)
Correct	Michael gave **his** car keys to Arnie.

PRONOUN SHIFTS IN NUMBER

A pronoun must agree in number with the noun it refers to, which is called the pronoun's **antecedent**. Singular nouns require singular pronouns; plural nouns require plural pronouns.

In the following examples, pronouns are printed in **boldface type**; the antecedents are printed in *italic* type.

- The dying *tree* lost all **its** leaves.
  The antecedent *tree* is singular, so the pronoun must be singular: *its*.

- When *Vic* was in the Army, **his** little brother wrote to **him** almost every day.
  The antecedent *Vic* is singular, so the pronouns must be singular: *his* and *him*.

- Do the *neighbors* know that **their** dog is loose?
  The antecedent *neighbors* is plural, so the pronoun must be plural: *their*.

- *Sarah and Greg* act like newlyweds, but **they** have been married for years.
  The antecedent *Sarah and Greg* is plural, so the pronoun must be plural: *they*.

Practice 1

In each blank space, write the noun or nouns that the given pronoun refers to.

Example   The ridges on our fingertips have a function. They help fingers to grasp things.

They refers to _____ridges_____.

1. The photographer realized her flash attachment wasn't working.
   Her refers to _____photographer_____.

2. The cat hid its kittens in the hayloft.
   Its refers to _____cat_____.

3. Kate and Barry don't get along with their stepfather.
   Their refers to _____Kate and Barry_____.

4. Martin never drinks coffee in the evening. It keeps him awake all night.
   It refers to _____coffee_____.

5. Onion and pineapple taste good on pizza, but they don't taste good on the same pizza.
   They refers to _____onion and pineapple_____.

Practice 2

In the spaces provided for each sentence, write **(a)** the pronoun used and **(b)** the noun or nouns that the pronoun refers to.

1. The movie started late, and it was badly out of focus.
   The pronoun _____it_____ refers to _____movie_____.

2. Marlene buys most of her clothing at thrift shops.
   The pronoun _____her_____ refers to _____Marlene_____.

3. As the horse neared the finish line, his energy ran out.
   The pronoun _____his_____ refers to _____horse_____.

4. A man was at the door a minute ago, but now he is gone.
   The pronoun _____he_____ refers to _____man_____.

5. Carla and Vicki are twins, but they don't look alike.
   The pronoun _____they_____ refers to _____Carla and Vicki_____.

Indefinite Pronouns

Most pronouns refer to one or more particular persons or things. However, **indefinite pronouns** do not refer to particular persons or things. The following indefinite pronouns are always singular:

anybody	either	neither	one
anyone	everybody	no one	somebody
anything	everyone	nobody	someone
each	everything	nothing	something

Something has left **its** muddy footprints on the hood of the car.

● *One* of my sisters has lost **her** job.

● *Everybody* is entitled to change **his** or **her** mind.

The indefinite pronouns *something, one,* and *everybody* are singular. The personal pronouns that refer to them must also be singular: *its, his,* or *her.*

Note on Gender Agreement Choose a pronoun that agrees in gender with the noun it refers to. Because *one of my sisters* is clearly feminine, use *her.* But *everybody* includes males and females, so use *his or her.* If *his or her* seems awkward in a sentence, try rewriting the sentence with a plural subject:

● People are entitled to change **their** minds.

The following indefinite pronouns are always plural:

both	many	several
few	other	

● *Both* of my brothers worked **their** way through college.
  Both, the subject of this sentence, is plural, so the plural pronoun *their* is used.

The following indefinite pronouns are singular or plural, depending on their context:

all	more	none
any	most	some

● *Some* of the pie is fine, but its crust is burnt.
  Some here refers to one thing—the pie, so the singular pronoun *its* is used.

● *Some* of the students forgot their books.
  Some here refers to several students, so the plural pronoun *their* is used.

Practice 3

In the spaces provided for each sentence, write **(a)** the pronoun or pronouns needed and **(b)** the word that the pronoun or pronouns refer to.

Example   Neither of the boys has had *(his / their)* measles shot yet.

The pronoun needed is _____*his*_____. The word it refers to is _____*neither*_____.

1. Everything in the office has *(its / their)* own place.

   The pronoun needed is _____*its*_____. The word it refers to is _____*everything*_____.

2. Neither of my uncles has ever smoked in *(his / their)* life.

   The pronoun needed is _____*his*_____. The word it refers to is _____*neither*_____.

3. Many restaurants in town post *(its / their)* menus in the window.

   The pronoun needed is _____*their*_____. The word it refers to is _____*restaurants*_____.

4. Don't eat any of those grapes until you've washed *(it / them)*.

   The pronoun needed is _____*them*_____. The word it refers to is _____*grapes*_____.

5. Is anyone brave enough to read *(their / his or her)* essay aloud to the class?

   The pronoun needed is _____*his or her*_____. The word it refers to is _____*anyone*_____.

6. Both of the girls invited *(her mother / their mothers)* to the mother-daughter luncheon.

   The pronoun needed is _____*their*_____. The word it refers to is _____*both*_____.

7. Everyone is waiting for *(their / his or her)* final grades to be posted online.

   The pronoun needed is _____*his or her*_____. The word it refers to is _____*everyone*_____.

8. Nobody can enter that factory without *(their / his or her)* security badge.

   The pronoun needed is _____*his or her*_____. The word it refers to is _____*nobody*_____.

9. Most of the room has been painted, and *(it looks / they look)* much brighter now.

   The pronoun needed is _____*it*_____. The word it refers to is _____*room*_____.

10. Most of the invitations have been addressed, but *(it still needs / they still need)* to be stamped.

    The pronoun needed is _____*they*_____. The word it refers to is _____*invitations*_____.

A Note on Collective Nouns

A **collective noun** refers to a group of persons or things considered to be a unit. Collective nouns are usually singular. Following are some examples.

audience	committee	group	quartet
band	couple	herd	society
class	family	jury	team

- The *class* started late, and **it** ended early.
  Class refers to a single unit, so the singular pronoun *it* is used.

However, if a collective noun refers to the individual members of the group, a plural pronoun is used.

- The *class* handed in **their** essays before vacation.

Many writers feel it is awkward to use a collective noun as a plural. They prefer to revise the sentence.

- The class *members* handed in **their** essays before vacation.

PRONOUN SHIFTS IN PERSON

A pronoun that refers to the person who is speaking is called a **first-person pronoun**. Examples of first-person pronouns are *I, me,* and *our.* A pronoun that refers to someone being spoken to, such as *you,* is a **second-person pronoun**. And a pronoun that refers to another person or thing, such as *he, she,* or *it,* is a **third-person pronoun**.

Following are the personal pronouns in first-, second-, and third-person groupings:

	First Person	**Second Person**	**Third Person**
Singular	I, me, my, mine	you, your, yours	he, him, his; she, her, hers; it, its
Plural	we, us, our, ours	you, your, yours	they, them, their, theirs

When a writer makes unnecessary shifts in person, the writing may become less clear. The sentences below, for example, show some needless shifts in person. (The words that show the shifts are **boldfaced**.)

- The trouble with **my** sending e-mails to friends is that sometimes **you** don't get a response.
  The writer begins with the first-person pronoun *my,* but then shifts to the second-person pronoun *you.*

- Though **we** like most of **our** neighbors, there are a few **you** can't get along with.
  The writer begins with the first-person pronouns *we* and *our,* but then shifts to the second-person pronoun *you.*

These sentences can be improved by eliminating the shifts in person:

- The trouble with **my** sending e-mails to friends is that sometimes **I** don't get a response.
- Though **we** like most of **our** neighbors, there are a few **we** can't get along with.

Practice 4

Write the correct pronoun in each space provided.

they, we 1. Whenever students are under a great deal of stress, __they__ often stop studying.

one, you 2. If you want to do well in this course, __you__ should plan on doing all the assignments on time.

you, me 3. When I took a summer job as a waitress, I was surprised at how rude some customers were to __me__.

we, you 4. It's hard for us to pay for health insurance, but __we__ don't dare go without it.

you, I 5. When __I__ drive on the highway, I get disgusted at the amount of trash I see.

I, you 6. Although I like visiting my Aunt Rita, __I__ always feel as if my visit has disrupted her life.

you, we 7. We don't answer the door after 10:00 at night, because __we__ never know what kind of danger might be lurking on the other side of the door.

I, one 8. I would like to go to a school where __I__ can meet many people who are different from me.

you, they 9. Dog owners should put tags on their dogs in case __they__ lose their pets.

we, they 10. People often take a first-aid course so that __they__ can learn how to help choking and heart-attack victims.

UNCLEAR PRONOUN REFERENCE

A pronoun must refer clearly to its **antecedent**—the word it stands for. If it is unclear which word a pronoun refers to, the sentence will be confusing. As shown below, some pronouns are unclear because they have two possible antecedents. Others are unclear because they have no antecedent.

Two Possible Antecedents

A pronoun's reference will not be clear if there are two possible antecedents.

- Eva told her mother that she had received a postcard from Alaska.
  Who received the postcard, Eva or her mother?
- I wrote a to-do list with my purple pen, and now I can't find it.
  What can't the writer find, the list or the pen?

An unclear sentence with two antecedents can sometimes be corrected by using the speaker's exact words.

- Eva told her mother, "**I** received (or: "**You** received) a postcard from Alaska."

For an explanation of how to use quotation marks, see pages 63–64 in "Quotation Marks."

In some cases, the best solution is to replace the pronoun with the word it was meant to refer to.

- I wrote a to-do list with my purple pen, and now I can't find **the list** (*or:* **the pen**).

No Antecedent

A pronoun's reference will not be clear if there is no antecedent.

- We just received our cable TV bill. **They** said the Disney Channel is providing a free preview next month.

  Who said there's a free preview? We don't know because *they* has no word to refer to.

- My older brother is a chemist, but **that** doesn't interest me.

  What doesn't interest the writer? The pronoun *that* doesn't refer to any word in the sentence.

To correct an unclear reference in which a pronoun has no antecedent, replace the pronoun with the word or words it is meant to refer to.

- We just received our cable TV bill. **The cable company** said the Disney Channel is providing a free preview next month.

- My older brother is a chemist, but **chemistry** doesn't interest me.

 Practice 5

In each sentence below, underline the correct word or words in parentheses.

1. At a local deli, (*they* / <u>*the owners*</u>) provide each table with a free bowl of pickles.

2. My cell phone must be somewhere in this apartment, but I have no idea just where (*it* / <u>*the phone*</u>) is.

3. Rita asked Paula (*if she could help with the dishes.* / , <u>*"Can I help with the dishes?"*</u>)

4. In a letter from Publisher's Clearing House, (*they* / <u>*the contest organizers*</u>) all but promise that I have already won ten million dollars.

5. When my cousins arrived at the picnic with the homemade pies, (<u>*my cousins*</u> / *they*) were very welcome.

Practice 6

Revise each sentence to eliminate the unclear pronoun reference.   *Wording of revisions may vary.*

1. When Nick questioned the repairman, he became very upset.

    When Nick questioned the repairman, the repairman [OR Nick] became very

    upset.

2. My parents are expert horseshoe players, but I've never become any good at it.

    My parents are expert horseshoe players, but I've never become any good at

    horseshoes.

3. Mary Alice told her sister that her boyfriend was moving to another state.

    Mary Alice told her sister, "My boyfriend is moving to another state." [OR

    "Your boyfriend is moving to another state."]

4. I bought a stationary bicycle that has a timer, but I never use it.

    I bought a stationary bicycle that has a timer, but I never use the timer. [OR

    I never use the bicycle.]

5. I went to the hardware store for 100-watt light bulbs, but they didn't have any.

    I went to the hardware store for 100-watt light bulbs, but the clerks didn't

    have any.

Name _____   Section _____   Date _____

Score: (Number right) _____ x 10 = _____ %

Pronoun Problems: TEST 1

A. In each blank space, write the pronoun that agrees in number with the word or words it refers to.

its, their   **1.** The school has asbestos in many of _____*its*_____ classrooms.

her, their   **2.** My mother and her sister often share _____*their*_____ clothing and jewelry.

his or her, their   **3.** No one in the computer lab could remember _____*his or her*_____ password.

her, their   **4.** Neither of the little girls wants to share _____*her*_____ toys.

B. For each sentence, cross out the pronoun that makes a shift in person. Then, in the space provided, write a pronoun that corrects the shift in person.

_____*them*_____   **5.** Two people in my family work at a store where the owners don't provide ~~you~~ with any health insurance.

_____*I*_____   **6.** I wanted to see the movie star, but ~~one~~ couldn't get past her security guard.

_____*their*_____ **7.** Members of that gang said they feel the gang is like ~~your~~ family.

C. In each sentence below, choose the correct word or words and write them in the space provided.

8. Lonnie stopped at the post office and asked _____*a postal worker*_____ to hold his mail while he was on vacation.
   a. a postal worker
   b. them

9. Carrie told Linda _____*, "You got four phone calls this afternoon."*_____
   _____
   a. that she had gotten four phone calls that afternoon.
   b. , "You got four phone calls this afternoon."

10. Andrea could be a cafeteria server again next semester, but she really hates _____
   _____*working in the cafeteria.*_____
   a. it.
   b. working in the cafeteria.

Name _____ Section _____ Date _____

Score: (Number right) _____ x 10 = _____ %

Pronoun Problems: TEST 2

A. In each blank space, write the pronoun that agrees in number with the word or words it refers to.

his, their   **1.** Each of my brothers has _____ his _____ own television.

its, their   **2.** Some of the businesses in town have a day-care center for the children of
_____ their _____ employees.

her, their   **3.** One of the hens has laid _____ her _____ egg on an old blanket in the shed.

his or her, their   **4.** Everybody in our apartment building was told to keep _____ his or her _____
door locked at all times.

B. For each sentence, cross out the pronoun that makes a shift in person. Then, in the space provided,
write a pronoun that corrects the shift in person.

_____ me _____   **5.** The constant ringing of my telephone often drives ~~one~~ crazy.

_____ they _____   **6.** If people want something from the kitchen, ~~you~~ have to go and get it.

__ he (OR she) __   **7.** The newspaper carrier didn't realize that ~~you~~ would have to deliver papers at 5 a.m.

C. In each sentence below, choose the correct word or words and write them in the space provided.

8. Jeanine is a devoted user of coupons at the supermarket, but I can't find the time for _____
_____ collecting coupons. _____
   a. it.
   b. collecting coupons.

9. Ian told his father _____ , "You're late for your doctor's appointment." _____

_____
   a. he was late for his doctor's appointment.
   b. , "You're late for your doctor's appointment."

10. In this letter from the bank, _____ the customer service manager says _____
my mother's account is overdrawn.
   a. the customer service manager says
   b. they say

Basics about Adjectives and Adverbs

This chapter explains the following:

1 How to identify adjectives and adverbs

- The **circular** *(adjective)* house is **unusual** *(adjective).*
- The **extremely** *(adverb)* small boy climbed the rope **very** *(adverb)* **quickly** *(adverb).*

2 How to use adjectives and adverbs in comparisons

- I'm a **worse** cook than my brother, but our sister is the **worst** cook in the family.

3 How to use two troublesome pairs: *good* and *well*, *bad* and *badly*

- I can usually work **well** and do a **good** job even when I don't feel **well**.
- In addition to his **bad** attitude, the outfielder has been playing **badly**.

4 How to avoid double negatives

Incorrect   I **can't hardly** wait for summer vacation.
Correct   I **can hardly** wait for summer vacation.

IDENTIFYING ADJECTIVES AND ADVERBS

Adjectives

An **adjective** describes a noun or pronoun. It generally answers such questions as "What kind of?" "Which one?" "How many?"

An adjective may come before the noun or pronoun it describes.

- The **weary** hikers shuffled down the **dusty** road.
  The adjective *weary* describes the noun *hikers*; it tells what kind of hikers. The adjective *dusty* describes the noun *road*; it tells what kind of road.

- The **green** car has **two** antennas.
  The adjective *green* tells which car has the antennas. The adjective *two* tells how many antennas there are.

- Don't go to the **new** movie at the mall unless you want a **good** nap.
  The adjective *new* tells which movie; the adjective *good* tells what kind of nap.

An adjective that describes the subject of a sentence may also come after a linking verb (such as *is, were, looks,* and *seem*).

- That dog's skin is **wrinkled** and **dry**.
  The adjectives *wrinkled* and *dry* describe the subject, *skin*. They follow the linking verb *is*.

For more information on linking verbs, see "Subjects and Verbs," pages 3 and 147–148.

Practice 1

Complete each sentence with an appropriate adjective. Then underline the noun or pronoun that the adjective describes.

Answers will vary.

Examples   My _____favorite_____ sweater had shrunk in the wash.

The school principal was _____strict_____.

1. This _____rainy_____ weather really bothers me.

2. I'm in the mood for a(n) _____action_____ movie.

3. I've never read such a(n) _____depressing_____ book.

4. A(n) _____selfish_____ person makes a poor boss.

5. My aunt has an unusually _____soft_____ voice.

6. That chocolate chip cheesecake is _____terrific_____.

7. My _____favorite_____ pants are at the cleaners.

8. It's too bad that you are so _____shy_____.

9. _____Rose_____ bushes are growing in front of the house.

10. Selena posted a(n) _____new_____ photo on her Facebook page.

Adverbs

An **adverb** is a word that describes a verb, an adjective, or another adverb. Many adverbs end in *-ly*. Adverbs generally answer such questions as "How?" "When?" "Where?" "How much?"

- The chef **carefully** spread raspberry frosting over the cake.
  The adverb *carefully* describes the verb *spread*. *Carefully* tells how the chef spread the frosting.

- Put the package **there**.
  The adverb *there* describes the verb *put*. *There* (meaning "in that place") tells where the package should be put.

- Ann was **extremely** embarrassed when she stumbled on stage.
  The adverb *extremely* describes the adjective *embarrassed*. It tells how much Ann was embarrassed.

- That lamp shines **very brightly**.
  The adverb *very* describes the adverb *brightly*. *Very* tells how brightly the lamp shines. The adverb *brightly* describes the verb *shines*; it tells how the lamp shines.

Adverbs with Action Verbs

Be careful to use an adverb—not an adjective—with an action verb. Compare the following:

Incorrect	Correct
The boss slept sound at his desk. *Sound* is an adjective.	The boss slept **soundly** at his desk.
The graduates marched proud. *Proud* is an adjective.	The graduates marched **proudly**.
The batter swung wild at all the pitches. *Wild* is an adjective.	The batter swung **wildly** at all the pitches.

Practice 2

Complete each sentence with the adverb form of the adjective in the margin. (Change each adjective in the margin to an adverb by adding -*ly*.)

Example   *quick*   Sandra read the book too _____quickly_____.

bright   **1.** The soap bubbles glistened _____brightly_____ in the midday sun.

helpless   **2.** The family watched _____helplessly_____ as their house burned.

hurried   **3.** The two teachers spoke _____hurriedly_____ between classes.

shy   **4.** The little girl peeked _____shyly_____ at her new neighbor.

honest   **5.** A good businessperson deals _____honestly_____ with everyone.

quiet   **6.** The old woman hummed _____quietly_____ as she did her shopping.

longing   **7.** The cat stared _____longingly_____ at the leftover tuna casserole.

frequent   **8.** Cable TV channels _____frequently_____ show the same movie ten or more times in one month.

soft   **9.** The police officer spoke _____softly_____ to the terrified children.

serious   **10.** Many teenagers complain that their parents don't take them _____seriously_____.

Practice 3

Complete each sentence correctly with either the adverb or adjective in the margin.

rapid, rapidly   1. Felipe spoke _____ rapidly _____ in Spanish to his grandfather.

rapid, rapidly   2. Their _____ rapid _____ conversation was difficult for me to follow.

quiet, quietly   3. The frog sat _____ quietly _____ on a lily pad.

patient, patiently   4. The mother is _____ patient _____ with her youngster.

patient, patiently   5. Ravi waited _____ patiently _____ for the elevator to arrive.

willing, willingly   6. How many of you are _____ willing _____ to sell tickets for the play?

prompt, promptly   7. The invitation asks for a _____ prompt _____ response.

quick, quickly   8. The helicopter descended _____ quickly _____ toward the hospital.

cheerful, cheerfully 9. Olga smiled _____ cheerfully _____ at the customer.

cheerful, cheerfully 10. Her _____ cheerful _____ smile warmed the room.

USING ADJECTIVES AND ADVERBS IN COMPARISONS
Comparing Two Things

In general, to compare two things, add *-er* to adjectives and adverbs of one syllable.

● Grilling food is **faster** than roasting.
  The adjective *faster* is used to compare two methods: grilling and roasting.

● My mother works **longer** each day than my father.
  The adverb *longer* is used to compare how long two people work each day.

For longer adjectives and adverbs, do not add *-er*. Instead, add the word *more* when comparing two things.

● My dog is **more intelligent** than my cat.
  The words *more intelligent* describe the subject *dog*; they are being used to compare two things, the dog and the cat.

● Marie sings **more sweetly** than I do.
  The words *more sweetly* describe the verb *sings*; they compare the ways two people sing.

Practice 4

Write in the correct form of the word in the margin by adding either *-er* or *more*.

Examples   **thin**   Kate is _____ thinner _____ than her twin sister.

        carefully   I prefer to ride with Dan. He drives _____ more carefully _____ than you.

cheap   1. This bag of potato chips is _____ cheaper _____ than that one.

affectionate 2. My dog is _____ more affectionate _____ than my boyfriend.

gray   **3.** This shirt looks _____grayer_____ than it did before I washed it.

neat   **4.** The inside of Ed's car is _____neater_____ than the inside of my apartment.

ridiculous **5.** There are no shows on TV _____more ridiculous_____ than those reality shows about bachelors and bachelorettes.

Comparing Three Things

In general, to compare three or more things, add *-est* to adjectives and adverbs of one syllable.

● Grilling food is faster than roasting, but microwaving is **fastest** of all.

  The adjective *fastest* is used to compare three methods: grilling, roasting, and microwaving. It indicates that microwaving is faster than the other two.

● My mother works longer each day than my father, but in my family, I work **longest**.

  The adverb *longest* is used to compare how long three or more people work each day. It indicates that of the three, I work the most number of hours.

For longer adjectives and adverbs, do not add *-est*. Instead, add the word *most* when comparing three or more things.

● My dog is more intelligent than my cat, but my parrot is the **most intelligent** pet I have ever had.

  Most intelligent is used to compare three animals. It shows which one is the smartest.

● Among the couples I know, my brother and sister-in-law are the **most happily** married of all.

  Most happily is used to compare how happy many married couples are. It indicates that my brother and sister-in-law are more happily married than any of the other couples I know.

 Practice 5

Write in the correct form of the word in the margin by adding either *-est* or *most*.

Examples cold   The _____coldest_____ it ever gets around here is about zero degrees Fahrenheit.

delightful   The _____most delightful_____ play of the year is now at the Morgan Theater.

young   **1.** Eliza is the _____youngest_____ of eight children.

important   **2.** The _____most important_____ thing in Julia's life is clothes.

fresh   **3.** The Metro Mart has the _____freshest_____ vegetables in town.

artistic   **4.** Of the eighteen students in my class, Juan is the _____most artistic_____.

difficult   **5.** My brother enjoys playing the _____most difficult_____ video games he can find.

Notes about Comparisons

1   Do not use both an *-er* ending and *more*, or an *-est* ending and *most*.

Incorrect   My uncle's hair is more curlier than my aunt's.

Correct   My uncle's hair is **curlier** than my aunt's.

2   Certain short adjectives and adverbs have irregular forms:

	Comparing two	Comparing three or more
bad, badly	worse	worst
good, well	better	best
little	less	least
much, many	more	most

● The grape cough syrup tastes **better** than the orange syrup, but the lemon cough drops taste the **best**.

● Sid is doing **badly** in speech class, but I'm doing even **worse**.

Practice 6

Cross out the incorrect word or words of comparison in each of the following sentences. Then write the correction on the line provided.

Example   _____easier_____   The test was ~~more easier~~ than I expected.

_____worst_____   **1.** That was the ~~baddest~~ accident I've ever seen.

_____better_____   **2.** It is ~~gooder~~ to try and fail than not to try at all.

_____older_____   **3.** My mother is ~~more older~~ than my father.

_____less_____   **4.** I use ~~littler~~ oil in my cooking than I used to.

_____sweeter_____   **5.** This grapefruit is actually ~~more sweeter~~ than that orange.

_____least_____   **6.** This year we had the ~~most little~~ rain we've had in years.

_____most beautiful_____   **7.** I think the peacock is the ~~most beautifulest~~ of all birds.

_____worse_____   **8.** The macaroni salad tastes ~~worser~~ than the potato salad.

_____most_____   **9.** Cheap Charlie's is the ~~more~~ expensive of all the variety stores in town.

_____less_____   **10.** I'm on a diet, so put ~~more little~~ mayonnaise on my sandwich than usual.

USING TWO TROUBLESOME PAIRS: GOOD AND *WELL*, *BAD* AND *BADLY*

Good is an adjective that often means "enjoyable," "talented," or "positive."

- I had a **good** day.
- Sue is a **good** skier.
- Think **good** thoughts.

As an adverb, *well* often means "skillfully" or "successfully."

- Sue skis **well**.
- The schedule worked **well**.
- Pedro interacts **well** with others.

As an adjective, *well* means "healthy."

- The patient is **well** once again.

Bad is an adjective. *Badly* is an adverb.

- I look **bad**.

  Bad is an adjective that comes after the linking verb *look*. It describes the appearance of the subject of the sentence, *I*.

- I need sleep **badly**.

  Badly is an adverb that describes the verb *need*. It explains how much the sleep is needed.

Practice 7

Complete the sentence with the correct word in the margin.

good, well   1. Ike hums really _____well_____.

good, well   2. Did you have a _____good_____ day at school?

bad, badly   3. I need a haircut _____badly_____.

bad, badly   4. My mother has a really _____bad_____ headache.

good, well   5. No student did very _____well_____ on the math test.

bad, badly   6. Luckily, no one was _____badly_____ hurt in the accident.

good, well   7. It is a very _____good_____ sign that Granddad is no longer coughing or running a temperature.

bad, badly   8. After a week on a liquids-only diet, Ben looks really _____bad_____.

good, well   9. Keep taking the antibiotic until it's gone, even if you think you are completely _____well_____.

good, well   10. Working in a nursing home was a _____good_____ experience for Tamika.

AVOIDING DOUBLE NEGATIVES

In standard English, it is incorrect to express a negative idea by pairing one negative with another. Common negative words include *not, nothing, never, nowhere, nobody,* and *neither.* To correct a double negative, either eliminate one of the negative words or replace a negative with a positive word.

Incorrect	I **shouldn't** go **nowhere** this weekend.
Correct	I **should** go **nowhere** this weekend.
Correct	I **shouldn't** go **anywhere** this weekend.

Shouldn't means *should not,* so the first sentence above contains two negatives: *not* and *nowhere.* In the first correct sentence, *not* has been eliminated. In the second correct sentence, *nowhere* has been replaced with the positive word: *anywhere.*

The words *hardly, scarcely,* and *barely* are also negatives. They should not be paired with other negatives such as *never* and *not.* Correct a double negative containing *hardly, scarcely,* or *barely* by eliminating the other negative word.

Incorrect	I **couldn't scarcely** recognize you.
Correct	I **could scarcely** recognize you.

 Practice 8

Correct the double negative in each sentence by crossing out one of the negative words and writing any additional correction above the line.

Example   I won't ~~never~~ go to that restaurant again.
                         ever

   OR   I ~~won't~~ never go to that restaurant again.
                    will

1. Don't ~~never~~ stick anything into an electrical outlet.
   ever [OR: ~~Don't~~]

2. The two sisters ~~don't~~ scarcely speak to one another.
   [OR: ~~scarcely~~]

3. I ~~won't~~ never believe a word that Vicky says.
   will [OR: ~~never~~ ever]

4. Some days I feel that I can't do ~~nothing~~ right.
   anything [OR: ~~can't~~ can]

5. Ken can't go ~~nowhere~~ without running into one of his ex-girlfriends.
   anywhere [OR: ~~can't~~ can]

6. It's so dark in this room that I ~~can't~~ scarcely read.
   can [OR: ~~scarcely~~]

7. My neighbor shouldn't ~~never~~ have tried to fix the roof on her own.
   ever [OR: ~~shouldn't~~ should]

8. My father ~~can't~~ hardly hear the TV unless he turns the volume all the way up.
   can [OR: ~~hardly~~]

9. Nobody ~~wouldn't~~ believe what happened to me in class today.
   would

10. That salesperson ~~won't~~ never stop trying, even when a customer starts walking away.
    will [OR: ~~never~~ ever]

Name _____   Section _____   Date _____

Score: (Number right) _____ x 10 = _____ %

Adjectives and Adverbs: TEST 1

Cross out the adjective or adverb error in each sentence, and write the correction in the space at the left.

Example _____*sweeter*_____   This peach is ~~more sweeter~~ than candy.

_____*suddenly*_____   **1.** We braked our car ~~sudden~~ to avoid a dog.

_____*good*_____   **2.** How did you get to be so ~~well~~ in math?

_____*calmly*_____   **3.** Let's try to settle our disagreement ~~calm~~.

_____*faster*_____   **4.** To get a job as a secretary, I will have to be able to type ~~more faster~~.

_____*nicest*_____   **5.** James is the ~~most nicest~~ of all the waiters.

_____*well*_____   **6.** I feel pretty good, but the doctor says I'm not ~~good~~ yet.

_____*carefully*_____   **7.** Sam printed his name ~~careful~~ across the top of the page.

_____*brightly*_____   **8.** Although it is cold, the sun is shining ~~bright~~.

_____*anything*_____   **9.** Nobody knows ~~nothing~~ about why the manager was fired.

_____*better*_____   **10.** My sister has a ~~more good~~ chance than I do of making the team.

Name _____   Section _____   Date _____

Score: (Number right) _____ x 10 = _____ %

Adjectives and Adverbs: TEST 2

Each short paragraph below contains **two** errors in adjective and/or adverb use. Find the errors and cross them out. Then write the correct form of each word or words in the space provided.

1. We eat three different kinds of cereal in my house. One teenager wants the ~~most sweetest~~ sugar-coated cereal he can find. The other doesn't like ~~nothing~~ sweet, so he eats shredded wheat instead. I eat hot oatmeal every morning.

   a. _____ *sweetest* _____

   b. _____ *anything* _____

2. Many people become ~~bad~~ depressed during the winter. Their mood improves ~~quick~~ when they receive natural-light therapy.

   a. _____ *badly* _____

   b. _____ *quickly* _____

3. I can't decide which book to read for my report. *The Old Man and the Sea* is ~~more short~~ than *The Great Gatsby*, so at first I thought I'd read that. But now that I've glanced through *Gatsby*, it seems the ~~most interesting~~ book.

   a. _____ *shorter* _____

   b. _____ *more interesting* _____

4. Mr. Kensington has the ~~goodest~~ sense of humor in his family. For instance, he'll say that his knee is stiff from a war injury. But if you ask him to explain, he'll tell you ~~cheerful~~ that he got old and his knee "wore out."

   a. _____ *best* _____

   b. _____ *cheerfully* _____

5. Nothing is ~~more good~~ on a cold day than cuddling up on the sofa with hot cocoa and a good magazine. But I've got so much studying to do lately that I ~~haven't scarcely~~ any time to read anything but textbooks.

   a. _____ *better* _____

   b. _____ *have scarcely* _____

Misplaced and Dangling Modifiers

Basics about Misplaced and Dangling Modifiers

This chapter explains two common modifier problems:

1 Misplaced modifiers

Incorrect   The man bought a tie at the department store **with yellow and blue stripes**.

Correct   The man bought **a tie with yellow and blue stripes** at the department store.

2 Dangling modifiers

Incorrect   **Biting my lip**, not laughing was difficult.

Correct   **Biting my lip, I found it difficult** not to laugh.

MODIFIERS

A **modifier** is one or more words that describe another word or word group. For example, the modifier below is **boldfaced**, and the word it modifies is <u>underlined</u>.

● My cousin has a <u>cat</u> **with all-white fur**.
  The modifier *with all-white fur* describes *cat*.

Here are a few more examples:

● The <u>woman</u> **behind the cash register** is the owner of the store.
● I have **nearly** <u>a thousand</u> baseball cards.
● He <u>printed</u> his name **neatly**.

MISPLACED MODIFIERS

A **misplaced modifier** is a modifier that is incorrectly separated from the word or words that it describes. Misplaced modifiers seem to describe words that the author did not intend them to describe. When modifiers are misplaced, the reader may misunderstand the sentence. Generally, the solution is to place the modifier as close as possible to the word or words it describes. Look at the following examples.

Misplaced modifier   Sam bought a used car from a local dealer with a smoky tailpipe.

Corrected version   Sam bought a used <u>car</u> **with a smoky tailpipe** from a local dealer.

In the first sentence above, the modifier *with a smoky tailpipe* is misplaced. Its unintentional meaning is that the local dealer has a smoky tailpipe. To avoid this meaning, place the modifier next to the word that it describes, *car*.

Misplaced modifier   The robin built a nest at the back of our house of grass and string.

Corrected version   The robin built a <u>nest</u> **of grass and string** at the back of our house.

In the first sentence above, the words *of grass and string* are misplaced. Because they are near the word *house*, the reader might think that the house is made of grass and string. To avoid this meaning, place the modifier next to the word that it describes, *nest*.

Misplaced modifier   Take the note to Mr. Henderson's office which Kim wrote.

Corrected version   Take the <u>note</u> **which Kim wrote** to Mr. Henderson's office.

In the first sentence above, the words *which Kim wrote* are misplaced. The words must be placed next to *note*, the word that they are clearly meant to describe.

Following is another example of a sentence with a misplaced modifier. See if you can correct it by putting the modifier in another place in the sentence. Write your revision on the lines below.

Misplaced modifier   I am going to New Orleans to visit my aunt on a train.

I am going on a train to New Orleans to visit my aunt.

_____

The original version of the sentence seems to say that the speaker will visit with his aunt on the train. However, the modifier *on a train* is meant to tell how the speaker is going to New Orleans. To make that meaning clear, the modifier needs to be placed closer to the words *am going*: "I <u>am</u> <u>going</u> **on a train** to New Orleans to visit my aunt."

Practice 1

Underline the misplaced words in each sentence. Then rewrite the sentence in the space provided, placing the modifier where its meaning will be clear.

1. I'm returning the swimsuit to the store <u>that makes me look fat</u>.

   I'm returning the swimsuit that makes me look fat to the store.

   _____

2. The plants by the lamp <u>with small purple blossoms</u> are violets.

   The plants with small purple blossoms by the lamp are violets.

   _____

3. We watched as our house burned to the ground <u>with helpless anger</u>.

   We watched with helpless anger as our house burned to the ground.

   _____

4. The woman in that boat <u>that is waving</u> is trying to tell us something.

   The woman that is waving in that boat is trying to tell us something.

   _____

5. The two students at the corner table <u>eating pizza</u> were laughing loudly.

   The two students eating pizza at the corner table were laughing loudly.

   _____

Certain Single-Word Modifiers

Certain single-word modifiers—such as *almost, only, nearly,* and *even*—limit the words they modify. Such single-word modifiers must generally be placed before the word they limit.

Misplaced modifier	Christie almost sneezed fifteen times last evening.
Corrected version	Christie sneezed **almost** <u>fifteen</u> times last evening.

Because the word *almost* is misplaced in the first sentence, readers might think Christie *almost sneezed* fifteen times, but in fact did not sneeze at all. To prevent this confusion, put *almost* in front of the word it modifies, *fifteen.* Then it becomes clear that Christie must have sneezed a number of times.

Practice 2

Underline the misplaced word in each sentence. Then rewrite the sentence in the space provided, placing the modifier where its meaning will be clear.

1. Carrie <u>nearly</u> has sixty freckles on her face.

   Carrie has nearly sixty freckles on her face.
   _____

2. I <u>only</u> studied one hour for my midterm test.

   I studied only one hour for my midterm test.
   _____

3. I didn't <u>even</u> make one mistake on the midterm test.

   I didn't make even one mistake on the midterm test.
   _____

4. The terrible fall <u>nearly</u> broke every bone in the skier's body.

   The terrible fall broke nearly every bone in the skier's body.
   _____

5. By the end of the war, twenty countries were <u>almost</u> involved in the fighting.

   By the end of the war, almost twenty countries were involved in the fighting.
   _____

DANGLING MODIFIERS

You have learned that a misplaced modifier is incorrectly separated from the word or words it describes. In contrast, a **dangling modifier** has no word in the sentence to describe. Dangling modifiers usually begin a sentence. When a modifier begins a sentence, it must be followed right away by the word or words it is meant to describe. Look at this example:

Dangling modifier	Sitting in the dentist's chair, the sound of the drill awakened Larry's old fears.

The modifier *sitting in the dentist's chair* is followed by *the sound of the drill.* This word order suggests that the sound of the drill was sitting in the dentist's chair. Clearly, that is not what the author intended. The modifier was meant to describe the word *Larry.* Since the word *Larry* is not in the sentence (*Larry's* is a different form of the word), it is not possible to correct the dangling modifier simply by changing its position in the sentence.

Here are two common ways to correct dangling modifiers.

Method 1   Follow the dangling modifier with the word or words it is meant to modify.

After the dangling modifier, write the word it is meant to describe, and then revise as necessary. Using this method, we could correct the sentence about Larry's experience at the dentist's office like this:

Correct version   Sitting in the dentist's chair, **Larry found that** the sound of the drill awakened **his** old fears.

Now the modifier is no longer dangling. It is followed by the word it is meant to describe, *Larry*.

Following is another dangling modifier. How could you correct it using the method described above? Write your correction on the lines below.

Dangling modifier   Depressed and disappointed, running away seemed the only thing for me to do.

Depressed and disappointed, I felt that running away was the only thing for me to do.

_____

The dangling modifier in the above sentence is *depressed and disappointed*. It is meant to describe the word *I*, but there is no *I* in the sentence. So you should have corrected the sentence by writing *I* after the opening modifier and then rewriting as necessary: "Depressed and disappointed, **I felt that** running away **was** the only thing for me to do."

Practice 3

Underline the dangling modifier in each sentence. Then, on the lines provided, revise the sentence, using the first method of correction.   *Revisions may vary.*

1. <u>Out of money</u>, my only choice was to borrow from a friend.
   Out of money, I decided that my only choice was to borrow from a friend.

   _____

2. <u>While jogging</u>, a good topic for Anton's English paper occurred to him.
   While jogging, Anton thought of a good topic for his English paper.

   _____

3. <u>Vacuuming the living room</u>, my cat frightened me by running around in frantic circles.
   Vacuuming the living room, I was frightened by my cat running around in frantic circles.

   _____

4. <u>Moving around the sun</u>, Earth's speed is more than 66,000 miles per hour.
   Moving around the sun, Earth travels at a speed of more than 66,000 miles per hour.

   _____

5. <u>Loudly booing and cursing</u>, the fans' disapproval of the call was clear.
   Loudly booing and cursing, the fans clearly showed their disapproval of the call.

   _____

Method 2   Add a subject and a verb to the opening word group.

The second method of correcting a dangling modifier is to add a subject and a verb to the opening word group, and revise as necessary. We could use this method to correct the sentence about Larry's experience at the dentist's office.

Dangling modifier   Sitting in the dentist's chair, the sound of the drill awakened Larry's old fears.

Correct version   **As Larry was** sitting in the dentist's chair, the sound of the drill awakened **his** old fears.

In this revision, the subject *Larry* and the verb *was* have been added to the opening word group.

Following is the dangling modifier that you revised using the first method of correction. How could you correct it using the second method? Write your revision on the lines below.

Dangling modifier   Depressed and disappointed, running away seemed the only thing for me to do.

Because I was depressed and disappointed, running away seemed like the only thing

for me to do.

You should have revised the sentence so that *I* and the appropriate verb are in the opening word group: "**Because I was** depressed and disappointed, running away seemed like the only thing for me to do."

Practice 4

Underline the dangling modifier in each sentence. Then, on the lines provided, revise the sentence, using the second method of correction.

1. While waiting for an important call, Peg's phone began making weird noises.
   While Peg was waiting for an important call, her phone began making weird noises.

2. After being shampooed, Trish was surprised by the carpet's new look.
   After the carpet was shampooed, Trish was surprised by its new look.

3. Still half asleep, the bright morning sun flooded Jen's room and woke her up in time for class.
   Although Jen was still half asleep, the bright morning sun flooded her room and woke her up in time for class.

4. After eating one too many corn dogs, Stella's stomach rebelled.
   After Stella ate one too many corn dogs, her stomach rebelled.

5. Born on the Fourth of July, Rob's birthday cake was always red, white, and blue.
   Because Rob was born on the Fourth of July, his birthday cake was always red, white, and blue.

Name _____ Section _____ Date _____

Score: (Number right) _____ x 10 = _____ %

Misplaced and Dangling Modifiers: TEST 1

In each sentence, underline the **one** misplaced or dangling modifier. (The first five sentences contain misplaced modifiers; the second five sentences contain dangling modifiers.) Then rewrite each sentence so that its intended meaning is clear. *Some revisions may vary.*

1. The customer demanded that the waiter take her order <u>rudely</u>.
   The customer rudely demanded that the waiter take her order.
   _____

2. I peeled the potatoes before I cooked them <u>with a paring knife</u>.
   I peeled the potatoes with a paring knife before I cooked them.
   _____

3. In one week, the cat <u>nearly</u> had caught every mouse in the house.
   In one week, the cat had caught nearly every mouse in the house.
   _____

4. The child playing on the jungle gym <u>with fuzzy orange hair</u> is my nephew.
   The child with fuzzy orange hair playing on the jungle gym is my nephew.
   _____

5. We discovered an Italian bakery a few miles from our house that <u>had just opened</u>.
   We discovered an Italian bakery that had just opened a few miles from our house.
   _____

6. After <u>visiting the bakery</u>, the aroma of freshly baked bread filled our car.
   After we visited the bakery, the aroma of freshly baked bread filled our car.
   _____

7. <u>Lying on the sunny beach</u>, thoughts of skin cancer began to enter my mind.
   As I lay on the sunny beach, thoughts of skin cancer began to enter my mind.
   _____

8. <u>Not meaning to be cruel</u>, George's careless remark hurt Jackie's feelings.
   Not meaning to be cruel, George hurt Jackie's feelings with his careless remark.
   _____

9. <u>Though not a fan of science fiction</u>, the *Star Trek* movies, to my surprise, have all been enjoyable.
   Though not a fan of science fiction, I found the Star Trek movies, to my surprise, all
   very enjoyable.

10. <u>Exhausted by his first day at school</u>, Sam's eyes closed in the middle of his favorite TV show.
   Exhausted by his first day at school, Sam closed his eyes in the middle of his favorite
   TV show.

Name _____   Section _____   Date _____

Score: (Number right) _____ x 10 = _____ %

Misplaced and Dangling Modifiers: TEST 2

Each group of sentences contains **one** misplaced modifier and **one** dangling modifier. Underline the two errors. Then, on the lines provided, rewrite the sentences that contain the errors so that the intended meanings are clear.   *Some revisions may vary.*

1. I mailed a letter to my cousin who lives in Alaska <u>without a stamp</u>. <u>Embarrassed</u>, the post office sent it back to me a week later.

    I mailed a letter without a stamp to my cousin who lives in Alaska. I was embarrassed

    when the post office sent the letter back to me a week later.

    _____

2. Lin's mother answered the door, and Jim asked if he could speak to Lin <u>politely</u>. <u>Impressed with Jim's manner</u>, the answer was "Certainly. Please come in."

    Lin's mother answered the door, and Jim asked politely if he could speak to Lin.

    Impressed with Jim's manner, her mother answered, "Certainly. Please come in."

    _____

3. The thunderstorm ended, and Shannon saw the sun burst through the clouds. <u>Searching the sky</u>, a glorious rainbow appeared. It <u>nearly</u> lasted a minute and then faded from view.

    . . . As she was searching the sky, a glorious rainbow appeared. It lasted nearly a

    minute and then faded from view.

    _____

4. <u>Not meaning to embarrass you</u>, but please answer a question about your birthday present. Will you wear the sweater that I bought for you <u>ever</u>? If you won't, I could exchange it for something else.

    I don't mean to embarrass you, but please answer a question about your birthday

    present. Will you ever wear the sweater that I bought for you?

    _____

5. Most of Ms. Nichol's students were gazing blankly into space one warm spring day. In fact, Ms. Nichol noticed that two students <u>only</u> were paying attention. <u>Clapping her hands together sharply</u>, the students woke up from their daydreams.

    . . . In fact, Ms. Nichol noticed that only two students were paying attention. When she

    clapped her hands together sharply, the students woke up from their daydreams.

    _____

21 Word Choice

Basics about Word Choice

Not all writing problems involve grammar. A sentence may be grammatically correct, yet fail to communicate well because of the words that the writer has chosen. This chapter explains three common types of ineffective word choice:

1 Slang

Slang	My sister is **something else**.
Revised	My sister is a very special person.

2 Clichés

Cliché	This semester, I have **bitten off more than I can chew**.
Revised	This semester, I have taken on more work than I can manage.

3 Wordiness

Wordy	It is **absolutely essential and necessary** that you borrow some folding chairs for the party.
Revised	It is essential that you borrow some folding chairs for the party.

SLANG

Slang expressions are lively and fun to use, but they should be avoided in formal writing. One problem with slang is that it's not always understood by all readers. Slang used by members of a particular group (such as teenagers or science-fiction fans) may be unfamiliar to people outside of the group. Also, slang tends to change rapidly. What was *cool* for one generation is *awesome* for another. Finally, slang is by nature informal. So while it adds color to our everyday speech, it is generally out of place in writing for school or work. Use slang only when you have a specific purpose in mind, such as being humorous or communicating the flavor of an informal conversation.

Slang	After a bummer of a movie, we pigged out on a pizza.
Revised	After a **disappointing** movie, we **devoured** a pizza.

Practice 1

Rewrite the slang expression (printed in *italic type*) in each sentence.   Revisions may vary.

1. Tiffany did not *have a clue about* what was being taught in her science class.
   _____ understand _____

2. When my parents see my final grades, I will be *dead meat*.
   _____ in trouble _____

3. Everyone was *grossed out* when the cat brought home a dead rat.

disgusted

_____

4. Exhausted by their trip, the twins *sacked out* as soon as they got home.

fell asleep

_____

5. Freddie is really *in la-la land* if he thinks he can make a living as a juggler.

unrealistic

_____

CLICHÉS

A cliché is an expression that was once lively and colorful. However, because it has been used too often, it has become dull and boring. Try to use fresh wording in place of predictable expressions. Following are a few of the clichés to avoid in your writing:

Common Clichés

avoid like the plague	last but not least	sick and tired
better late than never	light as a feather	sigh of relief
bored to tears	make ends meet	time and time again
easy as pie	pie in the sky	tried and true
in the nick of time	pretty as a picture	under the weather
in this day and age	sad but true	without a doubt

Cliché   Our new family doctor is as sharp as a tack.
Revised   Our new family doctor is **very insightful**.

Practice 2

Rewrite the cliché (printed in *italic type*) in each sentence.   Revisions may vary.

1. Although the box was *light as a feather*, Jeremy refused to carry it.

extremely light

_____

2. *In this day and age*, teenagers face many temptations.

Today

_____

3. Smoking cigarettes is *playing with fire*.

very risky

_____

4. On the first day of summer vacation, I felt *free as a bird*.

carefree

_____

5. Luke must really have been tired because he *slept like a log* all morning.

slept soundly

_____

WORDINESS

Some writers think that using more words than necessary makes their writing sound important. Actually, wordiness just annoys and confuses your reader. Try to edit your writing carefully.

First of all, remove words that mean the same as other words in the sentence, as in the following example.

Wordy   Though huge in size and blood red in color, the cartoon monster had a sweet personality.

Revised   Though **huge** and **blood red**, the cartoon monster had a sweet personality.

Huge refers to size, so the words *in size* can be removed with no loss of meaning. *Red* is a color, so the words *in color* are also unnecessary. Following is another example of wordiness resulting from repetition. The author has said the same thing twice.

Wordy   Scott finally made up his mind and decided to look for a new job.

Revised   Scott finally **decided** to look for a new job.

Secondly, avoid puffed-up phrases that can be expressed in a word or two instead.

Wordy   Due to the fact that the printer was out of paper, Renee went to a store for the purpose of buying some.

Revised   **Because** the printer was out of paper, Renee went to a store **to buy** some.

In general, work to express your thoughts in the fewest words possible that are still complete and clear. Notice, for example, how easily the wordy expressions in the box below can be replaced by one or two words. The wordy expressions in the box on the next page can be made concise by eliminating repetitive words.

Wordy Expression	Concise Replacement
a large number of	many
at an earlier point in time	before
at this point in time	now
be in possession of	have
due to the fact that	because
during the time that	while
each and every day	daily
in order to	to
in the event that	if
in the near future	soon
in this day and time	today
made the decision to	decided

> **Examples of Wordiness due to Repetition**
>
> few ~~in number~~   listened ~~with his ears~~
>
> green ~~in color~~   punched ~~with his fist~~
>
> postponed ~~until later~~   ~~the feeling of~~ sadness
>
> small ~~in size~~   ~~hurriedly~~ rushed
>
> the first paragraph ~~at the beginning~~ of the chapter

See if you can revise the following wordy sentence by

1 replacing one group of words and

2 eliminating two unnecessary words.

> *Wordy* Owing to the fact that I was depressed, I postponed my guitar lesson until later.
>
> Because I was depressed, I postponed my guitar lesson.
> _____

The wordy expression *owing to the fact that* can be replaced by the single word *because* or *since*. The words *until later* can be eliminated with no loss of meaning. Here's a concise version of the wordy sentence: "Because I was depressed, I postponed my guitar lesson."

Practice 3

Underline the **one** example of wordiness in each sentence that follows. Then rewrite the sentence as clearly and concisely as possible. *Revisions may vary.*

Example   I suddenly realized that my date <u>was not going to show up and had stood me up.</u>

I suddenly realized that my date was not going to show up.
_____

1. <u>Due to the fact that</u> Lionel won the lottery, he won't be coming to work today.
   Because Lionel won the lottery, he won't be coming to work today.
   _____

2. My sister <u>went ahead and made the decision</u> to take a job in Maryland.
   My sister decided to take a job in Maryland.
   _____

3. Jeff hid his extra house key and now has forgotten <u>the location where it is.</u>
   Jeff hid his extra house key and now has forgotten where it is.
   _____

4. I do not know <u>at this point in time</u> if I will be going to this school next year.
   I do not know now if I will be going to this school next year.
   _____

5. Daily exercise <u>every day of the week</u> gives me more energy.
   Daily exercise gives me more energy.
   _____

Name _____   Section _____   Date _____

Score: (Number right) _____ x 10 = _____ %

Word Choice: TEST 1

A. Each sentence below contains **one** example of slang or clichés. Underline the error and then rewrite it, using more effective language.   *Revisions may vary.*

1. All morning I have been <u>as nervous as a long-tailed cat in a room full of rocking chairs</u>.

    _____ *extremely nervous* _____

2. Maddie was <u>slow as molasses</u> getting ready for school this morning.

    _____ *very slow* _____

3. After our first science lab, I felt totally <u>clueless</u>.

    _____ *confused* _____

4. Public interest in the upcoming election seems <u>dead as a doornail</u>.

    _____ *to have died out* _____

5. Dad <u>freaked out</u> when I got home at 3 a.m.

    _____ *lost his temper* _____

B. Underline the **one** example of wordiness in each sentence that follows. Then rewrite the sentence as concisely as possible.

6. We were glad to hear the test had been postponed <u>until a later date</u>.

    We were glad to hear the test had been postponed.

7. Because <u>of the fact that</u> it was raining, we canceled our trip.

    Because it was raining, we canceled our trip.

8. Please call me <u>at the point in time</u> when you are ready to go.

    Please call me when you are ready to go.

9. The store opens at 10 a.m. <u>in the morning</u>.

    The store opens at 10 a.m.

10. Reba forgot her jacket and had to return <u>back again</u> to her house for it.

    Reba forgot her jacket and had to return to her house for it.

Name _____   Section _____   Date _____

Word Choice: TEST 2

Each item below contains **two** examples of ineffective word choice: slang, clichés, or wordiness. Underline the errors. Then rewrite each underlined part as clearly and concisely as possible.   *Revisions may vary.*

1. <u>In the event that</u> I get the part-time job, I <u>will heave a sigh of relief</u>.

   a. If _____

   b. be relieved _____

2. Thirty-seven students signed up for the creative writing class, but only twenty-four could be accepted. The other thirteen were really <u>bummed out</u>. They asked the teacher to consider opening a second section of the class, but he <u>gave them the cold shoulder</u>.

   a. disappointed _____

   b. ignored them _____

3. Wally assembled the big circular track for his son's model train. Then he <u>connected the cars, hooking them up together</u>. Finally, he threw the switch and watched the train glide around the track. He was <u>as pleased as punch</u> that it all worked perfectly.

   a. connected the cars _____

   b. very pleased _____

4. The microwave oven I bought from your store is <u>a loser</u>. Although I have followed the manufacturer's instructions, the oven has never worked properly. I expect you to replace the oven without delay <u>in the very near future</u>. If that is not possible, please return my money.

   a. defective _____

   b. very soon _____

5. The movie I saw last night was advertised as a comedy, but I didn't laugh once. Instead, it <u>completely weirded me out</u>. It showed married people who hated one another and parents who shouted at their children. Why do people <u>in this day and age</u> think it is funny for people to mistreat one another?

   a. made me feel uneasy _____

   b. today _____

Numbers and Abbreviations

Basics about Numbers and Abbreviations

This chapter explains the following:

1 When to write out numbers (*one, two*) and when to use numerals (*1, 2*)

2 When to use abbreviations and which ones to use

NUMBERS

Here are guidelines to follow when using numbers.

1 **Spell out any number that can be written in one or two words. Otherwise, use numerals.**

- When my grandmother turned **sixty-nine**, she went on a **fifteen**-day trip across **nine** states.

- The mail carrier delivered **512** pieces of mail today.

NOTE When written out, numbers twenty-one through ninety-nine are hyphenated.

2 **Spell out any number that begins a sentence.**

- **Eight hundred and seventy-one** dollars was found in the briefcase.

To avoid writing out a long number, you can rewrite the sentence:

- The briefcase contained **$871**.

3 **If one or more numbers in a series need to be written as numerals, write all the numbers as numerals.**

- The movie theater sold **137** tickets to a horror movie, **64** to a comedy, and **17** to a romance.

4 **Use numerals to write the following.**

a Dates

- My grandfather was born on July **4, 1949**.

b Times of the day

- The last guest left at **1:45** a.m.

But when the word *o'clock* is used, the time is spelled out:

- I got home at **six o'clock**.

Also spell out the numbers when describing amounts of time:

- Marian worked **fifty** hours last week.

c Addresses

- The bookstore is located at **1216** North **48th** Street.

d Percentages

- Nearly **70** percent of the class volunteered for the experiment.

e Pages and sections of a book
- Jeff read pages **9–57** of the novel, which includes chapters **2** and **3**.

f Exact amounts of money that include change
- My restaurant bill was **$28.49**.

g Scores
- The Sacramento Kings beat the Los Angeles Lakers **94–90**.
- People with an IQ over **145** are considered geniuses.

5 When writing numerals, use commas to indicate thousands.
- Angie has **1,243** pennies in a jar.
- The number that comes after **999,999** is **1,000,000**.

BUT Do not use commas in telephone numbers (1-800-555-1234), zip codes (08043), street numbers (3244 Oak Street), social security numbers (372-45-0985), or years (2015).

Practice 1

Cross out the **one** number mistake in each sentence. Then write the correction in the space provided.

_____50_____ **1.** No wonder these cookies cost $5.25—they're ~~fifty~~ percent butter!

_____two_____ **2.** The pro football player wore a gold earring and ~~2~~ diamond rings.

_____seven_____ **3.** By ~~7~~ o'clock, the temperature had dipped below freezing.

_____2001_____ **4.** Nelson began working at his present job in ~~two thousand and one~~.

_____40_____ **5.** For next week, please read pages 1 through ~~forty~~ in Chapter 1.

_____Twenty-six_____ **6.** ~~26~~ students helped out at the homeless shelter at 31 South Lake Street.

_____2:45_____ **7.** Last night I woke up at midnight and didn't fall asleep again until ~~two forty-five~~.

_____ten_____ **8.** Did you know that an official baseball weighs about five ounces and a regulation basketball hoop is ~~10~~ feet above the floor?

_____50_____ **9.** For their wedding, the couple invited 260 people—210 of the bride's friends and relatives and ~~fifty~~ of the groom's.

_____2,456_____ **10.** In the mayoral election, the winner received ~~two thousand four hundred and fifty-six~~ more votes than her nearest opponent.

ABBREVIATIONS

Abbreviations can save you time when taking notes. However, you should avoid abbreviations in papers you write for classes. The following are among the few abbreviations that are acceptable in formal writing.

1   Titles that are used before and after people's names
- **Ms.** Glenda Oaks
- **Dr.** Huang
- Keith Rodham, **Sr.**

2   Initials in a person's name
- Daphne **A.** Miller
- **T.** Martin Sawyer

3   Time and date references
- The exam ended at 4:45 **p.m.**
- Cleopatra lived from about 69 to 30 **B.C.**

4   Organizations, agencies, technical words, countries, or corporations known by their initials. They are usually written in all capital letters and without periods.
- YMCA
- FBI
- DVD
- AIDS
- USA
- NBC

Practice 2

Cross out the **one** abbreviation mistake in each sentence. Then write the correction in the space provided.

century   **1.** Buddhism was founded in the sixth ~~cent.~~ B.C. by Buddha.

Philadelphia   **2.** Dr. Diamond works for the YMCA in ~~Phila.~~

Canada   **3.** Mr. Ostrow emigrated from Russia to ~~Can.~~ in 1995.

Monday   **4.** On ~~Mon.~~, Tim has an appointment at IBM with Ms. Janice Grant.

Kansas   **5.** Dwight D. Eisenhower was born in Abilene, ~~Kan.~~, in 1890.

William   **6.** My brother ~~Wm.~~ uses TiVo to record all his favorite television shows.

retired   **7.** When my grandfather ~~retd.~~, he volunteered to work with a local AIDS group.

number   **8.** In 1970, the FBI expanded the ~~nmbr.~~ of criminals on its most-wanted list from ten to sixteen.

California   **9.** My cousin is getting married at 9:30 a.m. on the beach in Santa Cruz, ~~Calif.~~

college   **10.** According to an NBC reporter, many of today's ~~coll.~~ students drink in binges.

Name _____ Section _____ Date _____

Score: (Number right) _____ x 10 = _____ %

Numbers and Abbreviations: TEST 1

Cross out the **one** number or abbreviation mistake in each of the following sentences. Then write the correction on the line provided.

One hundred and two   **1.** ~~102~~ patients visited Dr. Jamison's clinic today.

three   **2.** I wrote ~~3~~ protest letters to CBS when my favorite show was canceled.

university   **3.** That ~~univ.~~ has 143 professors and 894 students.

population   **4.** Davenport, Iowa, has a ~~pop.~~ of over 100,000.

hospital   **5.** The ~~hosp.~~ has treated eighteen patients with AIDS.

superintendent   **6.** Mr. Pidora has been ~~supt.~~ of schools for the past nine years.

eight   **7.** We finally reached the outskirts of New York City at ~~8~~ o'clock.

_13_   **8.** Only ~~thirteen~~ percent of the customers preferred the new brand of cereal.

_$1,220_   **9.** The IRS says my aunt owes ~~one thousand, two hundred and twenty dollars~~ in back taxes.

sandwich   **10.** I got up at 2:30 a.m. and made myself a tuna ~~sand.~~ on rye.

Name _____ Section _____ Date _____

Score: (Number right) _____ x 10 = _____ %

Numbers and Abbreviations: TEST 2

Cross out the **one** number or abbreviation mistake in each of the following sentences. Then write the correction on the line provided.

_____five_____ **1.** Ms. Bradley begins her day at ~~5~~ o'clock.

_____January_____ **2.** An officer of the NAACP will speak on campus in ~~Jan.~~

_____thirty_____ **3.** Shelly watched a program on PBS for ~~30~~ minutes before going to work.

_____reference_____ **4.** I listed Dr. Keenan as a ~~ref.~~ on my resumé.

_____80_____ **5.** The vendors sold ~~eighty~~ soft pretzels, 145 soft drinks, and 106 hot dogs.

_____Francisco_____ **6.** While in San ~~Fran.,~~ we were part of a six-car accident on the Golden Gate Bridge.

_____America_____ **7.** The twenty-seven students in Mrs. Greene's class are learning about South ~~Amer.~~

_____Boulevard_____ **8.** The YWCA on Waverly ~~Blvd.~~ is having an open house in two weeks.

_____$1.50_____ **9.** Since the meal was about ten dollars, the tip should be at least ~~one dollar and fifty cents.~~

_____11_____ **10.** On September ~~eleven,~~ 2001, terrorists attacked the World Trade Center and the Pentagon.

23 More about Subjects and Verbs

More about Subjects

THE SUBJECT AND DESCRIPTIVE WORDS

A subject is often accompanied by one or more words that describe it. See if you can find the subjects of the following sentences and the words that describe them.

- A very large truck stalled on the bridge.
- Some tomatoes are yellow.
- Two young boys were playing catch in the alley.

In the first sentence, *truck* is the subject. The words *a*, *very*, and *large* describe the word *truck*. In the second sentence, *tomatoes* is the subject, and *some* and *yellow* describe it. In the third sentence, the subject is *boys*; the words describing that subject are *two* and *young*.

For more information on descriptive words (also known as adjectives and adverbs), see "Adjectives and Adverbs," pages 115-124, and "Parts of Speech," pages 251–262.

Practice 1

Insert an appropriate word into each of the following blanks. The word that you add will be the subject of the sentence. It will tell who or what the sentence is about.   Answers will vary.

1. A _____burglar_____ crept through the dark house.

2. Only three _____apples_____ are left in the refrigerator.

3. A _____tourist_____ approached me on the street corner.

4. David's gold _____chains_____ glittered in the sunlight.

5. _____Fran_____ reminded me to eat some lunch.

6. Several _____kittens_____ were crowded into the small cage.

7. _____Julie_____ ate the raspberries right from the box.

8. _____English_____ is my favorite school subject.

9. Without a sound, a _____hawk_____ grabbed the field mouse by the neck.

10. My mother never went to college. _____She_____ has always felt bad about that.

THE SUBJECT AND PREPOSITIONAL PHRASES

The subject of a sentence is never part of a prepositional phrase. As explained on page 4, a **prepositional phrase** is a group of words that begins with a preposition (a word like *in*, *from*, *of*, or *with*) and ends with a noun or pronoun (the object of the preposition). Following are some common prepositions:

about	before	down	like	to
above	behind	during	of	toward
across	below	except	off	under
after	beneath	for	on	up
among	beside	from	over	with
around	between	in	since	without
at	by	into	through	

Here are a few examples of prepositional phrases:

- in the house
- of the world
- from the bakery
- with your permission

Now look at the sentence below. What is the subject? Write your answer here: _____ *bunch* _____

- A bunch of green grapes fell onto the supermarket floor.

   The answer is *bunch*, but many people would be tempted to choose *grapes*. In this case, however, *grapes* is part of the prepositional phrase *of green grapes*, so it cannot be the subject.

As you look for the subject of a sentence, it may help to cross out the prepositional phrases. For example, look at the following sentences. In each sentence, find the prepositions and cross out the prepositional phrases. Then underline the subject. After finding each subject, read the explanation that follows.

- The sick <u>man</u>, ~~with shaking hands~~, poured the pills ~~from the brown bottle~~.

   The prepositions are *with* and *from*. Cross out *with shaking hands* and *from the brown bottle*, and you are left with the sentence *The sick man poured the pills*. Ask yourself, "Who poured the pills?" The answer, *man*, is the subject of the sentence.

- A <u>student</u> ~~in the class~~ fell asleep ~~during the long lecture~~.

   In and *during* are prepositions. You should have crossed out the prepositional phrases *in the class* and *during the long lecture*. When you do this, you are left with the sentence *A student fell asleep*. Ask yourself, "Who fell asleep?" The answer, *student*, is the subject of the sentence.

For more information on prepositions, see "Parts of Speech," pages 251–262.

Practice 2

Cross out the **one** prepositional phrase in each sentence. Then underline the subject of the sentence.

Example The pack ~~of cookies~~ disappeared quickly.

1. The blueberries ~~in this pie~~ are bitter.

2. ~~On weekends~~, Troy works overtime.

3. The woman ~~with a pierced nose~~ is my hair stylist.

4. Leaves ~~from our neighbor's tree~~ covered our lawn.

5. ~~During the school play~~, the lead actress lost her voice.

6. Some ~~of the used books~~ have missing pages.

7. ~~Like her father~~, Abby adores baseball.

8. The dust ~~under your bed~~ contains tiny creatures.

9. One ~~of my best friends~~ is a computer programmer.

10. ~~From my bedroom window~~, I can watch my neighbor's TV.

A Note on Singular and Plural Subjects

In addition to finding subjects, you should note whether a subject is **singular** (one) or **plural** (more than one). Most plural subjects simply end in *s*:

Singular	The **car** in front of us is speeding.
Plural	The **cars** in front of us are speeding.

Some plural subjects are irregular:

Singular	The **child** was crying.
Plural	The **children** were crying.

A **compound subject** is two or more subjects connected by a joining word such as *and*. Compound subjects are usually plural.

Compound	The **car** and the **truck** in front of us are speeding.

For more information on compound subjects, see "Subject-Verb Agreement," pages 15–20.

Practice 3

Underline the subject or subjects of each sentence. Then in the space on the left, write **S** if the subject is singular and **P** if the subject is plural.

Example ___P___ Love and hate are closely related emotions.

___P___ **1.** The leaves on our new houseplant are turning yellow.

___P___ **2.** Books are often my best companions.

___P___ **3.** A cat and a dog sometimes become best friends.

___P___ **4.** The guitarist and drum player do not like each other.

___S___ **5.** The aroma of barbecued ribs tempts almost everyone.

___P___ **6.** Three men in my family are named Michael.

___S___ **7.** This envelope has a postmark from Chicago.

___P___ **8.** Our oven and refrigerator are both out of order right now.

___S___ **9.** A deck of cards is useful for many different games.

___P___ **10.** Every summer, tourists and mosquitoes descend on the Florida coast.

More about Verbs

Every complete sentence contains a verb. In general, as explained briefly on page 3, there are two types of verbs: **action verbs** and **linking verbs**.

FINDING ACTION VERBS

See if you can double-underline the action verb in the following two sentences. Then read the explanations.

- The moon disappeared behind the clouds.
- The impatient customer tapped her fingers on the counter.

In looking for the verb in the first sentence, you can eliminate the prepositional phrase *behind the clouds*. That leaves the words *the moon disappeared*. The *moon* is what did something, so it is the subject of the sentence. What did the moon do? It *disappeared*. So *disappeared* is the action verb.

In the second sentence, you can also eliminate a prepositional phrase: *on the counter*. That leaves *The impatient customer tapped her fingers*. The subject is *customer*—that's who did something. What did the customer do? She *tapped* (her fingers). So *tapped* is the action verb in that sentence.

Just as a sentence can contain a compound subject, a sentence can contain a **compound verb**: two or more verbs that have the same subject or subjects. For example, here's another version of one of the sentences above:

- The impatient customer tapped her fingers on the counter and cleared her throat.

In this version, the customer did two things: *tapped* (her fingers) and *cleared* (her throat). Therefore, the subject *customer* has a compound verb: *tapped* and *cleared*.

In case you have trouble finding the verb of a sentence, here is one other way to identify a verb: Try putting a pronoun such as *I, you, he, she, it,* or *they* in front of the word you suspect is a verb. If the word is a verb, the resulting sentence will make sense. Notice, for instance, that for the sentences on the previous page, *it disappeared* and *she tapped* make sense.

Practice 4

Double-underline the action verb or verbs in each sentence. You may find it helpful to first identify and underline the subject and to cross out any prepositional phrases.

1. Members ~~of the audience~~ applauded loudly.

2. ~~Before the party,~~ I took a short nap ~~on the living-room couch.~~

3. ~~Without warning,~~ the can ~~of red paint~~ slid ~~off the ladder.~~

4. Wesley tripped ~~on the steps~~ and dropped all his packages.

5. The huge tree ~~on the front lawn~~ shades our front porch ~~in the afternoon.~~

6. Aunt Lois opened the package and gasped ~~in delight.~~

7. A German shepherd waited patiently ~~for his owner~~ to return.

8. The angry bull snorted loudly and charged ~~at the red blanket.~~

9. ~~Because of her fear of zombies,~~ my little sister sleeps ~~with a light on.~~

10. ~~By 7 a.m.,~~ impatient shoppers were gathering ~~at the front entrance of the mall for a special sale.~~

LINKING VERBS

Linking verbs do not show action. **Linking verbs** join (or link) the subject to one or more words that describe the subject. Look at the following examples.

- Before the race, the runners were anxious.

  The subject of this sentence is *runners*. The sentence has no action verb—the runners did not **do** anything. Instead, the verb *were* links the subject to a word that describes it: *anxious.* (*Before the race* is a prepositional phrase, so it cannot contain the subject or the verb.)

- Cara's boyfriend is a good mechanic.

  The subject of this sentence is *boyfriend*. The linking verb *is* joins that subject with words that describe it: *a good mechanic.*

Most linking verbs are forms of the verb *be*. Here are forms of *be*, which is the most used verb in the English language:

am	were	had been
is	will be	will have been
are	have been	
was	has been	

Here are other common words that can be linking verbs.

appear	feel	seem	sound
become	look	smell	taste

Now see if you can double-underline the linking verbs in the following two sentences.

- George <u>looks</u> uncomfortable in a suit and tie.
- Sometimes anger <u>is</u> a healthy emotion.

If you underlined *looks* in the first sentence, you were right. *Looks* links the subject, *George*, to words that describe him: *uncomfortable in a suit and tie.*

If you underlined *is* in the second sentence, you were right. *Is* links the subject, *anger*, to words that describe it: *a healthy emotion.*

 Practice 5

Double-underline the **one** word that is a linking verb in each sentence. You may find it helpful to first identify and underline the subject and to cross out any prepositional phrases.

1. That <u>nurse</u> <u>was</u> kind.
2. The <u>kitchen</u> <u>smells</u> spicy.
3. <u>Trisha</u> and <u>Suki</u> <u>are</u> roommates.
4. <u>Velvet</u> <u>feels</u> soft and silky.
5. The chocolate <u>cookies</u> <u>taste</u> salty and dry.
6. ~~After jogging~~, <u>I</u> <u>am</u> always hungry.
7. Those <u>dishes</u> ~~from the dishwasher~~ still <u>look</u> dirty.
8. ~~Since his divorce~~, <u>Nate</u> <u>seems</u> unhappy.
9. The <u>cashier</u> ~~at our supermarket~~ <u>is</u> a student ~~at Jefferson High School~~.
10. ~~During the hot, dry summer~~, the <u>farmers</u> <u>were</u> uneasy ~~about their crops~~.

MAIN VERBS AND HELPING VERBS

Most of the verbs you have looked at so far have been just one word—*wrote, drifted, is, look,* and so on. But many verbs consist of a main verb plus one or more **helping verbs**.

Look at the following two sentences and explanations.

- My sister is joining a book club.

Sister is the subject of this sentence. She is the person who is doing something. What is she doing? She *is joining* (a book club). Here, *is* is a helping verb, and *joining* is the main verb.

Joining by itself would not make sense as a verb. It would be incorrect to say, "My sister joining a book club." Words that end in *-ing* cannot be the verb of a sentence unless they are accompanied by a helping verb.

- Mikey should have given his dog a bath before the pet contest.

In this sentence, *Mikey* is the subject. What should he have done? He *should have given* (his dog a bath). *Should* and *have* are helping verbs. The next word, *given*, is the main verb.

Given by itself could not be the verb. We would not say, "Mikey given his dog a bath . . ."

The helping verbs are listed in the box below.

Forms of *be*:	be, am, is, are, was, were, being, been
Forms of *have*:	have, has, had
Forms of *do*:	do, does, did
Special verbs:	can, could, may, might, must, ought (to), shall, should, will, would
	These special verbs are also known as ***modals***.

The **modals**, unlike the other helping verbs, do not change form to indicate tense. In other words, they do not take such endings as *-ed*, *-s*, and *-ing*. After the modals, always use the basic form of a verb, the form in which a verb is listed in the dictionary (*go*, *see*, *work*, and so on).

● You *can* turn in the paper tomorrow.
● We *should* visit Dee in the hospital.

Now see if you can underline the main verbs and the helping verbs in the following two sentences. Then read the explanations.

● Gwen <u>has visited</u> the learning skills lab.
● I <u>will be running</u> in the school's five-mile race.

In the first sentence, *Gwen* is the subject. She is the one who has done something. To find the verb, we can ask, "What did Gwen do?" The answer is *has visited*. *Has* is the helping verb, and *visited* is the main verb.

In the second sentence, *I* is the subject. What will that subject be doing? He or she *will be running*. So in this sentence, *will* and *be* are helping verbs, and *running* is the main verb.

Practice 6

Fill in the blanks under each sentence.

1. As usual, my brother was complaining about his homework.

Helping verb(s): _____was_____   *Main verb:* _____complaining_____

2. The students will decorate the classroom for the teacher's surprise party.

Helping verb(s): _____will_____   *Main verb:* _____decorate_____

3. The dental appointment should take about an hour.

Helping verb(s): _____should_____   *Main verb:* _____take_____

4. Surprisingly, I do enjoy learning grammar.

Helping verb(s): _____do_____   *Main verb:* _____enjoy_____

5. Margaret has planted parsley and other herbs in her backyard.

Helping verb(s): _____has_____   *Main verb:* _____planted_____

6. You should have called your mother on her birthday.

Helping verb(s): _____should have_____   *Main verb:* _____called_____

7. The video-game machine will accept only quarters.

Helping verb(s): _____will_____   *Main verb:* _____accept_____

8. That drunk driver could have killed Aunt Esther.

Helping verb(s): _____could have_____   *Main verb:* _____killed_____

9. My girlfriend must have forgotten our date this evening.

Helping verb(s): _____must have_____   *Main verb:* _____forgotten_____

10. The star basketball player at our college might have injured himself seriously.

Helping verb(s): _____might have_____   *Main verb:* _____injured_____

WORDS THAT ARE NOT VERBS

Here is some added information that will help when you look for verbs in a sentence.

1   The verb of a sentence never begins with the word *to*.

- The instructor **agreed** to provide ten minutes for study before the quiz.
  Although *provide* is a verb, *to provide* cannot be the verb of a sentence. The verb of this sentence is *agreed*.

2   Certain words—such as *always, just, never, not,* and *only*—may appear between the main verb and the helping verb. Such words are **adverbs**. They describe the verb, but they are never part of it.

- Our canary **does** not **sing** in front of visitors.
- We **will** never **eat** at that restaurant again.
- You **should** always **wear** your seat belt in a moving vehicle.

For more information on adverbs, see "Adjectives and Adverbs," pages 115–124, and "Parts of Speech," pages 251–262.

Practice 7

In the space provided, write the complete verb (main verb plus helping verb) in each sentence.

1. My uncle is not wearing his toupee anymore.

Complete verb: _____is wearing_____

2. The children hurried to finish their art projects by the end of the class.

Complete verb: _____hurried_____

3. Those noodles should never be boiled more than seven minutes.

Complete verb: _____should be boiled_____

4. Unfortunately, gas prices have risen a lot this summer.

Complete verb: _____have risen_____

5. Reba will always love her ex-husband.

Complete verb: _____will love_____

Name _____ Section _____ Date _____

Score: (Number right) _____ x 5 = _____ %

More about Subjects and Verbs: TEST 1

For each sentence, cross out any prepositional phrases. Then, on the lines provided, write the subject(s) and verb(s), including any helping verb(s).

1. The parrot ~~with the bright green head~~ can say more than fifty words.

   Subject(s): _____parrot_____   *Verb(s):* _____can say_____

2. My cousins ~~in Louisiana~~ formed a gospel music group.

   Subject(s): _____cousins_____   *Verb(s):* _____formed_____

3. ~~At exactly noon~~, my summer vacation will begin.

   Subject(s): _____vacation_____   *Verb(s):* _____will begin_____

4. A warm sweatshirt ~~with a hood~~ feels good ~~on a chilly day~~.

   Subject(s): _____sweatshirt_____   *Verb(s):* _____feels_____

5. The source ~~of heating and cooling for the house~~ is a heat pump.

   Subject(s): _____source_____   *Verb(s):* _____is_____

6. The cardboard boxes ~~by the river~~ are home ~~to several people~~.

   Subject(s): _____boxes_____   *Verb(s):* _____are_____

7. ~~For my little brother and sister~~, happiness is a McDonald's restaurant.

   Subject(s): _____happiness_____   *Verb(s):* _____is_____

8. Retrievers and sheepdogs do not bite very often.

   Subject(s): __Retrievers . . . sheepdogs__   *Verb(s):* _____do . . . bite_____

9. The rug-cleaning people should have been here ~~by now~~.

   Subject(s): _____people_____   *Verb(s):* _____should have been_____

10. ~~After work~~, Dena and her boyfriend ate dinner and studied ~~at her apartment~~.

    Subject(s): __Dena . . . boyfriend__   *Verb(s):* _____ate . . . studied_____

Name _____ Section _____ Date _____

Score: (Number right) _____ x 10 = _____ %

More about Subjects and Verbs: TEST 2

In each of the ten sentences in this paragraph, cross out any prepositional phrases. Then, underline all the subjects once and the verbs twice. Remember to include any helping verb(s) and also all parts of compound subjects and verbs.

¹<u>Sharks</u>, ~~with their pointed snouts and fearsome teeth~~, <u>terrify</u> most people. ²However, ~~of the 375 or so different types of sharks~~, <u>few</u> <u>have attacked</u> people. ³Most <u>sharks</u> <u>will attack</u> only when ~~in danger~~. ⁴The great white <u>shark</u> <u>is</u> one ~~of the most dangerous sharks to humans~~. ⁵Many <u>people</u> <u>know</u> and <u>fear</u> this shark ~~from its role in the movie *Jaws*~~. ⁶<u>It</u> <u>can grow</u> ~~to over twenty feet in length~~. ⁷The <u>coloring</u> ~~of the great white shark~~ <u>is</u> a camouflage ~~in the water~~. ⁸The <u>color</u> ~~of its belly~~ <u>is</u> white. ⁹~~From underneath~~, the white <u>belly</u> <u>blends</u> ~~with the bright sky overhead~~. ¹⁰<u>Seals</u>, smaller <u>fish</u>, and <u>people</u> often <u>do</u> not <u>see</u> the great white shark ~~in time~~.

You have already reviewed (on pages 15–20) two situations that affect subject-verb agreement:

1 **Words between the subject and the verb**

2 **Compound subjects**

This section will cover five other situations that affect subject-verb agreement:

3 **Verb coming before the subject**

4 **More about compound subjects**

5 **Collective nouns**

6 **Indefinite pronoun subjects**

7 **Relative pronoun subjects:** *who, which, that*

VERB COMING BEFORE THE SUBJECT

The verb follows the subject in most sentences:

- *Hector* **passed** the course.
- A *rabbit* **lives** in my backyard.
- The *plane* **roared** overhead.

However, in some sentences, the verb comes *before* the subject. To make the subject and verb agree in such cases, look for the subject after the verb. Then decide if the verb should be singular or plural. Sentences in which the verb comes first include questions.

- What **was** your *score* on the test?

  The verb *was* is singular. It agrees with the singular subject *score*. *On the test* is a prepositional phrase. The subject of a sentence is never in a prepositional phrase. (See page 144.)

The verb also comes first in sentences that begin with such words as *there is* or *here are*.

- There **are** *ants* in the sugar bowl.

  The verb of this sentence is the plural verb *are*, so the subject should be plural as well. You can find the subject by asking, "What are in the sugar bowl?" The answer, *ants*, is the subject.

- Here **is** the *menu*.

  The subject of this sentence is *menu*, which needs a singular verb.

The verb may also come before the subject in sentences that begin with a prepositional phrase.

- On that shelf **are** the *reports* for this year.

  The sentence begins with the prepositional phrase *on that shelf*, which is followed by the plural verb *are*. You can find the subject by asking, "What are on that shelf?" The answer is the subject of the sentence: *reports*. The subject and verb agree—they are both plural.

Here's another helpful way to find the subject when the verb comes first: Try to rearrange the sentence so that the subject comes first. The subject may be easier to find when the sentence is in the normal order. For the sentences on the previous page, you would then get:

● Your *score* on the test **was** what?

● *Ants* **are** in the sugar bowl.

● The *menu* **is** here.

● The *reports* for this year **are** on that shelf.

Practice 1

Underline the subject of each sentence. Then, in the space provided, write the form of the verb that agrees with the subject. (If you have trouble finding the subject, try crossing out any prepositional phrases.)

is, are   1. Here _____are_____ some messages ~~for you~~.

is, are   2. What _____is_____ your middle name?

stands, stand 3. ~~Beside the stream~~ _____stands_____ a low wooden fence.

grows, grow   4. ~~In that little garden~~ _____grow_____ twenty herbs.

was, were   5. There _____were_____ black clouds ~~in the sky~~ this morning.

is, are   6. Where _____is_____ the box ~~for these crayons~~?

lies, lie   7. ~~On the table in the dining room~~ _____lies_____ a letter ~~for you~~.

is, are   8. There _____are_____ good reasons to hire older workers.

is, are   9. Why _____are_____ all those people running ~~down the street~~?

rests, rest   10. ~~On the bench outside of the mall~~ _____rest_____ two tired shoppers.

MORE ABOUT COMPOUND SUBJECTS

As explained on page 15, a **compound subject** is made up of two nouns connected by a joining word. Subjects joined by *and* generally take a plural verb.

However, when a compound subject is connected by *or, nor, either . . . or,* or *neither . . . nor,* the verb must agree with the part of the subject that is closer to it.

● My *aunts* or my *mother* usually **hosts** our family gatherings.

The singular noun *mother* is closer to the verb, so the singular verb *hosts* is used.

● Either *he* or *his parents* **were** home that night.

● Either *his parents* or *he* **was** home that night.

In the first sentence, the plural noun *parents* is closer to the verb, so the verb is plural. In the second sentence, the singular noun *he* is closer to the verb, so the verb must be singular.

● Neither the *teacher* nor the *students* **are** to blame for the shortage of textbooks.

The plural noun *students* is closer to the verb, so the verb is plural.

Practice 2

In each sentence, underline the compound subject. Then, in the space provided, write the correct form of the verb in the margin.

smells, smell   1. Either the trash <u>can</u> or your <u>socks</u> _____*smell*_____ horrible.

tastes, taste   2. Neither the <u>fish</u> nor the <u>vegetables</u> _____*taste*_____ fresh in this restaurant.

donates, donate   3. Her <u>sisters</u> or <u>she</u> usually _____*donates*_____ a cake or cookies to the community bake sale.

seems, seem   4. Neither <u>Polly</u> nor her <u>brothers</u> _____*seem*_____ surprised by their parents' announcement.

washes, wash   5. "On Father's Day, either the <u>children</u> or my <u>wife</u> _____*washes*_____ the family car," Don said.

COLLECTIVE NOUNS

A **collective noun** refers to a group of persons or things that are thought of as one unit. Collective nouns are usually considered singular. Following are some examples.

● The **family** *lives* on Russell Avenue.

Family refers to a single unit, so the singular verb *lives* is used. However, if a collective noun refers to the individual members of the group, a plural verb is used.

● The **family** *are* Republicans, Democrats, and Independents.

Since one unit cannot have three different political views, *family* in this sentence clearly refers to the individual members of the group, so the plural verb *are* is used. To emphasize the individuals, some writers would use a subject that is clearly plural:

● The **members** of the family *are* Republicans, Democrats, and Independents.

Practice 3

In each sentence, underline the subject and decide if it needs a singular or plural verb. Then fill in the correct form of the verb in the margin.

is, are   1. The <u>jury</u> _____*is*_____ going to announce its verdict this morning.

has, have   2. The <u>faculty</u> _____*have*_____ not been able to agree on one book for everyone in the school to read.

is, are   3. This noisy <u>audience</u> _____*is*_____ spoiling the movie for me.

takes, take   4. The <u>couple</u> _____*take*_____ separate vacations: she likes to hike, and he likes to lie on the beach.

marches, march   5. Every year, the <u>band</u> _____*marches*_____ in the town's Thanksgiving parade.

INDEFINITE PRONOUN SUBJECTS

Indefinite pronouns are pronouns that do not refer to a specific person or thing. The ones in the box below are always singular:

anybody	either	neither	one
anyone	everybody	no one	somebody
anything	everyone	nobody	someone
each	everything	nothing	something

In the following sentences, the subjects are singular indefinite pronouns. Each of the verbs is therefore also singular.

- *Each* of the puppies **is** cute in its own way.
- *Neither* of the boys **wants** to walk the dog.
- Despite the rules, nearly *everyone* in my apartment building **owns** a pet.

Note that the indefinite pronoun *both* is always plural:

- *Both* of the puppies **are** cute in their own ways.

The indefinite pronoun *most* is singular or plural, depending on its context:

- *Most* of the cake **has** been cut.
  Most here refers to one thing—the cake, so the singular verb *has* is used.

- *Most* of the pieces **are** very small.
  Most here refers to several pieces, so the plural verb *are* is used.

Practice 4

Underline the subject of each sentence. Then, in the space provided, write the form of the verb that agrees with the subject.

is, are   1. <u>Everybody</u> at my new school _____*is*_____ friendly.

feels, feel   2. <u>Neither</u> of those mattresses _____*feels*_____ comfortable.

knows, know 3. <u>Nobody</u> in my family _____*knows*_____ how to swim.

is, are   4. <u>Both</u> of my parents _____*are*_____ allergic to peanuts.

has, have   5. <u>Most</u> of the house _____*has*_____ been painted.

needs, need   6. <u>Each</u> of the children _____*needs*_____ some attention.

seem, seems 7. <u>Either</u> Monday or Friday _____*seems*_____ like a good day for the meeting.

goes, go   8. <u>Everything</u> in that box _____*goes*_____ to the neighborhood garage sale.

is, are   9. <u>Both</u> of my best friends _____*are*_____ older than I.

has, have   10. <u>Most</u> of the wedding invitations _____*have*_____ been addressed and mailed.

RELATIVE PRONOUN SUBJECTS: *WHO, WHICH, THAT*

The relative pronouns *who, which,* and *that* are singular when they refer to a singular noun. They are plural when they refer to a plural noun.

- I met a woman *who* **is** from China.

- I met two women *who* **are** from China.

    In the first sentence above, *who* refers to the singular word *woman,* so the verb is singular too. In the second sentence, *who* refers to the plural word *women,* so the verb must be plural.

- Our car, *which* **is** only a year old, already needs a new battery.

    Which refers to *car,* a singular noun, so the singular verb *is* is used.

- My father's boss collects old wind-up toys *that* still **work**.

    That refers to the plural noun *toys,* so the plural verb *work* is used.

For more information on relative pronouns, see "Parts of Speech," page 254.

Practice 5

In each sentence, underline the noun that the relative pronoun refers to. Then fill in the correct form of the verb in the margin.

gives, give   1. We have planted several <u>shrubs</u>, which _____*give*_____ some privacy to our backyard.

gives, give   2. We have planted a <u>hedge</u>, which _____*gives*_____ some privacy to our backyard.

is, are   3. Rhoda dislikes all <u>foods</u> that _____*are*_____ good for her.

is, are   4. Rhoda dislikes all <u>food</u> that _____*is*_____ good for her.

was, were   5. The <u>soles</u> of my shoes, which _____*were*_____ covered with mud, left black footprints on the sidewalk.

was, were   6. The <u>sole</u> of my right shoe, which _____*was*_____ covered with mud, left black footprints on the sidewalk.

is, are   7. Lenny plays basketball with a <u>man</u> who _____*is*_____ twice his age.

is, are   8. Lenny plays basketball with <u>men</u> who _____*are*_____ twice his age.

speaks, speak   9. My niece's favorite playmate is a little <u>girl</u> who _____*speaks*_____ no English.

speaks, speak   10. My niece's favorite playmates are two little <u>girls</u> who _____*speak*_____ no English.

Name _____ Section _____ Date _____

More about Subject-Verb Agreement: TEST 1

For each sentence, fill in the correct form of the verb in the margin.

needs, need   1. The house or the barn _____needs_____ to be painted this year.

is, are   2. Also, both buildings, which _____are_____ very old, need repairs.

itches, itch   3. Each of these sweaters _____itches_____.

gets, get   4. That group _____gets_____ together every Friday night to play poker.

was, were   5. There _____were_____ sad expressions on the students' faces.

is, are   6. In my English class, either a novel or short stories _____are_____ assigned every week.

hurries, hurry   7. Through the airport _____hurry_____ travelers from all over the world.

likes, like   8. Our neighbors are people who _____like_____ their privacy.

is, are   9. Why _____are_____ the lights flickering?

knows, know   10. No one _____knows_____ how long the rain delay will continue.

Name _____   Section _____   Date _____

More about Subject-Verb Agreement: TEST 2

For each sentence, fill in the correct form of the verb in the margin.

is, are   1. There _____are_____ three fast-food restaurants in the next block.

was, were   2. What _____were_____ the reasons for the workers' strike?

plays, play 3. Someone in the apartment upstairs _____plays_____ a guitar late at night.

is, are   4. Some cookies or a cake _____is_____ needed for dessert.

was, were   5. Among the guests _____was_____ a private detective.

has, have   6. The jury _____have_____ conflicting opinions.

was, were   7. The students and their teacher _____were_____ sitting in a circle.

is, are   8. There _____are_____ many hungry people in America's cities.

makes, make 9. The mayor is a woman who _____makes_____ things happen in our town.

was, were   10. Neither the children nor their father _____was_____ aware that someone was at
                       the door.

25 More about Verbs: Tenses

Verb Tenses

All verbs have various **tenses**—forms that indicate the time the sentence is referring to. This chapter explains the following about verb tenses:

1 **The four principal verb parts that are the basis for all of the tenses**

2 **The most common verb tenses in English**

Six main tenses	present, past, future
	present perfect, past perfect, future perfect
Three progressive tenses	present progressive, past progressive,
	future progressive

THE FOUR PRINCIPAL PARTS OF VERBS

Each verb tense is based on one of the four principal parts of verbs. Following are explanations of each of those verb parts.

1 **Basic Form** The basic form is the form in which verbs are listed in the dictionary. It is used for the present tense for all subjects except third-person singular subjects.

● I **ask** questions in class.

Third-person singular verbs are formed by adding *-s* to the basic form.

● Sue **asks** questions in class.

2 **Past Tense Form** The past tense of most verbs is formed by adding *-ed* or *-d* to the basic form.

● We **asked** the teacher to postpone the test.

● I **amused** the children by doing magic tricks.

3 **Present Participle** The present participle is the *-ing* form of a verb. It is used in the progressive tenses, which you will learn about later in the chapter.

● Jack is **asking** the teacher something in the hallway.

● I am **amusing** the children while their mother does errands.

4 **Past Participle** The past participle of a verb is usually the same as its past tense form. The past participle is the form that is used with the helping verbs *have, has,* and *had* and with *am, is, are, was,* or *were*.

● The teachers have **asked** us to study in groups.

● I was **amused** when the children asked if I could stay forever.

Here are the principal parts of three regular verbs:

Basic Form	Past Tense Form	Present Participle	Past Participle
work	worked	working	worked
smile	smiled	smiling	smiled
wonder	wondered	wondering	wondered

SIX MAIN TENSES

There are six main tenses in English. They are **present, past, future, present perfect, past perfect,** and **future perfect**.

Look at the following chart. It shows the six basic tenses of the verb *work*.

Tense	Example
Present	I **work**.
Past	I **worked**.
Future	I **will work**.
Present Perfect	I **have worked**.
Past Perfect	I **had worked**.
Future Perfect	I **will have worked**.

These tenses are explained in more detail below and on the pages that follow.

Present Tense

Verbs in the **present tense** express present action or habitual action. (A habitual action is one that is often repeated.)

- Our dog **smells** the neighbor's barbecue.

  Smells expresses a present action.

- Jay **works** as a waiter on weekends.

  Works expresses a habitual action.

The forms of present tense verbs are shown with the verb *work* in the box below. Notice the difference between the singular third-person form and the other present tense forms.

	Singular	Plural
First person	I work	we work
Second person	you work	you work
Third person	he, she, it works	they work

Present tense verbs for the third-person singular end with an *s*. Here are some other sentences in the present tense with subjects that are third-person singular:

● She **reads** a book a week.

● It **takes** me a month to read a book.

● Dan **drives** an hour to school every day.

● His old car **averages** only ten miles a gallon.

NOTE A third-person subject is *he, she, it*, or any single person or thing other than the speaker (first person) or the person spoken to (second person).

Practice 1

A. Fill in the present tense of *smile* for each of the following:

	Singular		**Plural**
First person	I ____smile____	we ____smile____
Second person	you ____smile____	you ____smile____
Third person	he, she, it ____smiles____	they ____smile____

B. Fill in each space with the present tense form of the verb shown in the margin.

drill   **1.** The dentist ____drills____ the cavity as his assistant watches.

practice   **2.** Ling ____practices____ her typing every day.

ring   **3.** Those church bells ____ring____ on the hour.

make   **4.** He suddenly ____makes____ a U-turn.

dig   **5.** Some workers ____dig____ through the stones and rubble.

trim   **6.** I ____trim____ my fingernails before playing the piano.

clean   **7.** Dinah ____cleans____ her apartment every Saturday.

tell   **8.** The nurse ____tells____ the patient to make a fist.

discover   **9.** My sister often ____discovers____ loose change in her coat pockets.

remember   **10.** Children often ____remember____ what they got for their last birthday.

Past Tense

Verbs in the **past tense** express actions that took place in the past.

● Last year, Jay **worked** as a messenger.

● One day our dog **chased** a raccoon.

The past tense is usually formed by adding *-ed* or *-d* to the end of the basic form of the verb. In the above sentences, the *-ed* and *-d* endings are added to the basic forms of the verbs *work* and *chase*.

NOTE People sometimes drop the *-ed* or *-d* ending in their everyday speech. They then tend to omit those endings in their writing as well. For example, someone might say

● I finish the paper an hour before class.

instead of

● I **finished** the paper an hour before class.

In written English, however, the *-ed* or *-d* ending is essential.

Practice 2

Fill in each space with the past tense form of the verb shown in the margin.

seem   **1.** The movie _____seemed_____ to end suddenly.

sail   **2.** The ship _____sailed_____ to the Bahamas last week.

wonder   **3.** Alisha _____wondered_____ where she had put her car keys.

knock   **4.** Last night someone _____knocked_____ on the door at 3 a.m.

name   **5.** Jean _____named_____ the spotted puppy Freckles.

jump   **6.** My little brother _____jumped_____ up when I entered the room.

talk   **7.** The students _____talked_____ easily with the new instructor.

check   **8.** Bert _____checked_____ the air in his car tires before he went on vacation.

wipe   **9.** The man _____wiped_____ the lipstick off his cheek with his shirt sleeve.

play   **10.** Stan _____played_____ his guitar in a concert last summer.

Future Tense

Verbs in the **future tense** describe future actions.

● Next summer, Jay **will work** at a camp.

The future tense is formed by adding the word *will* or *shall* to the basic form of the verb.

Practice 3

Fill in the space with the future tense form of the verb shown in the margin.

play   **1.** Stan _____will play_____ his guitar in a concert tonight.

plant   **2.** The lumberjacks _____will plant_____ new trees here next spring.

iron   **3.** Ramon _____will iron_____ his shirt before going to the interview.

attend   **4.** Penny _____will attend_____ San Antonio College in the fall.

circle   **5.** The teacher _____will circle_____ any errors she finds in your paper.

Present Perfect Tense (*have* or *has* + past participle)

The **present perfect** tense describes an action that began in the past and either has been finished or is continuing at the present time.

● I **have written** five pages of notes on the textbook chapter.

● Jay **has worked** at a number of jobs over the years.

The present perfect tense is formed by adding the correct form of the helping verb *have* to the past participle of the verb (which is usually the same as its past tense form). Here are the present tense forms of *have*:

	Singular	Plural
First person	I have	we have
Second person	you have	you have
Third person	he, she, it has	they have

Practice 4

Fill in each space with the present perfect tense form of the verb shown in the margin. One is done for you as an example.

pour   **1.** The hostess _____*has poured*_____ iced tea for most of her guests.

live   **2.** I _____*have lived*_____ in three different countries.

check   **3.** Because Bert will be driving a long distance, he _____*has checked*_____ the air in his car tires.

boil   **4.** The chef _____*has boiled*_____ the eggs for the salad and is now slicing them.

mix   **5.** The children _____*have mixed*_____ together in one box the pieces of three different puzzles.

Past Perfect Tense (*had* + past participle)

The **past perfect** tense describes an action that was completed in the past before another past action.

● Jay **had worked** as a messenger before he located a better job as a waiter.

The past perfect tense is formed by adding *had* to the past participle of a verb.

Practice 5

Fill in the space with the past perfect tense form of the verb shown in the margin. Add *had* to the past participle of the verb. One is done for you as an example.

promise   **1.** Zora _____*had promised*_____ to go to the meeting before she realized it was on her birthday.

struggle   **2.** My brother _____*had struggled*_____ in several part-time jobs before returning to college.

ask   **3.** Jill _____*had asked*_____ two other men to the dance before inviting Dan.

intend   **4.** I _____*had intended*_____ to go to the library to get material for my report, but then I realized I could use the Internet instead.

invite   **5.** Hector _____*had invited*_____ his friends to his apartment before he knew that his roommate was ill.

Future Perfect Tense (*will have + past participle*)

The **future perfect** tense describes an action that will be completed before some time in the future.

- Jay **will have worked** at a half dozen different jobs before college graduation.

The future perfect tense is formed by adding *will have* to the past participle of a verb.

Practice 6

Fill in the space with the future perfect tense form of the verb shown in the margin. Add *will have* to the past participle of the verb. One is done for you as an example.

complete 1. I _____will have completed_____ five exams by the end of finals week.

attend 2. By graduation day, I _____will have attended_____ five parties.

finish 3. You eat so slowly that I _____will have finished_____ my ice cream before you begin your spaghetti.

learn 4. After ten weeks, you _____will have learned_____ how to rebuild a car's engine.

design 5. By the end of the summer, my mother _____will have designed_____ and sewed my sister's wedding dress.

THE PROGRESSIVE TENSES

As their names suggest, the **progressive tenses** express actions still in progress at a particular time. They are made by adding a form of the helping verb *be* to the present participle, the *-ing* form of the verb.

Present Progressive Tense (*am, are, or is* + present participle)

The **present progressive** tense expresses an action taking place at this moment or that will occur sometime in the future.

- Jay **is working** at the restaurant today.

- I **am going** to get home late tonight.

The present progressive tense is formed by adding the correct present tense form of the helping verb *be* to the *-ing* form of the verb.

Present Tense Forms of the Verb *Be*

	Singular	**Plural**
First person	I am	we are
Second person	you are	you are
Third person	he, she, it is	they are

Practice 7

Below are five sentences with verbs in the present tense. Cross out each verb and change it to the present progressive in the space provided. One is done for you as an example.

1. The child ~~plays~~ with the puppy. _____ *is playing*
2. The microwave ~~beeps~~ loudly. _____ *is beeping*
3. The roses in the garden ~~bloom~~. _____ *are blooming*
4. I ~~practice~~ my speech tonight. _____ *am practicing*
5. The visitors ~~pace~~ in the hospital lobby. _____ *are pacing*

Past Progressive Tense (*was* or *were* + present participle)

The **past progressive** tense expresses an action that was in progress at a certain time in the past.

- Jay **was working** yesterday.

The past progressive tense is formed by adding the correct past tense form of *be* to the *-ing* form of the verb.

Past Tense Forms of the Verb *Be*

	Singular	Plural
First person	I was	we were
Second person	you were	you were
Third person	he, she, it was	they were

Practice 8

Below are five sentences with verbs in the past tense. Cross out each verb and change it to the past progressive in the space provided. One is done for you as an example.

1. The child ~~played~~ with the puppy. _____ *was playing*
2. The microwave ~~beeped~~ loudly. _____ *was beeping*
3. The roses in the garden ~~bloomed~~. _____ *were blooming*
4. I ~~practiced~~ my speech last night. _____ *was practicing*
5. The visitors ~~paced~~ in the hospital lobby. _____ *were pacing*

Future Progressive Tense (*will be* + present participle)

The **future progressive** tense expresses an action that will be in progress at a certain time in the future.

- Jay **will be working** tomorrow.

The future progressive tense is formed by adding *will be* to the *-ing* form of the verb.

Practice 9

Below are five sentences with verbs in the future tense. Cross out each verb and change it to the future progressive in the space provided. One is done for you as an example.

1. The child ~~will play~~ with the puppy. _____ will be playing _____
2. The microwave ~~will beep~~ loudly. _____ will be beeping _____
3. The roses in the garden ~~will bloom~~. _____ will be blooming _____
4. I ~~will practice~~ my speech tonight. _____ will be practicing _____
5. The visitors ~~will pace~~ in the hospital lobby. _____ will be pacing _____

A Note on *-ing* Verbs

Look at the following word groups:

- Jay working tonight.
- The visitors pacing in the hospital lobby.

The above word groups express incomplete thoughts because their verbs are incomplete. The *-ing* form of a verb cannot stand by itself as the verb of a sentence—it must be accompanied by a helping verb:

- Jay **is working** tonight.
- The visitors **were pacing** in the hospital lobby.

Practice 10

The verb in each of the following sentences is incomplete. Correct each incomplete verb by adding *is, are, was,* or *were* in the space provided.

1. Oscar _____ is _____ playing the clarinet in his school band this year.
2. You _____ were _____ giggling in your sleep last night.
3. Even though I _____ was _____ sneezing and coughing, no one thought I was sick.
4. The scars from my father's recent operation _____ are _____ fading, but I can still see them.
5. The customers _____ were _____ complaining about the long wait until a waitress offered them free cups of coffee.

A SUMMARY OF THE NINE MOST COMMON VERB TENSES

Using the regular verb *call*, the chart below illustrates the nine most common tenses in English.

The Nine Most Common Verb Tenses

Present	I **call** my grandmother Nana. My mother **calls** her Babe.
Past	A number of employees **called** in sick today.
Future	Because the flu is going around, more **will** probably **call** in sick tomorrow.
Present perfect	Rebecca **has called** the radio station at least ten times to request her favorite song.
Past perfect	No one **had called** Mitchell "Shorty" for years until he attended his grade-school reunion.
Future perfect	When you finish your first day as a telemarketer, you **will have called** forty potential customers.
Present progressive	Ken **is calling** the restaurant right now to make a reservation for dinner.
Past progressive	He **was calling** a different restaurant when I came in, but I urged him to call my favorite one.
Future progressive	Mom **will be calling** when she arrives at work and realizes she left her purse here.

Name _____ Section _____ Date _____

More about Verbs: TEST 1

A. In each space, write the **present tense** form of the verb in the margin.

Examples   **plan**   Carl _____*plans*_____ to enter the contest.

attend   The students _____*attend*_____ a meeting on the new dress code.

soar   **1.** A hawk _____*soars*_____ above the cornfield.

listen   **2.** The jurors _____*listen*_____ to the witness.

think   **3.** Leona _____*thinks*_____ she passed her English exam.

B. In each space, write the **past tense** form of the verb in the margin.

Example   **promise**   My brother _____*promised*_____ to wash our car on Saturday.

scratch   **4.** The prisoner _____*scratched*_____ his initials on the cell wall.

doze   **5.** As the lecturer continued talking, several students _____*dozed*_____ off.

float   **6.** Five orange slices _____*floated*_____ on top of the red punch.

struggle   **7.** The campers _____*struggled*_____ through the thick underbrush near the camp.

C. In each space, write the **future tense** form of the verb in the margin.

Example   **check**   The nurse _____*will check*_____ your blood pressure each day.

become   **8.** Those funny-looking caterpillars _____*will become*_____ gorgeous blue and yellow butterflies.

stand   **9.** Everyone _____*will stand*_____ when the judge enters the courtroom.

wear   **10.** Johnny _____*will wear*_____ a dinosaur costume to the party.

Name _____ Section _____ Date _____

Score: (Number right) _____ x 10 = _____ %

More about Verbs: TEST 2

A. In each space, write the **present perfect tense** form of the verb in the margin.

Examples **walk** Bernice ___has walked___ over twenty miles this week.

look I ___have looked___ all over for my glasses.

wash **1.** The students ___have washed___ nearly seventy cars to raise money for their class trip.

learn **2.** We ___have learned___ about the civil rights movement in our history class this semester.

gain **3.** Rodney ___has gained___ ten pounds in his first year of college.

notice **4.** I ___have noticed___ changes in you since you started going to the gym.

B. In each space, write the **past perfect tense** form of the verb in the margin.

Example **walk** Before her heart attack, Bernice seldom ___had walked___ for exercise.

argue **5.** Fritz ___had argued___ with a friend before the car accident.

warn **6.** Before she left for her hair appointment, Jenna ___had warned___ us that she would soon be looking very different.

manage **7.** Chelsea ___had managed___ to clean the entire house by the time her parents got home last evening.

C. In each space, write the **future perfect tense** form of the verb in the margin.

Example **walk** By the end of this month, Bernice ___will have walked___ over one hundred miles.

work **8.** Paco ___will have worked___ fifty-five hours by the end of the week.

interview **9.** By the time she writes her paper, Jodi ___will have interviewed___ six nurses.

watch **10.** By the end of the day, the children ___will have watched___ five hours of television.

More about Verb Tenses

This chapter explains three other things you should know about verb tense:

1 Consistent verb tense

Inconsistent verb tense   We **parked** the car and **head** toward the movie theater.

Consistent verb tense   We **parked** the car and **headed** toward the movie theater.

2 The passive and active voices

Passive voice   I **was visited** last week by a former neighbor.

Active voice   A former neighbor **visited** me last week.

3 Nonstandard and standard verbs

Nonstandard verbs   Every week, Mandy **volunteer** at a nursing home near her apartment. She often **read** to residents there.

Standard verbs   Every week, Mandy **volunteers** at a nursing home near her apartment. She often **reads** to residents there.

CONSISTENT VERB TENSE

In your writing, avoid illogical or needless shifts in tense. For example, if you are writing a paper with the action in the past tense, don't shift suddenly to the present. Look at the examples below:

Inconsistent verb tense   In my nightmare, a hairy spider **crawled** up the side of my bed and **races** quickly onto my pillow.

There is no reason for the writer to shift suddenly from the past tense (*crawled*) to the present tense (*races*). The inconsistency can be corrected by using the same tense for both verbs:

Consistent verb tense   In my nightmare, a hairy spider **crawled** up the side of my bed and **raced** quickly onto my pillow.

 Practice 1

In each short passage, there is **one** illogical change in verb tense. Cross out the incorrect verb. Then write the correct form of that verb on the line provided.

_____crashed_____   **1.** The ice skater moved smoothly through her routine. On her last jump, however, she lost her balance and ~~crashes~~ to the ice with a thud.

_____heat_____   **2.** On many farms, machines milk the cows. The farmers then send the fresh milk to a processing plant. Workers there ~~heated~~ the milk at high temperatures. The intense heat removes bacteria.

_____picked_____ **3.** When Tina saw flames and smoke coming from her kitchen, she reacted quickly. She ~~picks~~ up her kitten and her purse. Then she rushed out into the fresh air.

_____crossed_____ **4.** Soldiers in the Civil War fought in bloody battles during the day. But at night, they often ~~cross~~ "enemy" lines for a friendly visit.

_____prepared_____ **5.** Melba took an inexpensive vacation this summer. She called parks and museums in the area to find out the cheapest times to visit. To save money, she ~~prepares~~ picnic lunches for her visits.

_____fertilizes_____ **6.** Tony and Lola do their gardening on weekends. While Tony digs out weeds, Lola ~~fertilized~~ plants and flowers.

_____delivers_____ **7.** Arlo works for a small greeting-card company. He writes poems for the wedding cards. Then he ~~delivered~~ the cards to the art department, where an artist sketches pictures of wedding bells or flowers.

_____surged_____ **8.** Last summer, my father went water skiing. After about five attempts, he skied around the entire lake. But when a large wave from another boat ~~surges~~ by, he flipped into the water headfirst.

_____stays_____ **9.** My sister complains at the drop of a hat. She often runs to her room in a rage. She ~~stayed~~ there for hours feeling sorry for herself.

_____disappeared_____ **10.** Last night, Lita went on the worst date ever. Her date, Mario, showed up an hour late. During dinner, all he talked about was himself. Then, just before the waitress brought the check, he ~~disappears~~. Lita unhappily paid the bill and took a taxi home.

THE PASSIVE AND ACTIVE VOICES

The subject of a sentence usually performs the action of the verb. In such cases, the verb is in the **active voice**. For example, look at the following sentence:

● My father **planted** the Japanese maple tree in the front yard.

> The verb in this sentence is *planted*. Who performed that action? The answer is *father*, the subject of the sentence. (He planted the tree.) Therefore, the verb is in the **active voice**.

Now look at this version of that sentence:

● The Japanese maple tree in the front yard **was planted** by my father.

> The verb in this sentence is *was planted*. The subject of the sentence, *tree*, did not perform the action. It received the action; the tree was planted by the father. When the subject of a sentence is acted upon, the verb is in the **passive voice**.

Passive verbs are formed by combining a helping verb—a form of *to be (am, is, are, was, were)*—with the past participle of a verb (which is usually the same as its past tense form). For example, in the sentence above, *was* plus the past participle of *plant* results in the passive verb *was planted*.

Here are some other passive verbs:

Form of to be	+	past participle	=	passive verb
am	+	pushed	=	am pushed
is	+	surprised	=	is surprised
was	+	delayed	=	was delayed

In general, write in the active voice. Because it expresses action, it is more energetic and effective than the passive voice. Use the passive voice when you wish to emphasize the receiver of the action or when the performer of the action is unknown.

Here are some more examples of sentences with active and passive verbs:

Active   Our landlord's son **mows** our backyard every week.
             The subject of the sentence, *son*, performs the action of the sentence, *mows*.

Passive   Our backyard **is mowed** every week by our landlord's son.
             The subject of the sentence—*backyard*—does not act. Instead, it is acted upon. (The passive verb is a combination of *is* plus the past participle of *mow*.)

Active   My sister **wrecked** her new car in an accident last night.
             The subject of the sentence, *sister*, is the one who acted—she *wrecked* the car.

Passive   My sister's new car **was wrecked** in an accident last night.
             The subject of this sentence, *car*, does not do anything. Something is done to it.

Practice 2

Underline the verb in each sentence. Then circle the **A** in the margin if the verb is active. Circle the **P** in the margin if the verb is passive.

Example   A   (P)   The car window was shattered by a poorly aimed baseball.

(A) P   **1.** My grandmother Skypes me almost every day.

A (P)   **2.** Rice is consumed every day by people all over Asia.

(A) P   **3.** Certain breeds of dog bite more often than others.

(A) P   **4.** The cashier counted the change out carefully.

A (P)   **5.** The injured man was rushed to the emergency room.

A (P)   **6.** The parade was headed by two young girls twirling batons.

(A) P   **7.** The audience cheered at the play's end.

A (P)   **8.** Several flights were delayed because of a snowstorm.

(A) P   **9.** The Yellow Pages provide lots of useful information.

A (P)   **10.** The words "No Trespassing" were painted in red letters on the fence.

Rewriting from the Passive to the Active Voice

Keep in mind that in the active voice, the subject performs the action. Here's a sentence with a passive verb. See if you can rewrite the sentence using the active voice.

Passive voice   Our roof was damaged by the storm.

Active voice   ___The storm damaged our roof._____

In the passive version of the sentence, the subject *(roof)* was acted upon by the storm. The storm is what did the action. To write an active version of the sentence, you should have made *storm* the subject: *The storm damaged our roof.*

Practice 3

The following sentences are written in the passive voice. For each sentence, underline the verb. Then rewrite the sentence in the active voice, changing the wording as necessary.

Example   Fruits and vegetables <u>are painted</u> often by artists.

Artists often paint fruits and vegetables.

1. The cat <u>was named</u> Leo by my brother.
   My brother named the cat Leo.

2. Soccer <u>is played</u> by children all over the world.
   Children all over the world play soccer.

3. The pizza party <u>was arranged</u> by the team's coaches.
   The team's coaches arranged the pizza party.

4. Some students <u>were pushed</u> around by the gym teacher.
   The gym teacher pushed around some students.

5. Shipping labels <u>are printed</u> quickly by the computer.
   The computer prints shipping labels quickly.

6. A nest <u>was constructed</u> in our mailbox by some robins.
   Some robins constructed a nest in our mailbox.

7. The alarm clock <u>was invented</u> by an American.
   An American invented the alarm clock.

8. The pizza restaurant <u>was closed</u> by the health inspector.
   The health inspector closed the pizza restaurant.

9. My telephone <u>was used</u> for a long-distance call by Jana without permission.
   Jana used my telephone for a long-distance call without permission.

10. Many annoying insects, such as mosquitoes, <u>are consumed</u> by spiders.
    Spiders consume many annoying insects, such as mosquitoes.

NONSTANDARD AND STANDARD VERBS

Nonstandard expressions such as *they ain't, we has, I be* or *he don't* are often part of successful communication among family members and friends. In both school and the working world, however, standard English is widely accepted as the norm for speaking and writing.

The chart below shows both nonstandard and standard forms of the regular verb *like*. Practice using the standard forms in your speech and writing.

	Nonstandard Forms		**Standard Forms**	
Present Tense	I likes	we likes	I like	we like
	you likes	you likes	you like	you like
	he, she, it like	they likes	he, she, it likes	they like
Past Tense	I like	we like	I liked	we liked
	you like	you like	you liked	you liked
	he, she, it like	they like	he, she, it liked	they liked

NOTES

1 In standard English, always add *-s* or *-es* to a third-person singular verb in the present tense.

| *Nonstandard* | Rex dislike his new job in Utah, and he miss his San Diego friends. |
| *Standard* | Rex **dislikes** his new job in Utah, and he **misses** his San Diego friends. |

2 Always add the ending *-ed* or *-d* to a regular verb to show it is past tense.

| *Nonstandard* | When they were children, Mona and her brother enjoy their piano lessons but hate practicing. |
| *Standard* | When they were children, Mona and her brother **enjoyed** their piano lessons but **hated** practicing. |

 Practice 4

In each blank below, write the standard form of the verb in parentheses.

1. When the skinny boxer saw his huge opponent, he (*decide / decided*) _____decided_____ he was against violent sports.

2. At the family reunion last week, people (*greet / greeted*) _____greeted_____ each other with kisses.

3. Every week, Betty (*make / makes*) _____makes_____ soup from the leftovers she finds in her refrigerator.

4. The movie was so bad that everyone (*laugh / laughed*) _____laughed_____ at the "scary" parts.

5. The twins (*wish / wishes*) _____wish_____ that their parents would get back together.

6. Lester (*play / plays*) _____ plays _____ the saxophone better than anyone else I've ever heard.

7. Two nights a week, my mother and aunt (*attend / attends*) _____ attend _____ night classes.

8. Before she left on her vacation, Cindy (*water / watered*) _____ watered _____ her plants, stopped delivery of her newspaper, and ate the leftovers in her refrigerator.

9. In bed, my brother always (*pull / pulls*) _____ pulls _____ the covers over his head.

10. At high tide during yesterday's violent storm, powerful waves (*pound / pounded*) _____ pounded _____ the shore.

Name _____ Section _____ Date _____

Score: (Number right) _____ x 10 = _____ %

Even More about Verbs: TEST 1

A. In each short passage, there is **one** illogical shift in verb tense. Cross out the incorrect verb. Then write the correct form of that verb on the line provided.

_____ended_____ **1.** The gangster movie started with a car chase, featured a half dozen gun fights, and ~~ends~~ with the death of half the characters.

_____worked_____ **2.** Josh wanted to attend college, but his parents couldn't afford to send him. So he ~~works~~ for two years after high-school graduation. With the money he saved, he attended a community college.

_____watched_____ **3.** Officer McFry worked the night shift last night. He patrolled the western part of the city. He also ~~watches~~ traffic at the intersection on Front Street. McFry returned home around 6:30 a.m.

_____play_____ **4.** Our service group meets at a nursing home once a month. We visit with the patients and plan fun activities for them. We sing, ~~played~~ card games, and do craft projects.

B. The following sentences are written in the passive voice. In each sentence, underline the verb. Then rewrite the sentence in the active voice, changing the wording as necessary.

5. That delicious chocolate cake <u>was baked</u> by Sidney.
   Sidney baked that delicious chocolate cake. _____

6. Rock music <u>is played</u> at top volume by our neighbors.
   Our neighbors play rock music at top volume. _____

7. The highest score on the test <u>was earned</u> by Clarita.
   Clarita earned the highest score on the test. _____

C. In each blank below, write the standard form of the verb in parentheses.

8. The children (*look / looked*) _____looked_____ under the sofa cushions and found eighty-three cents.

9. At home, Vicky is always in jeans, but she (*wear / wears*) _____wears_____ suits and dresses to work.

10. When he was younger, my uncle (*play / played*) _____played_____ saxophone with a dance band.

Name _____   Section _____   Date _____

Score: (Number right) _____ x 10 = _____ %

Even More about Verbs: TEST 2

A. In each short passage, there is **one** illogical shift in verb tense. Cross out the incorrect verb. Then write the correct form of that verb on the line provided.

_____sprayed_____   **1.** As we walked into the department store, a well-dressed woman from the cosmetics department approached us. Before we could protest, she ~~sprays~~ a cloud of musky-smelling perfume in our direction.

_____delivered_____   **2.** My friends worked at odd jobs this past summer. Carlos worked at a zoo, cleaning out the bird cages. Jenny worked at Pizza Hut. She ~~delivers~~ pizzas every night of the week.

_____appear_____   **3.** White flowers blossom on the apple trees every spring. Then tiny green apples ~~appeared~~. Finally, the apples turn into sweet red fruit.

_____included_____   **4.** On the first Thanksgiving, pilgrims celebrated their survival through the winter. They served many foods, but turkey was not one of them. The menu ~~includes~~ duck, goose, seafood, and eels.

B. Each of the following sentences is written in the passive voice. Rewrite each in the active voice, changing the wording as necessary.

5. Directions to the hotel were provided by a taxi driver.

_A taxi driver provided directions to the hotel._____

6. The dinner table was always cleared by the children.

_The children always cleared the dinner table._____

7. Much air pollution is caused by cars and factories.

_Cars and factories cause much air pollution._____

C. In each blank below, write the standard form of the verb in parentheses.

8. Before he leaves for work each morning, Duncan (*make / makes*) _____makes_____ coffee and pours it into a thermos.

9. When they were teenagers, Kate and Nellie often (*trade / traded*) _____traded_____ secrets.

10. My cat (*know / knows*) _____knows_____ which bedroom window is mine, and he scratches at it when he wants to be let in.

You have already reviewed (on pages 39–50) the most common ways of correcting run-on sentences and comma splices:

1 **Use a period and a capital letter.**

2 **Use a comma and a joining word.**

3 **Use a dependent word.**

This section will describe one other method of correction.

ANOTHER METHOD OF CORRECTING A RUN-ON: USE A SEMICOLON

Run-on sentences and comma splices may be corrected by putting a **semicolon (;)** between the two complete thoughts. A semicolon is made up of a period and a comma. It is used between two closely related complete thoughts.

Run-on	The fish was served with its head still on Carlo quickly lost his appetite.
Comma splice	The fish was served with its head still on, Carlo quickly lost his appetite.
Correct version	The fish was served with its head still on; Carlo quickly lost his appetite.

Practice 1

Draw a line (|) between the two complete thoughts in each run-on or comma splice that follows. Then rewrite the item, using a semicolon to connect the two complete thoughts. Note the example below.

Example   The exam was not easy | there were two hundred multiple-choice items.

The exam was not easy; there were two hundred multiple-choice items.

1. Dogs run in packs | cats are more solitary animals.

   Dogs run in packs; cats are more solitary animals.

2. The stack of books was too high, | it fell with a crash.

   The stack of books was too high; it fell with a crash.

3. I peered through the front-door peephole | a strange man was standing outside.

   I peered through the front-door peephole; a strange man was standing outside.

4. Steve drank the hot coffee too quickly, | the top of his mouth felt burned.

   Steve drank the hot coffee too quickly; the top of his mouth felt burned.

5. The auditorium was packed with angry people | the meeting would be an ugly one.

   The auditorium was packed with angry people; the meeting would be an ugly one.

Semicolon with a Transitional Word or Words

A semicolon is sometimes used with a transitional word (or words) and a comma to join two complete thoughts.

Run-on	The fish was served with its head still on as a result, Carlo quickly lost his appetite.
Comma splice	The fish was served with its head still on, as a result, Carlo quickly lost his appetite.
Correct version	The fish was served with its head still on**; as a result,** Carlo quickly lost his appetite.

Below are some common transitional words that may be used when correcting a run-on or comma splice.

Common Transitional Words

afterward	however	moreover
also	in fact	nevertheless
as a result	in addition	on the other hand
consequently	instead	otherwise
furthermore	meanwhile	therefore

Practice 2

Draw a line (|) between the two complete thoughts in each item. Then write out each sentence, using a semicolon to connect the two thoughts.

Example   The air is very stale in the library|moreover, the lighting is poor.

<u>The air is very stale in the library; moreover, the lighting is poor.</u>

1. I don't usually like desserts|however, this pumpkin pie is delicious.

    <u>I don't usually like desserts; however, this pumpkin pie is delicious.</u>

2. Our dog barks all the time,|as a result, the landlord has refused to renew our lease.

    <u>Our dog barks all the time; as a result, the landlord has refused to renew our lease.</u>

3. The house needs a new septic system,|in addition, it should have a new roof.

    <u>The house needs a new septic system; in addition, it should have a new roof.</u>

4. I almost never write to my brother|however, I post updates on his Facebook wall.

    <u>I almost never write to my brother; however, I post updates on his Facebook wall.</u>

5. You should eat a good breakfast|otherwise, you'll be out of energy before noon.

    <u>You should eat a good breakfast; otherwise, you'll be out of energy before noon.</u>

Name _____ Section _____ Date _____

Score: (Number right) _____ x 20 = _____ %

More about Run-Ons and Comma Splices: TEST 1

Draw a line (|) between the two complete thoughts in each run-on or comma splice. Then rewrite each sentence, using a semicolon to connect the two complete thoughts.

1. The milk was sour|it had been in the refrigerator for two weeks.

   The milk was sour; it had been in the refrigerator for two weeks.

   _____

2. Many people send fruitcake as a holiday gift|few people really like it.

   Many people send fruitcake as a holiday gift; few people really like it.

   _____

3. The wind knocked over a ladder|the ladder then broke a window.

   The wind knocked over a ladder; the ladder then broke a window.

   _____

4. We decided to leave the restaurant|the food was too expensive.

   We decided to leave the restaurant; the food was too expensive.

   _____

5. The slumber party was over|the house looked as if a wrecking crew had been there.

   The slumber party was over; the house looked as if a wrecking crew had been there.

   _____

Name _____   Section _____   Date _____

Score: (Number right) _____ x 20 = _____ %

More about Run-Ons and Comma Splices: TEST 2

Draw a line (|) between the two complete thoughts in each run-on or comma splice. Then rewrite each sentence, using a semicolon to connect the two complete thoughts. Note that a transitional word or phrase is part of each sentence.

1. The job applicant was an hour late for his interview|as a result he was not hired.

The job applicant was an hour late for his interview; as a result, he was not hired.

_____

2. The weatherman predicted a sunny day|however, it is cold and cloudy.

The weatherman predicted a sunny day; however, it is cold and cloudy.

_____

3. The engine has cooled|therefore, you can add more water to the radiator.

The engine has cooled; therefore, you can add more water to the radiator.

_____

4. These raisin cookies are delicious|nevertheless, I can't eat another one.

These raisin cookies are delicious; nevertheless, I can't eat another one.

_____

5. The floor must be swept and mopped|in addition, the carpets must be vacuumed.

The floor must be swept and mopped; in addition, the carpets must be vacuumed.

_____

A comma often marks a slight pause, or break, in a sentence. These pauses or breaks occur at the point where one of the six main comma rules applies. When you read a sentence aloud, you can often hear the points where slight pauses occur.

In general, use a comma only when a comma rule applies or when a comma is otherwise needed to help a sentence read clearly.

You have already reviewed (on pages 51–56) three main uses of the comma:

1 The comma is used to separate three or more items in a series.

2 The comma is used to separate introductory material from the rest of the sentence.

3 The comma is used between two complete thoughts connected by the joining words *and, but,* or *so.* (*Or, nor, for,* and *yet* are also joining words.)

This chapter will consider three other uses of the comma:

4 Around words that interrupt the flow of a sentence

5 For words of direct address and short expressions

6 In dates, addresses, and letters

AROUND WORDS THAT INTERRUPT THE FLOW OF A SENTENCE

Sentences sometimes contain material that interrupts the flow of thought. Such words and word groups should be set off from the rest of the sentence by commas. For example:

- Our minivan**, which has stickers from every state we've visited,** seems like part of the family.

If you read this sentence out loud, you can hear that the words *which has stickers from every state we've visited* interrupt the flow of thought.

Here are some other examples of sentences with interrupters:

- Liza**, who was wearing a new dress,** yelled at the waiter who spilled wine on her.
- The waiter**, however,** was not very apologetic.
- The restaurant manager**, afraid that Liza might cause a scene,** rushed to help.

More about Interrupters

A word group that identifies another word in the sentence is not always an interrupter. Sometimes it is needed for the full meaning of the sentence. If so, it should not be set off with commas.* For instance, consider the boldfaced words in the following sentences:

- The man **who came to the party with Joy** says he was kidnapped by aliens.
- Harvey, **who came to the party with Joy,** says he was kidnapped by aliens.

*Grammar books sometimes refer to interrupters as "nonrestrictive elements" and essential descriptions as "restrictive elements."

In the first sentence, the boldfaced words are needed to identify the man. Without them, we would not know who said he was kidnapped by aliens. Such essential words are not interrupters and should not be set off with commas. In the second sentence, however, we know who said he was kidnapped by aliens even without the boldfaced words. (It was Harvey.) In that case, the boldfaced words are not essential to the main message of the sentence. So in the second sentence, *who came to the party with Joy* is an interrupter and should be set off by commas.

To find out whether a word group is an interrupter, try reading the sentence without it. The first sentence above would then read: "The man says he was kidnapped by aliens." This version makes us ask, "Which man?" The boldfaced words are essential to answer that question. If we read the second sentence without the boldfaced words, we would not be omitting essential information: "Harvey says he was kidnapped by aliens."

Practice 1

Four of the following five sentences contain interrupters. Insert commas around the interrupting word groups. One sentence includes a word group that provides essential information and should not be enclosed by commas.

1. Penguins' wings,which are short and thick,are not designed for flight.
   ^   ^

2. King Arthur,according to legend,will return some day to rule Britain.
   ^   ^

3. Our basketball coach,it is rumored,is about to be fired.
   ^

4. The woman who sat in front of me at the concert was wearing strong perfume.

5. Grandfather likes to joke that his hometown,which has only one traffic light and two gas stations,could be missed if a traveler blinked. ^
   ^

Practice 2

Write three sentences using the suggested interrupters. Add words both before and after the interrupting words. Then add the necessary commas.   Answers will vary.

1. Use the words *who is my best friend* in the middle of a sentence.
   Lisa, *who is my best friend,* always has time to listen to my problems.
   _____

2. Use the words *which is my favorite snack* in the middle of a sentence.
   Frozen yogurt, *which is my favorite snack,* is low in calories.
   _____

3. Use the words *wearing an all-white outfit* in the middle of a sentence.
   Dolores, *wearing an all-white outfit,* posed at the top of the stairs.
   _____

FOR WORDS OF DIRECT ADDRESS AND SHORT EXPRESSIONS

For words of direct address Use commas to set off names or other words used to address directly the person or people being spoken to.

- You, **Mr. Gimble,** are the lucky winner of a ballpoint pen.
- Ladies and gentlemen, the sword-swallower is unable to perform tonight due to a bad sore throat.

For short expressions Use commas to set off words such as *well, yes, no,* and *oh.*

- No, you cannot have a raise.
- Well, I thought I would at least ask.

IN DATES, ADDRESSES, AND LETTERS

Within a date Place commas after the day of the week (if used), the date, and the year.

- Friday, October 13, 2003, was the date of my sister's wedding.
- On March 7, 1876, Alexander Graham Bell received a patent for the telephone.

In an address within a sentence Place a comma after each part of the address *except* between the state and the ZIP code.

- Send your comments about *English Essentials: What Everyone Needs to Know about Grammar, Punctuation, and Usage* to Townsend Press, 439 Kelley Drive, West Berlin, NJ 08091-9284.

In informal letters Place a comma after the opening and closing.

- Dear Grandma, ● With love, ● Fondly,

NOTE In business letters, a colon is used after the opening, but a comma is still used after the closing.

- Dear Mr. Cramer: ● Dear Homeowner: ● Yours truly,

Practice 3

Insert commas where needed **a)** to set off words of direct address and short expressions and **b)** in dates and addresses.

1. Why are you studying so late, Kimberly?

2. Well, look who's coming in our direction.

3. My sister lives at 2 Dog Lane, Canine, SC 09999.

4. It's about time that you woke up, sleepyhead, and got out of bed.

5. San Franciscans were surprised on the morning of April 18, 1906, by a major earthquake.

Practice 4

Complete each sentence as indicated, inserting commas where needed.

1. _____ Answers will vary. _____ is my home address.
    (Fill in your address.)

2. _____ Answers will vary. _____ is the date that I was born.
    (Fill in your complete date of birth.)

3. Dear _Susan,_____

    Meet me at the fountain in the mall tomorrow.

               Sincerely, _____

               Marco

    (Complete the heading of the above letter with the word *Susan*, and add as a closing the
    word *Sincerely*.)

**Another use of the comma is to set off direct quotations from the rest of a sentence, as explained
in "Quotation Marks" on page 63.**

Name _____   Section _____   Date _____

Score: (Number right) _____ x 10 = _____ %

More about Commas: TEST 1

On the lines provided, write the word or words in each sentence that need to be followed by a comma. Include each missing comma as well.

1. In my opinion Jesse you owe Jeff an apology.

opinion, Jesse, _____

2. Poison ivy which grows almost everywhere in North America is not welcome anywhere.

ivy, . . . America, _____

3. The first battle of the American Civil War occurred on April 12 1861 in South Carolina.

12, 1861, _____

4. Hey get away from our car!

Hey, _____

5. Oh I'm afraid this isn't what I ordered.

Oh, _____

6. It is important fellow union members to stick together during this strike.

important, . . . members, _____

7. You can write to the president at The White House 1600 Pennsylvania Avenue Washington DC 20500.

House, 1600 Pennsylvania Avenue, Washington, DC _____

8. The fact is Your Honor that the wrong man is on trial.

is, . . . Honor, _____

9. The sick child a blanket draped over his shoulders slumped in his chair.

child, . . . shoulders, _____

10. The models looking bored and unfriendly strolled down the runway.

models, . . . unfriendly, _____

Name _____ Section _____ Date _____

Score: (Number right) _____ x 10 = _____ %

More about Commas: TEST 2

In each space, write the letter of the **one** comma rule that applies to the sentence. Then insert one or more commas where they belong in the sentence.

> **a** Around interrupting words
> **b** To set off words of direct address and short expressions
> **c** In dates, addresses, and letters

_____B_____ **1.** I'm sorry, sir, but the diner is now closing.

_____B_____ **2.** This coffee shop, my friends, is a non-smoking area.

_____C_____ **3.** I'm already planning my fiftieth birthday party for Friday, March 10, 2045, at Disney World.

_____B_____ **4.** No, you may not have a third piece of chocolate cake.

_____A_____ **5.** The sofa, heaped with magazines and folded laundry, did not seem like a comfortable place to sit.

_____C_____ **6.** Eric jokingly gave his address as 25 Main Street, Elmhurst, Illinois, United States of America, North America, Planet Earth.

_____C_____ **7.** Our final exam will be given on Wednesday, June 2.

_____B_____ **8.** Yes, I have dated both Sophia and her sister.

_____A_____ **9.** Diamonds, the most expensive jewels on Earth, are closely related to lumps of coal.

_____C_____ **10.** Many visitors take the tour of the NBC Studios at 3000 West Alameda Avenue, Burbank, California 91505.

REVIEW OF THE APOSTROPHE IN POSSESSIVES

To show that something belongs to someone, we could say, for example, *the stereo owned by Rita.* But it's much simpler to say:

● *Rita's stereo*

To make most nouns possessive, add an apostrophe plus an *s*. To help you decide which word to make possessive, ask yourself the following:

1 **What is owned?**
2 **Who is the owner?**

Then put the apostrophe plus an *s* after the name of the owner.

Here's an example:

What is owned? *The stereo*
Who is the owner? *Rita*

When an apostrophe plus an *s* is added to the name of the owner, the result is the possessive form of the word: *Rita's.* That word is then followed by what is owned: *Rita's stereo.*

Here is another example:

● the waiting room belonging to the doctor

Again, ask yourself, "What is owned?" The answer is *waiting room.* Then ask, "Who is the owner?" The answer is *the doctor.* So add an apostrophe plus *s* after the name of the owner and add what is owned: *the doctor's waiting room.* The apostrophe plus *s* shows that the waiting room belongs to the doctor.

Here is a third example:

● the hopes of everyone

Again, ask yourself, "What is owned?" The answer is *hopes.* Then ask, "Who is the owner?" The answer is *everyone.* So add an apostrophe plus *s* after the name of the owner and add what is owned: *everyone's hopes.* The apostrophe plus *s* shows that the hopes belong to everyone.

Practice 1

Rewrite the items below as possessives with an apostrophe plus *s*. In the first column, write the name of the owner. In the second column, write the possessive form plus what is owned. One is done for you as an example.

	Who is the owner?	Possessive form plus what is owned
1. the bike belonging to Randy	Randy	Randy's bike
2. the purr of the cat	cat	cat's purr
3. the temper of our neighbor	neighbor	neighbor's temper
4. the ending of the story	story	story's ending
5. the mummy belonging to the museum	museum	museum's mummy

Practice 2

Underline the word in each sentence that needs an apostrophe plus *s*. That word is the owner. Then write the word correctly, along with what is owned, in the space provided. The first one is done for you as an example.

1. I tracked mud on my <u>mother</u> white rug.   *mother's white rug*
2. <u>Vietnam</u> climate is hot and damp.   *Vietnam's climate*
3. A <u>gorilla</u> diet is mainly vegetarian.   *gorilla's diet*
4. The <u>photographer</u> camera was stolen.   *photographer's camera*
5. The <u>bride</u> wedding dress was knee-length.   *bride's wedding dress*

Practice 3

Write three sentences that include words ending in an apostrophe plus *s*.   *Answers will vary.*

1. _____
   _____
2. _____
   _____
3. _____
   _____

Showing Possession with Singular and Plural Nouns That End in *s*

An apostrophe plus *s* is used to show possession even with a singular noun that already ends in *s*:

- Gus**'s** computer (the computer belonging to Gus)
- The boss**'s** secretary (the secretary belonging to the boss)

However, an apostrophe alone is used to show possession with a plural noun that ends in s:

- the contestant**s'** answers (the answers of a number of contestants)
- the three lawyer**s'** office (the office belonging to three lawyers)

Practice 4

Underline the word that needs an apostrophe in each sentence below. Then write that word, adding the **'** or the **'s**, in the space provided.

bass's   1. Adam carefully removed the fishhook from the <u>bass</u> mouth.

lions'   2. The <u>lions</u> keeper has worked with them from birth.

Otis's   3. <u>Otis</u> story about being kidnapped by a flying saucer is hard to believe.

twins'   4. The <u>twins</u> mother was a twin herself.

Olsons'   5. The <u>Olsons</u> home has a secret passageway.

WHEN *NOT* TO USE AN APOSTROPHE

Do Not Use an Apostrophe in Plurals and with Verbs

People sometimes confuse possessive and plural forms of nouns. Remember that a plural is formed simply by adding an *s* to a noun; no apostrophe is used. Look at the sentence below to see which words are plural and which word is possessive:

● Lola's necklace has pearls and diamond chips.

The words *pearls* and *chips* are plurals—there is more than one pearl, and there is more than one diamond chip. But *Lola's*, the word with the apostrophe plus *s*, is possessive. Lola owns the necklace.

Also, many verbs end with an *s*. Do not use an apostrophe in a verb.

● Jenny **plays** poker once a week.

● She often **wins**.

Practice 5

In the spaces provided under each sentence, correctly write the **one** word that needs an apostrophe. Also, explain why the other word or words ending in *s* do not get apostrophes.

Example   The patients eyes opened slowly after surgery.

patients: _____patient's, meaning "belonging to the patient"_____

eyes: _____eyes, meaning "more than one eye"_____

1. In a new version of the fairy tale, the princes wife rescues him from fire-breathing dragons.

   princes: prince's, meaning "belonging to the prince"

   rescues: rescues—a verb

   dragons: dragons, meaning "more than one dragon"

2. The chocolates in the silver box are a gift from my mothers best friend.

   chocolates: chocolates, meaning "more than one chocolate"

   mothers: mother's, meaning "belonging to my mother"

3. Everyone wonders how the magicians feet got freed from the chains.

   wonders: wonders—a verb

   magicians   magician's, meaning "belonging to the magician"

   chains: chains, meaning "more than one chain"

4. Sheer white curtains and fresh lilacs added to the rooms simple charm.

   curtains: curtains, meaning "more than one curtain"

   lilacs: lilacs, meaning "more than one lilac"

   rooms: room's, meaning "belonging to the room"

5. Studies show that a rooms color affects our moods.

Studies: *Studies, meaning "more than one study"*

rooms: *room's, meaning "belonging to the room"*

affects: *affects—a verb*

moods: *moods, meaning "more than one mood"*

Do Not Use an Apostrophe with Possessive Pronouns

Do not use an apostrophe in the possessive pronouns *his, hers, its, yours, ours, theirs,* and *whose.*

- Those seats are **ours**.

- **His** car is purple.

People often confuse certain possessive pronouns with contractions. For instance, *its* is often confused with *it's*. The following sentence includes both words:

- **It's** sad that our old tree is losing **its** leaves.

The word *it's* is a contraction meaning *it is*. Contractions, of course, do have apostrophes. *Its* means *belonging to it*—the leaves belong to it (the tree). *Its* is a possessive pronoun and does not have an apostrophe.

Following are examples of other possessive pronouns and the contractions they are confused with.

- The Pratts rarely mow **their** lawn. **They're** not concerned about the looks of the neighborhood.
  Their means *belonging to them* (the lawn belongs to them). *They're* is a contraction that means *they are*.

- **You're** going to fall if you do not tie **your** shoelaces.
  You're is a contraction that means *you are*. *Your* means *belonging to you* (the shoelaces belong to you).

- **Who's** the person **whose** car is blocking ours?
  Who's is a contraction meaning *who is*. *Whose* means *belonging to whom* (the car belonging to whom).

 Practice 6

Underline the correct word within each pair of parentheses.

1. We arranged with two neighborhood boys to mow our lawn, but now (*they're* / *their*) father tells me (*they're* / *their*) going to camp for a month.

2. Darryl told his son, "If (*you're* / *your*) homework is not done by seven o'clock, (*you're* / *your*) not going to watch the movie."

3. (*Who's* / *Whose*) turn is it to wash the dishes, and (*who's* / *whose*) going to dry them?

4. (*It's* / *Its*) difficult, if not impossible, to get toothpaste back into (*it's* / *its*) tube.

5. The fruit salad on the table is (*hers'* / *hers*), and the freshly baked bread is (*ours'* / *ours*).

Name _____   Section _____   Date _____

Score: (Number right) _____ x 10 = _____ %

More about Apostrophes: TEST 1

Each of the sentences below contains **one** word that needs an apostrophe. Write the word, with its apostrophe, in the space provided.

1. Susans eyes were glassy with fatigue.

    _____ Susan's _____

2. There is no bread, so well have crackers with our soup.

    _____ we'll _____

3. Fixing drippy faucets is the landlords job.

    _____ landlord's _____

4. Joanne hasnt ever gone on a roller coaster, and she insists she never will.

    _____ hasn't _____

5. Four tiny packages arrived in Saturdays mail.

    _____ Saturday's _____

6. Leo knows his girlfriend is angry at him, but hes not sure why.

    _____ he's _____

7. Many presents have been delivered to the brides home.

    _____ bride's _____

8. The keyboards plastic cover protects the keys from crumbs and dust.

    _____ keyboard's _____

9. There are about 100,000 hairs on the average persons head.

    _____ person's _____

10. The soft moans in the classroom made it clear that students werent expecting the test.

    _____ weren't _____

Name _____   Section _____ Date _____

Score: (Number right) _____ x 10 = _____ %

More about Apostrophes: TEST 2

Each of the sentences below contains **one** word that needs an apostrophe. Write the word, with its apostrophe, in the space provided.

1. We didnt recognize our teacher at first without his beard.

    _____didn't_____

2. Both of Janes husbands were named Andrew.

    _____Jane's_____

3. Half-finished paintings filled the artists studio.

    _____artist's_____

4. Someone will be taking in our mail and packages while were away on vacation.

    _____we're_____

5. Floridas neighbors are Alabama and Georgia.

    _____Florida's_____

6. The snowflakes glittered in the flashlights glare.

    _____flashlight's_____

7. The farmers may lose their entire wheat crop if it doesnt rain soon.

    _____doesn't_____

8. Someday Ill tell you about the day Uncle Harry was chased by some mad chickens.

    _____I'll_____

9. The two brothers relationship has remained strong through the years.

    _____brothers'_____

10. The critics were careful not to give away the movies surprise ending.

    _____movie's_____

REVIEW OF QUOTATIONS WITH SPLIT SENTENCES

In a direct quotation, one sentence may be split into two parts:

● "Add the eggs to the sauce," said the TV chef, "blending them together."

Note that the chef's exact words are set off by two sets of quotation marks. The words *said the TV chef* are not included in the quotation marks since they were not spoken by the chef.

The words *blending them together* begin with a small letter because they are a continuation of a sentence, not a new sentence. (The full sentence spoken by the instructor is "Add the eggs to the sauce, blending them together.")

Commas are used to set off the quoted parts from the rest of the sentence:

● "Add the eggs to the sauce**,**" said the TV chef**,** "blending them together."

QUOTATIONS OF MORE THAN ONE SENTENCE

A direct quotation can be divided into separate sentences:

● "I really hate my job," Stan told his wife. "I think I'd better start looking for a new one."
The words *Stan told his wife* are not part of the direct quotation.

At times, a direct quotation will be more than one sentence:

● Our minister always says, "It's every citizen's responsibility to vote. If you don't vote, you shouldn't complain."

Note that only one pair of quotation marks is used. Do not use quotation marks for each new sentence as long as the quotation is not interrupted.

Practice 1

Insert quotation marks where needed in the following sentences.

1. "The wait for a table," said the restaurant hostess, "will be about forty minutes."

2. "I don't mind if you borrow my new sweater," said my sister, "but I don't expect to find it rolled up in a ball under your bed."

3. The newspaper editor said to the new reporter, "I'm sorry to have to tell you this. I can't use the article that you spent two weeks writing."

4. "Why is it," asked Sara, "that the monthly charges on my cell phone are so high?"

5. "Our math teacher is unfair," complained James. "He assigns four hours of homework for each class. Does he think we have nothing else to do?"

QUOTATIONS WITH QUESTION MARKS AND EXCLAMATION POINTS

If a direct quotation is a question, place the question mark within the quotation marks:

● "Where are my red shoes?" asked Lana.

After a question mark, no comma is used to set off the direct quotation.

If the entire sentence is a question, place the question mark after the quotation marks:

● Did you say "Thank you"?

An exclamation point also goes within quotation marks unless it applies to the whole sentence.

● The kids shouted, "Let's go to the pool!"

INDIRECT QUOTATIONS

Often we express someone's spoken or written thoughts without repeating the exact words used. When we use an **indirect quotation**, we put the message into our own words. Indirect quotations do not require quotation marks.

The following example shows how the same material could be handled as either a direct or an indirect quotation.

Direct Quotation

● The baker said, **"I forgot** to put yeast in the dough."

The words *I forgot* tell us that the baker's exact words are being used—he's referring to himself. Since his exact words are being used, they must be put in quotation marks.

Indirect Quotation

● The baker said **that he had forgotten** to put yeast in the dough.

The sentence refers to the baker as *he*, so we know that the baker's exact words are not being quoted. Quotation marks are not used for indirect quotations. The word *that* often signals an indirect quotation.

Here are a few more examples of indirect quotations:

● The boss said that workers could have a day off on their birthdays.
● Mom told us not to answer the front door.
● The park rangers warned us to keep our windows closed.

Practice 2

Rewrite each of the following indirect quotations as a direct quotation. The direct quotation will include the words that someone actually spoke.

Note that you will have to change some of the words as well as add capital letters, quotation marks, and any other punctuation needed. The first one is done for you as an example.

1. The child asked if the Milky Way candy bar was really full of milk.

The child asked, "Is the Milky Way candy bar really full of milk?"

2. My sister said that she would help me do the report if she could wear my new blouse.

   <u>My sister said, "I will help you do the report if I can wear your new blouse."</u>

3. The bookstore manager grumbled that he couldn't take back books with writing in them.

   <u>The bookstore manager grumbled, "I can't take back books with writing in them."</u>

4. The teacher warned us a surprise quiz was coming soon.

   <u>The teacher warned us, "A surprise quiz is coming soon."</u>

5. The officer asked me if I was lost.

   <u>The officer asked me, "Are you lost?"</u>

QUOTATION MARKS FOR TITLES OF SHORT WORKS

Use quotation marks to set off the titles of short stories, newspaper or magazine articles, songs, poems, episodes of TV series, book chapters, and other parts of longer works.

- Our teacher assigned the short story "The Open Boat" by Stephen Crane.
- The familiar song "For He's a Jolly Good Fellow" is over two hundred years old.
- The witty poet Ogden Nash wrote a poem titled "Never Mind the Overcoat; Button Up That Lip."

NOTE The titles of longer works, such as books, newspapers, magazines, plays, movies, TV series, and record albums, should be underlined when handwritten. When typed on a computer, such titles should appear in *italic type*.

- Our assignment was to read the chapter titled "The Traits of Happy People" in a book by David Meyers, <u>The Pursuit of Happiness</u>.
- "Three Words That Can Change Your Life" was the first article I turned to in the current issue of <u>Reader's Digest</u>.

Practice 3

Insert quotation marks or underlines where needed in the sentences below.

1. The chapter titled "Extrasensory Perception" in the textbook <u>Psychology Today</u> says there is no evidence that ESP actually exists.

2. The article "Quick Exercise Routines" in <u>Prevention</u> magazine is about working out during lunch.

3. The beloved song "Over the Rainbow" was first heard in the movie <u>The Wizard of Oz</u>.

4. The editor of the <u>Daily Tribune</u> has received many letters supporting and opposing her editorial "Let's Ban Proms in Schools."

Name _____ Section _____ Date _____

Score: (Number right) _____ x 10 = _____ %

More about Quotation Marks: TEST 1

Add opening and closing quotation marks or underlines where needed. One sentence does not need additional punctuation.

1. "Somebody has stuck gum all over my computer keyboard," Coco said angrily.

2. "One lucky caller wins a trip to Disneyland," the radio announcer promised.

3. "I bought a truck," Julie stated, "because I sit higher and feel safer."

4. "When you see me next," laughed the brunette, "I'll be a blonde."

5. The racecar driver said he wanted a quart of milk waiting for him at the finish line.

6. An article about online bullying called "When the Bullies Turned Faceless" recently appeared in the New York Times.

7. An hour after lunch, Rudy said, "I'm starving. I hope dinner will be ready soon."

8. The park ranger said, "Watch out for ticks."

9. "I need to move back home," said Wally to his parents.

10. The Monopoly card that I drew said, "Do not pass Go. Do not collect $200."

Name _____   Section _____   Date _____

Score: (Number right) _____ x 10 = _____ %

More about Quotation Marks: TEST 2

On the lines provided, rewrite the following sentences, adding quotation marks or underlines as needed. One sentence does not need additional punctuation.

1. Our coach said to us, I received some wonderful news this morning.
    Our coach said to us, "I received some wonderful news this morning."

2. The Secret Life of Trees is the title of a recent article in Time magazine.
    "The Secret Life of Trees" is the title of a recent article in Time magazine.

3. Aren't you going to do the dishes? It's your turn, my brother reminded me.
    "Aren't you going to do the dishes? It's your turn," my brother reminded me.

4. My friends asked me to meet them at the mall.
    No quotation marks needed.

5. Abraham Lincoln said, When I do good, I feel good. When I do bad, I feel bad. And that's my religion.
    Abraham Lincoln said, "When I do good, I feel good. When I do bad, I feel bad. And that's my religion."

6. Sleet has made the roads very icy, the TV announcer warned. If you don't need to go out, stay home.
    "Sleet has made the roads very icy," the TV announcer warned. "If you don't need to go out, stay home."

7. A poem by Shel Silverstein begins with the words, I am writing these poems from inside a lion.
    A poem by Shel Silverstein begins with the words, "I am writing these poems from inside a lion."

8. This vacation was lots of fun, said the woman, but after all of this sightseeing, I'm going to need a vacation from my vacation.
    "This vacation was lots of fun," said the woman, "but after all of this sightseeing, I'm going to need a vacation from my vacation."

9. If you have finished complaining, my father said quietly, you may go clean your room now.
    "If you have finished complaining," my father said quietly, "you may go clean your room now."

10. The handmade poster had a photograph of a cocker spaniel and the words, Curly has been missing since Sunday night. Please call us if you've seen him.
    The handmade poster had a photograph of a cocker spaniel and the words, "Curly has been missing since Sunday night. Please call us if you've seen him."

31

More about Homonyms

You have already reviewed a number of common homonyms (words that sound alike). This section identifies some other homonyms as well as other confusing words.

OTHER HOMONYMS

buy   to purchase
by   (1) close to; (2) no later than; (3) through the action of

● **Buy** furniture from Sofas Inc. **by** the end of the year, and you won't have to pay until March.

   Spelling hint   I'd like to b**uy** something for **U**.

Fill in each blank with either *buy* or *by*.

1. Why must you _____buy_____ something just because it's on sale?
2. The beautiful mural in the lobby was painted _____by_____ a student.
3. An old dog was sleeping on the front porch _____by_____ the screen door.
4. We have to turn in our research papers _____by_____ the end of the month.
5. My sister is hoping to _____buy_____ a home of her own this year.

passed   (the past tense of *pass*) (1) handed to; (2) went by; (3) completed successfully
past   (1) the time before the present; (2) by

● In the **past**, I have **passed** all my courses, but I may not pass them all this semester.

   Spelling hint   If you need a verb, use **passed**. The *-ed* at its end shows it is the past tense of the verb *pass*.

Fill in each blank with either *passed* or *past*.

1. Only five minutes have _____passed_____ since I last looked at the clock.
2. A bumblebee just flew _____past_____ my head.
3. Mick _____passed_____ his driver's test on the third try.
4. Unfortunately, one of the cars that Marylou _____passed_____ on the highway was a police car.
5. Life was not always as carefree in the _____past_____ as some people would like to believe.

principal   (1) main; (2) the person in charge of a school
principle   a guideline or rule

● Our **principal** believes in the **principle** of giving teachers a great deal of freedom.

   Spelling hint   Ideally, a school princi**pal** should be a **pal**.

Fill in each blank with either *principal* or *principle*.

1. My aunt is the _____principal_____ owner of a beauty shop on Mill Avenue.
2. I try to live by the _____principle_____ of treating others as I want to be treated.
3. Mr. Larson became _____principal_____ of Coles High School after teaching there for years.
4. The _____principal_____ reason the Butlers are moving to California is to be near their grandchildren.
5. Our basketball coach taught us to follow the _____principle_____ of being gracious in defeat as well as in victory.

OTHER CONFUSING WORDS

Here are some words that are not homonyms but are still confusing words. In most cases they have similar sounds and are often misused and misspelled.

a   used before words that begin with a consonant sound
an   used before words that begin with a vowel or a silent *h* (as in *an hour*).

● Would you like **an** ice-cream cone or **a** shake?

Fill in each blank with either *a* or *an*.

1. _____An_____ insect has six legs and a three-part body.
2. I left _____a_____ note on the kitchen counter saying when I'd be back.
3. Is that _____an_____ alligator you are petting in that photograph?
4. A hush fell over the circus audience when _____a_____ tightrope walker fell.
5. Although she worked hard, Louise was shocked to receive such _____an_____ honor as "Employee of the Year."

accept   (1) to receive; (2) to agree to take; (3) to believe in
except   (1) excluding or leaving out; (2) but

● All the employees **except** the part-timers were willing to **accept** the new contract.

Fill in each blank with either *accept* or *except*.

1. Mrs. Carlotti says she will _____accept_____ an appointment to the school board.
2. My little sister likes all types of food _____except_____ meat, fish, dairy products, and vegetables.
3. Whatever your decision is, I will _____accept_____ it.
4. All of my relatives attended our family reunion _____except_____ for an elderly aunt.
5. At the company dinner, Meredith will _____accept_____ the award on behalf of her department.

advice   opinion meant to be helpful

advise   to give an opinion meant to be helpful

● Never take the **advice** of someone who **advises** you to act against your conscience.

Fill in each blank with either *advice* or *advise*.

1. "I _____advise_____ you to replace your fan belt," the gas station attendant said.

2. Don't seek _____advice_____ from anybody you don't admire.

3. Employment experts _____advise_____ people to get training throughout their lives.

4. There's so much conflicting _____advice_____ about diet that it's no wonder people are confused about what they should eat.

5. The kindergarten teacher said the best _____advice_____ she could give parents is to read regularly to their children.

affect   to influence

effect   a result

● Divorce **affects** an entire family, and its **effects**—both good and bad—last for years.

Fill in each blank with either *affect* or *effect*.

1. Your actions _____affect_____ those around you, whether you're aware of them or not.

2. The child spattered red paint on the paper and then stepped back to admire the _____effect_____.

3. According to psychologists, the color of the clothes we wear _____affect_____s our moods.

4. What will be the economic _____effect_____s if the factory closes?

5. The referees did not allow the obnoxious behavior of some fans to _____affect_____ their decisions.

desert   (1) a verb meaning "to leave or abandon"; (2) a noun meaning "a dry region with little or no plant growth"

dessert   a sweet course eaten at the end of a meal

● The children were willing to **desert** the TV set only when **dessert** was served.

Fill in each blank with either *desert* or *dessert*.

1. For me, a real _____dessert_____ must contain chocolate.

2. As a result of irrigation, this area is now farmland instead of _____desert_____.

3. What causes a parent to _____desert_____ his or her children?

4. If I'm not very hungry, I skip the meal and eat _____dessert_____.

5. Certain medications can make your mouth feel as dry as a _____desert_____.

fewer used for items that can be counted
less   used for general amounts

● As our congregation ages, our church is left with **fewer** members and **less** financial support.

Fill in each blank with either *fewer* or *less*.

1. By the 1920s, there were _____fewer_____ horses and more cars on the road.

2. When I get too little sleep, I have _____less_____ patience than usual.

3. Whose car had _____fewer_____ miles on it, yours or Carl's?

4. Two-percent milk has _____less_____ fat in it than whole milk.

5. Two-percent milk also contains _____fewer_____ calories.

loose (1) not tight; (2) free; not confined
lose   (1) to misplace; (2) to not win; (3) to be deprived of something one has had

● If you don't fix that **loose** steering wheel, you could **lose** control of your car.

Fill in each blank with either *loose* or *lose*.

1. I _____lose_____ my keys at least once a week.

2. A _____loose_____ shutter was banging against the side of the house.

3. I always _____lose_____ when I play chess against my computer.

4. Clyde was warned that he would _____lose_____ his job if he was late for work one more time.

5. In our town, it's illegal to allow cats and dogs to run _____loose_____.

quiet (1) silent; (2) relaxing and peaceful
quite (1) truly; (2) very; (3) completely
quit   (1) to stop doing something; (2) to resign from one's job

● Giselle was **quiet** after saying she might want to **quit** her job but that she wasn't **quite** sure.

Fill in each blank with either *quiet, quite,* or *quit.*

1. The rain had frozen, and the roads were _____quite_____ slippery.

2. Let's spend a _____quiet_____ evening at home tonight.

3. The waitress began to take my dish, but I wasn't _____quite_____ finished.

4. My speech teacher told me to _____quit_____ saying the word *like* so much, but, like, what's wrong with that word?

5. Our neighbors had enjoyed the glitter and noisy excitement of Las Vegas, but they were glad to be back home in our _____quiet_____ little town.

than   a word used in comparisons
then   (1) at that time; (2) next

● First Dad proved he was a better wrestler **than** I am; **then** he helped me improve.

Fill in each blank with either *than* or *then*.

1. I scrubbed the potatoes, and _____*then*_____ I poked holes in them with my fork.

2. Crossword puzzles are more difficult _____*than*_____ word searches.

3. My grandparents were born in the 1950s. There were no cell phones or websites _____*then*_____.

4. Every eligible voter should learn about the candidates and _____*then*_____ go and vote.

5. The tiny family-owned shop is always more crowded _____*than*_____ the huge supermarket.

use   to make use of
used (to)   accustomed to; was in the habit of; did previously

● I am **used to** very spicy food, but when I cook for others, I **use** much less hot pepper.

   Spelling hint   Do not forget to include the *d* with *used to*.

Fill in each blank with either *use* or *used*.

1. After spending six years in Alaska, I am _____*used*_____ to cold weather.

2. Should I _____*use*_____ a paste or liquid wax on the car?

3. After you get married, will you _____*use*_____ your husband's last name?

4. Since she is the youngest of four girls, Elaine is _____*used*_____ to wearing hand-me-downs.

5. When she was little, Maureen _____*used*_____ to bite her fingernails, but she doesn't any more.

were   the past tense of *are*
we're   contraction of *we are*

● **We're** going to visit the town in Florida where my grandparents **were** born.

Fill in each blank with either *were* or *we're*.

1. Where _____*were*_____ you when I needed you?

2. _____*We're*_____ having a quiz on Friday.

3. Our relatives _____*were*_____ not surprised to hear of my brother's divorce.

4. I don't think _____*we're*_____ going to have to wait more than five minutes to get seated.

5. The Beatles _____*were*_____ once known as Long John and the Silver Beatles.

Name _____   Section _____   Date _____

Score: (Number right) _____ x 5 = _____ %

More about Homonyms: TEST 1

In the space provided, write the word that correctly fits each sentence.

by, buy   1. At first the motion of the airplane bothered Randall, but _____*by*_____ the
use, used   time the flight was over, he was _____*used*_____ to it.

advice, advise   2. Even people who won't usually take _____*advice*_____ somehow _____*accept*_____
except, accept   it from Rosalie.

principal, principle 3. The _____*principal*_____ of my old school _____*quit*_____ his job to stay
quit, quite, quiet   home and take care of his grandchildren.

effects, affects 4. Despite the terrible _____*effects*_____ of the earthquake, people didn't
loose, lose   _____*lose*_____ their sense of humor.

less, fewer   5. One benefit of watching _____*less*_____ TV is that you are exposed to
less, fewer   _____*fewer*_____ commercials.

past, passed   6. When Sarita learned that she had _____*passed*_____ her GED exam, she
quiet, quite, quit   disturbed her usually _____*quiet*_____ house with a shout of joy.

we're, were   7. Tonight _____*we're*_____ going to see _____*an*_____ old movie called
a, an   *The Three Faces of Eve.*

principal, principle 8. A basic _____*principle*_____ that _____*a*_____ student doctor learns
a, an   in training is "First, do no harm."

lose, loose   9. In order to _____*lose*_____ weight, it's better to exercise and eat sensibly
then, than   _____*than*_____ to starve yourself.

use, used   10. I am more _____*used*_____ to spending an evening watching TV
than, then   _____*than*_____ I am to reading or exercising.

Name _____   Section _____   Date _____

Score: (Number right) _____ x 5 = _____ %

More about Homonyms: TEST 2

In the space provided, write the word that correctly fits each sentence.

were, we're   1. The students _____*were*_____ hoping to be given _____*an*_____
a, an   opportunity to do extra-credit work.

dessert, desert   2. Gina likes to hike into the _____*desert*_____ because of the sense of
piece, peace   _____*peace*_____ she feels there.

advice, advise   3. Some of the best _____*advice*_____ I ever got was this: "When you
lose, loose   _____*lose*_____ your temper, count to ten before you speak."

then, than   4. First we'll have salad, _____*then*_____ a main course, and finally
desert, dessert   _____*dessert*_____.

were, we're   5. Because _____*we're*_____ going to be traveling in a hot climate, I
loose, lose   packed clothes that were _____*loose*_____ and cool.

quite, quit, quiet   6. Some medications, unfortunately, have _____*quite*_____ a few
affects, effects   unpleasant side _____*effects*_____.

fewer, less   7. More than half of today's college students are female; far _____*fewer*_____
passed, past   women went to college in the _____*past*_____.

quit, quiet, quiet   8. The boy was a poor sport who would _____*quit*_____ the game early if
lose, loose   he saw he was going to _____*lose*_____.

advise, advice   9. Even though the job doesn't pay much now, I strongly _____*advise*_____
accept, except   you to _____*accept*_____ it. It's a wonderful opportunity.

principal, principle   10. Until my graduation, I had never seen our _____*principal*_____ wearing
than, then   anything other _____*than*_____ a suit and tie.

32

More about Capital Letters

Other Rules for Capital Letters

You have already reviewed (on pages 75–80) the following uses of capital letters:

1 The first word in a sentence or direct quotation
2 The word "I" and people's names
3 Names of specific places, institutions, and languages
4 Product names
5 Calendar items
6 Titles

This chapter will consider other uses of capitals:

7 **Capitalize a word that is used as a substitute for the name of a family member. Also, capitalize words like *aunt, uncle,* and *cousin* when they are used as part of people's names.**

● My biggest fan at the dirt-bike competitions was **M**om.

● Go help **G**randfather carry those heavy bags.

● Phil is staying at **U**ncle Raymond's house for the holidays.

BUT Do not capitalize words such as *mom* or *grandfather* when they come after possessive words such as *my, her,* or *our.*

● My grandmother lives next door to my parents.

● Phil and his uncle are both recovered alcoholics.

8 **Capitalize the names of specific groups: races, religions, nationalities, companies, clubs, and other organizations.**

● Edward, who is **P**olish **A**merican, sometimes cooks **C**hinese dishes for his **N**orthside **C**hess **C**lub meetings.

● Arlene, the local president of **M**others **A**gainst **D**runk **D**riving, is a part-time real estate agent for **C**entury 21.

9 **Capitalize the names of specific school courses.**

● This semester, Jody has **D**ance 101, **G**eneral **P**sychology, and **E**conomics 235.

BUT The names of general subject areas are not capitalized.

● This semester, Jody has a gym class, a psychology course, and a business course.

10 **Capitalize the names of specific periods and famous events in history.**

- During the **M**iddle **A**ges, only the nobility and the clergy could read and write.
- The act of protest in which 342 tea chests were thrown into the ocean came to be known as the **B**oston **T**ea **P**arty.

11 **Capitalize the opening and closing of a letter.**

Capitalize words in the salutation of a letter.

- **D**ear **M**s. **A**xelrod:
- **D**ear **S**ir or **M**adam:

Capitalize only the first word of the closing of a letter.

- **S**incerely yours,
- **Y**ours truly,

12 **Capitalize common abbreviations made up of the first letters of the words they represent:**

- **YMCA**
- **ABC**
- **FBI**
- **AIDS**
- **UFO**
- **NASA**
- **AWOL**

Name _____ Section _____ Date _____

More about Capital Letters: TEST 1

Underline the **two** words that need capitalizing in each sentence. Then write those words correctly in the spaces provided.

1. Dear <u>sir</u>: Please tell me who played the character <u>aunt</u> Bea on the old *Andy Griffith Show*.
   Sincerely yours,
   Clint Hart

   _____Sir_____   _____Aunt_____

2. In today's <u>history</u> 201 class, we learned about the founding of the <u>naacp</u>.

   _____History_____   _____NAACP_____

3. In front of the <u>vfw</u> hall, there's a memorial to all the World <u>war</u> II veterans.

   _____VFW_____   _____War_____

4. During the period known as the <u>dark</u> <u>ages</u>, the rate of literacy fell in Europe.

   _____Dark_____   _____Ages_____

5. My mother is Mexican and a <u>baptist</u>, while my dad is <u>italian</u> and a Catholic.

   _____Baptist_____   _____Italian_____

6. When <u>grandma</u> retired from Blooming <u>valley</u> Nursery, her employers gave her a dozen rosebushes.

   _____Grandma_____   _____Valley_____

7. Dear <u>aunt</u> Sally,

   Thank you so much for your generous birthday check. I can certainly put it to good use!
   <u>with</u> love,
   Rachel

   _____Aunt_____   _____With_____

8. Uncle Leonardo is active in the local <u>sons</u> of <u>italy</u> social club.

   _____Sons_____   _____Italy_____

9. In our offices at <u>townsend</u> <u>press</u>, we communicate every day by e-mail.

   _____Townsend_____   _____Press_____

10. The Art <u>league</u> of Middletown is sponsoring a show of paintings by the artist known as <u>grandma</u> Moses.

    _____League_____   _____Grandma_____

Name _____ Section _____ Date _____

Score: (Number right) _____ x 5 = _____ %

More about Capital Letters: TEST 2

Underline the **two** words that need capitalizing in each sentence. Then write those words correctly in the spaces provided.

1. Our neighborhood has many <u>asian</u>-language newspapers and a <u>buddhist</u> temple.

   _____ Asian _____ _____ Buddhist _____

2. The event known as the <u>march</u> on <u>washington</u>, which took place August 26, 1963, brought together more than 250,000 people to demonstrate for civil rights.

   _____ March _____ _____ Washington _____

3. Rodrigo has <u>social</u> <u>issues</u> 101 at the same time that his brother has a history class.

   _____ Social _____ _____ Issues _____

4. To her surprise, <u>mom</u> still remembers every word of the <u>gettysburg</u> Address, which she memorized as a fifth-grader.

   _____ Mom _____ _____ Gettysburg _____

5. Because <u>uncle</u> Josh talked so little about what he did at work, we joked that he was really a spy for the <u>cia</u>.

   _____ Uncle _____ _____ CIA _____

6. As a project for her 4-<u>h</u> club, Melinda is raising a <u>vietnamese</u> potbellied pig.

   _____ H _____ _____ Vietnamese _____

7. Dear <u>sir</u>:
   Your microwave has been repaired and can be picked up at your convenience.
       <u>sincerely</u>,
   Rick's Repairs

   _____ Sir _____ _____ Sincerely _____

8. The <u>italian</u> <u>renaissance</u>, which took place from 1420 to 1600, is known as a time of great artistic accomplishment.

   _____ Italian _____ _____ Renaissance _____

9. Because yesterday was a <u>jewish</u> holiday, our <u>chemistry</u> 101 class did not meet.

   _____ Jewish _____ _____ Chemistry _____

10. The <u>great</u> <u>depression</u> began in 1929 on Black Tuesday, the day the stock market crashed.

   _____ Great _____ _____ Depression _____

33 The Basics of Writing

What, in a nutshell, do you need to become a better writer? You need to know the basic goals in writing and to understand the writing process—as explained on the pages that follow.

Two Basic Goals in Writing

When you write a paper, your two basic goals should be (1) to make a point and (2) to support that point. Look for a moment at the following cartoon:

PEANUTS © 1974 Peanuts Worldwide LLC. Dist. by UNIVERSAL UCLICK.
Reprinted by permission. All rights reserved.

See if you can answer the following questions:

- What is Snoopy's point in his paper?
  Your answer: His point is that _____ dogs are superior to cats. _____

- What is his support for his point?
  Your answer: _____ No support is given. _____

Explanation Snoopy's point, of course, is that dogs are superior to cats. But he offers no support whatsoever to back up his point! There are two jokes here. First, he is a dog and so is naturally going to believe that dogs are superior. The other joke is that his evidence ("They just are, and that's all there is to it!") is a lot of empty words. His somewhat guilty look in the last panel suggests that he knows he has not proved his point. To write effectively, you must provide real support for your points and opinions.

Writing Paragraphs

A **paragraph** is a series of sentences about one main idea, or **point**. A paragraph typically starts with a point (often called the **topic sentence**), and the rest of the paragraph provides specific details to support and develop that point.

A student named Michael wrote the following paragraph in response to this assignment:

> Write about three kinds of changes that could make our country a better place. You might want to consider changes on three different levels: national, social, and personal.

Three Helpful Changes

Three changes could help make our country a better place in which to live. First of all, on the national level, all Americans should be asked to pay a fair share of taxes. At present, many people who are very wealthy pay little income tax because of deductions and write-offs, and many corporations pay no taxes at all. If millionaires and companies paid the same tax rate as everyday people, our country would be more democratic. Next, on the social level, there should be less rudeness and more kindness. Examples of rudeness are all around us. Some people are rude while talking. They interrupt each other or have loud private conversations on their cell phones while others are sitting nearby. Others rudely get in the way—they block the aisle in the market while deciding just what they want to buy, or they drive too slowly or too quickly, putting other drivers at risk. And we've all seen, even at nice restaurants, parents who ignore their children's rude behavior. They let the kids run noisily around the tables, spoiling the experience for the other diners. Finally, on the personal level, people should stop watching TV commercials that make human beings seem like idiots. Countless commercials feature men and women who are smiling, bubbly, and apparently very happy because of a mattress, luggage, or furniture sale or a cereal purchase or an automobile bargain—or because they are all enjoying a particular beer with their attractive, sexy, and party-loving friends. Of course, there are many changes large and small that could improve our country; these are three of them.

- What is the point of the above paragraph? _____
  The author discusses three changes that could make our country a better place to live.

- What are the three kinds of changes that Michael has provided to support his point?
  1. *On national level—everyone should pay a fair share of taxes.*
  2. *On social level—there should be less rudeness and more kindness.*
  3. *On personal level—stop watching TV commercials that make people look like idiots.*

The above paragraph, like many effective paragraphs, starts by stating a main idea, or point. In this case, the clear point is that three changes could help make our country a better place in which to live. An effective paragraph must not only make a point but also support it with **specific evidence**—reasons, examples, and other details. Such specifics help prove to readers that the point is a reasonable one. Even if readers do not agree with the writer, at least they have the writer's evidence in front of them. Readers are like juries: they want to see the evidence for themselves so that they can make their own judgments.

To write an effective paragraph, always aim to do what the author has done: begin by making a point, and then go on to back up that point with strong specific evidence.

Writing Essays

Like a paragraph, an essay starts with a point and then goes on to provide specific details to support and develop that point. However, a paragraph is a series of sentences about one main idea or point, while an **essay** is a series of paragraphs about one main idea or point—called the **central point** or **thesis**. Since an essay is much longer than one paragraph, it allows a writer to develop a topic in more detail.

Look at the following essay, written by Michael after he was asked to develop more fully his paragraph about changes in America.

Three Helpful Changes

Introductory Paragraph

What is a single change on the national level that could make a difference in the lives of many Americans? What is one change in how we relate to each other on a day-to-day level that could make our country a kinder place in which to live? And on a personal level, what is a change that might help us think better about ourselves and our value and worth as human beings? Three changes—in our tax structure, in our daily relationships, and in our TV watching—would all serve a good purpose in our lives.

First Supporting Paragraph

On the national level, all Americans should be asked to pay a fair share of taxes. At present, many people who are very wealthy pay little income tax because of deductions and write-offs, and many corporations pay no taxes at all. Billionaire Warren Buffet pointed out several years ago that he was paying taxes at a lower rate than his secretary. He recommended changes in the tax law so that the very wealthy would no longer get tax breaks but would have to pay a minimum tax. Unfortunately, many wealthy contributors to Congress have not wanted the tax laws changed to make the tax rate more democratic and fair, and because of their influence, Buffet's recommendations have been ignored. But our government is supposed to represent all the people—the 100% and not the wealthiest 1%— and the tax reform needed will hopefully become law some day.

Second Supporting Paragraph

Along with a tax change on the national level, we need a change on the social level: less rudeness and more kindness. Examples of rudeness are all around us. Some people are rude when they talk, interrupting each other or having loud private conversations on their cell phones while others are sitting nearby. Others rudely get in the way—they block the aisle in the market while deciding just what they want to buy, or they drive too slowly or too quickly, putting other drivers at risk. And we've all seen, even at nice restaurants, parents who ignore their children's rude behavior. They let the kids run noisily around the tables, spoiling the experience for the other diners. In addition, rudeness abounds on the Internet, where people use the cloak of anonymity to say mean and ugly things to each other. Finally, in popular TV shows, a rude and hurtful spirit is often present. After one team member gets kicked off a reality show, another member says, "It's easy to say goodbye to Tyler. Not even one ounce of me wants him around." On another show, participants reveal how they have lied to a friend or partner, and the audience hoots and cheers when the former couple starts hitting one another. Rude and ugly behavior has become a source of entertainment.

Third Supporting Paragraph

Finally, on the personal level, people should stop watching TV commercials that make human beings seem like idiots. Countless commercials feature men and women who are apparently very happy because of a mattress, luggage, or furniture sale or a cereal purchase or an automobile bargain. In one real-world commercial, for example, a series of people of many different ethnic backgrounds all appear on the screen for a second or two, smiling and saying "Thank you!" to the friendly auto dealer who has sold them a car. Equally popular are commercials about upbeat young people who are having the time of their life enjoying a particular beer with their attractive, sexy, and party-loving friends. Surely achieving real happiness is more challenging—and more rewarding—than this!

Concluding Paragraph

There are many changes, large and small, that could improve our country. The three described here would work well on the national, social, and personal level. They are changes that would make us more fair, more kind, and more sane—all of which would clearly be changes for the good!

- Which sentence in the introductory paragraph expresses the central point of the essay? The final sentence

- How many supporting paragraphs are provided to back up the central point? ___Three___

The Parts of an Essay

Each of the parts of an essay is explained below.

INTRODUCTORY PARAGRAPH

A well-written introductory paragraph will normally do the following:

- Gain the reader's interest by using one of several common methods of introduction.

- Present the thesis statement. The **thesis statement** expresses the central point of an essay, just as a topic sentence states the main idea of a paragraph. The central idea in Michael's essay is expressed in the last sentence of the introductory paragraph.

Four Common Methods of Introduction

Four common methods of introduction are (1) telling a brief story, (2) asking one or more questions, (3) shifting to the opposite, or (4) going from the broad to the narrow. Following are examples of all four.

1 **Telling a brief story.** An interesting anecdote is hard for a reader to resist. In an introduction, a story should be no more than a few sentences, and it should relate meaningfully to the central idea. The story can be an experience of your own, of someone you know, or of someone you have heard about. For example, the author of an essay on teenagers tells a story as part of his opening paragraph:

> The other day I was in the store where I work and a young guy, probably about 17, asked me where he could find the door locks. I wasn't sure—I'm new on the job—but I went to ask someone and found out. Then I went back to find the guy and tell him. The problem was, there were several guys about his age in the store, and at first I didn't know which one had asked me for help. They were all dressed almost alike, and I thought to myself, "Teenagers!" Teens are at the stage in their lives where the most important thing in the universe is being accepted by their peers. This need for acceptance leads them to make some ridiculous choices. At the high school my younger brother goes to, I've observed three such ridiculous behaviors.

2 **Asking one or more questions.** These questions may be ones that you intend to answer in your essay, or they may indicate that your topic is of relevance and importance to readers. Michael uses this method of introduction in his essay:

> What is a single change on the national level that could make a difference in the lives of many Americans? What is one change in how we relate to each other on a day-to-day level that could make our country a kinder place in which to live? And on a personal level, what is a change that might help us think better about ourselves and our value and worth as human beings? Three changes, in our tax structure, in our daily relationships, and in our TV watching, would all serve a good purpose in our lives.

3 Shifting to the opposite. Another way to gain the reader's interest is to first present an idea that is the opposite of what will be written about. A student who wrote an essay about anger in everyday life begins her essay with an opposite idea:

> Some people never get extremely upset or raise their voices or say a single word in anger. No matter what happens, they are able to remain calm. In contrast, I do get angry, and I have realized that problems with time, technology, and tension often make me lose my temper.

4 Going from the broad to the narrow. Broad, general observations can capture your reader's interest; they can also introduce your topic and provide helpful background information. For instance, the author of an essay on memorable school classmates goes from the broad to the narrow in his opening paragraph.

> There are some classmates that you just never forget. In many ways, I probably remember a lot more about some of the people in my classes than I do about what was taught! Looking through yearbooks and seeing the faces of certain fellow students, I'm right back in that year and that class. From first grade through high school, there have been some pretty memorable classmates, and three in particular stand out in my memory.

SUPPORTING PARAGRAPHS

The traditional school essay has three supporting paragraphs. But some essays will have two supporting paragraphs, and others will have four or more. Each supporting paragraph should have its own topic sentence stating the point to be developed in that paragraph.

Notice that the essay on three helpful changes has clear topic sentences for each of the three supporting paragraphs.

TRANSITIONAL WORDS AND SENTENCES

In a paragraph, **transitional words** like *First, Another, Also, In addition*, and *Finally* are used to help connect supporting ideas. In an essay, **transitional sentences** are used to help tie the supporting paragraphs together. Such transitional sentences often occur at the beginning of a supporting paragraph.

● Look at the topic sentence for the second supporting paragraph in the essay on helpful changes. Explain how that sentence is also a transitional sentence.

The first nine words of the topic sentence of the second supporting paragraph refer to the paragraph immediately before it.

CONCLUDING PARAGRAPH

The concluding paragraph often summarizes the essay by briefly restating the thesis and, at times, the main supporting points. It may also provide a closing thought or two as a way of bringing the paper to a natural and graceful end.

- Look again at the concluding paragraph of the essay on helpful changes. Which sentence summarizes the essay? _____ Second _____ Which sentence provides a closing thought? _____ Third _____

A Note on a Third Goal in Writing

A third important goal in writing (see page 211 for the first two goals) is to organize the supporting material in a paper. Perhaps the most common way to do so is to use a **listing order**. In other words, provide a list of three or more reasons, examples, or other details. Use signal words such as *First of all, Another, Secondly, Also,* and *Finally* to mark the items in your list. Signal words, better known as **transitions**, let your reader know that you are providing a list of items.

- Turn back to page 212 and look again at the paragraph on changes. What signal words does Michael use to mark each of the three helpful changes?

  _____ First of all _____   _____ Next _____   _____ Finally _____

You'll note that he uses "First of all" to introduce the first change, "Next" to introduce the second change, and "Finally" to introduce the last change.

Practice 1: USING A LISTING ORDER

Read the paragraph below and answer the questions that follow.

Drunk Drivers

People caught driving while drunk—even first offenders—should be jailed. For one thing, drunk driving is more dangerous than carrying a loaded gun. Drunk drivers are in charge of three-thousand-pound weapons at a time when they have little coordination or judgment. Instead of getting off with a license suspension, the drunk driver should be treated as seriously as someone who walks into a crowded building with a ticking time bomb. In addition, views on drunk driving have changed. We are no longer willing to make jokes about funny drunk drivers, to see drunk driving as a typical adolescent stunt, or to overlook repeat offenders who have been lucky enough not to hurt anybody—so far. Last of all, a jail penalty might encourage solutions to the problem of drinking and driving. People who go out for an evening that includes drinking would be more likely to select another person as the driver. That person would stay completely sober. Bars might promote more tasty and trendy nonalcoholic drinks such as fruit daiquiris and "virgin" piña coladas. And perhaps beer and alcohol advertising would be regulated so that young people would not learn to associate alcohol consumption with adulthood. By taking drunk driving seriously enough to require a jail sentence, we would surely save lives.

- What is the writer's point in this paragraph? _____
  _____ People caught driving drunk should be jailed. _____

- What transition introduces the first supporting reason for the point? _____For one thing_____
- What transition introduces the second supporting reason? _____In addition_____
- What transition introduces the third supporting reason? _____Last of all_____

The author's list of reasons and use of transitions—*For one thing, In addition,* and *Last of all*—both help the author organize the supporting material and help the reader clearly and easily understand the supporting material.

Another common way to organize supporting details is to use a time order. In **time order**, supporting details are presented in the order in which they occurred. *First* this happened; *next,* this; *after* that, this; *then* this; and so on. The events that make up a story are organized in time order.

Practice 2: USING A TIME ORDER

Read the paragraph below, which is organized in a time order. In the spaces provided, write appropriate transitions showing time relationships. Use each of the following transitions once: *Before, Then, When, As, After.*

An Upsetting Incident

An incident happened yesterday that made me very angry. I got off the bus and started walking the four blocks to my friend's house. _____As_____ I walked along, I noticed a group of boys gathered on the sidewalk about a block ahead of me. _____When_____ they saw me, they stopped talking. A bit nervous, I thought about crossing the street to avoid them. But as I came nearer and they began to whistle, a different feeling came over me. Instead of being afraid, I was suddenly angry. Why should I have to worry about being hassled just because I was a woman? I stared straight at the boys and continued walking. _____Then_____ one of them said, "Oooh, baby. Looking fine today." _____Before_____ I knew what I was doing, I turned on him. "Do you have a mother? Or any sisters?" I demanded. He looked astonished and didn't answer me. I went on, "Is it OK with you if men speak to them like that? Shouldn't they be able to walk down the street without some creeps bothering them?" _____After_____ I spoke, he and the other boys looked guilty and backed away. I held my head up high and walked by them. An hour later, I was still angry.

The writer makes the main point of the paragraph in her first sentence: "An incident happened yesterday that made me very angry." She then supports her point with a specific account of just what happened. Time words that could be used to help connect her details include the following: "As I walked along," "When they saw me," "Then one of them said," "Before I knew," "After I spoke."

The Writing Process

Even professional writers do not sit down and write a paper in a single draft. Instead, they have to work on it one step at a time. Writing a paper is a process that can be divided into the following five steps:

Step 1 **Getting Started through Prewriting**

Step 2 **Preparing a Scratch Outline**

Step 3 **Writing the First Draft**

Step 4 **Revising**

Step 5 **Editing**

STEP 1   GETTING STARTED THROUGH PREWRITING

What you need to learn, first, are methods that you can use to start working on a writing assignment. These techniques will help you think on paper. They'll help you figure out both the point you want to make and the support you need for that point. Here are three helpful prewriting techniques:

- Freewriting
- Questioning
- List making

Freewriting

Freewriting is just sitting down and writing whatever comes into your mind about a topic. Do this for ten minutes or so. Write without stopping and without worrying in the slightest about spelling, grammar, and the like. Simply get down on paper all the information that occurs to you about the topic.

Below is part of the freewriting done by Michael for his paragraph on three changes that could make our country a better place. Michael had been given the assignment, "Write about three kinds of changes that could make our country a better place. You might want to consider changes on three different levels: national, social, and personal."

Example of Freewriting

How to make the US a better place Well we need more jobs, many of us are out of work even colege grads. Its tough with not enough money coming in. You know, whats really unfair about the US these days is that just a few people have most of the money. Their the ones that dont even pay a fair share of taxes, like the boss I read about who pays less inkome tax than his secritery. Thats on the national level so lets look at the social one next, what really ticks me off is rude people. I see them all the time. Talking loud on cell phones in the libery, shoving ahead of you in line, even driving to fast or to slow, aksidents waiting to happen . . .

Notice that there are lots of problems with spelling, grammar, and punctuation in Michael's freewriting. Michael is not worried about such matters, nor should he be—at this stage. He is just concentrating on getting ideas and details down on paper. He knows that it is best to focus on one thing at a time. At this point, he just wants to write out thoughts as they come to him, to do some thinking on paper.

You should take the same approach when freewriting: explore your topic without worrying at all about writing "correctly." Figuring out what you want to say should have all your attention in this early stage of the writing process.

Practice 3: FREEWRITING

On a sheet of paper, freewrite for at least ten minutes on the best or worst job or chore you ever had. Don't worry about grammar, punctuation, or spelling. Try to write—without stopping—about whatever comes into your head concerning your best or worst job or chore.

Questioning

Questioning means that you generate details about your topic by writing down a series of questions and answers about it. Your questions can start with words like *what, when, where, why,* and *how.*

Here are just some of the questions that Michael might have asked while developing his paper. Note that after he came up with the first few ideas, he then started to ask further questions about those ideas:

Example of Questioning

- What is a change needed on the national level?
- What is a change needed on the social level?
- What is a change needed on the personal level?
- Who would make these changes?
- How would the changes improve our lives?
- How could taxes be more fair?
- What are examples of how we are rude?
- Why are TV commercials so insulting?

Practice 4: QUESTIONING

On a sheet of paper, answer the following questions about your best or worst job or chore.

- When did you have the job (or chore)?
- Where did you work?
- What did you do?
- Whom did you work for?
- Why did you like or dislike the job? (Give one reason and some details that support that reason.)
- What is another reason you liked or disliked the job? What are some details that support the second reason?
- Can you think of a third reason you liked or did not like the job? What are some details that support the third reason?

List Making

In **list making** (also known as **brainstorming**), you make a list of ideas and details that could go into your paper. Simply pile these items up, one after another, without worrying about putting them in any special order. Try to accumulate as many details as you can think of.

After Michael did his freewriting about changes, he make up a list of details, part of which is shown below.

Example of List Making

~~national—more jobs~~
~~college grads working at car wash~~
national—rich people pay lower taxes than most people
rich people have more tax deductions
some companies don't pay taxes
social—some people are rude
talk loud on cell phones
shove in front of you in line
drive fast or slow
personal—stupid TV commercials
cereals, cars, beer make us happy?

One detail led to another as Michael expanded his list. (Note that he crossed out one idea and detail—"national—more jobs" and "college grads working at a car wash"—when he realized he wanted to focus on tax reform.) Slowly but surely, more supporting material emerged that he could use in developing his paper. By the time Michael had finished his list, he was ready to plan an outline of his paragraph and to write his first draft.

Practice 5: LIST MAKING

On a separate piece of paper, make a list of details about the job (or chore). Don't worry about putting them in a certain order. Just get down as many details about the job as occur to you. The list can include specific reasons you liked or did not like the job and specific details supporting those reasons.

STEP 2 PREPARING A SCRATCH OUTLINE

A **scratch outline** is a brief plan for a paragraph. It shows at a glance the point of the paragraph and the support for that point. It is the logical framework on which the paper is built.

This rough outline often follows freewriting, questioning, list making, or all three. Or it may gradually emerge in the midst of these strategies. In fact, trying to outline is a good way to see if you need to do more prewriting. If a solid outline does not emerge, then you know you need to do more prewriting to clarify your main point or its support. And once you have a workable outline, you may realize, for instance, that you want to do more list making to develop one of the supporting details in the outline.

In Michael's case, he knew what his three supporting points would be.

Example of a scratch outline

> Three changes that would make the US a better place
> 1. National: everyone pays fair share of taxes
> 2. Social: less rudeness, more kindness
> 3. Personal: stop watching stupid TV commercials

After all his preliminary writing, Michael sat back pleased. He knew he had a promising paper—one with a clear point and solid support. He was now ready to write the first draft of his paper, using his outline as a guide.

Practice 6: SCRATCH OUTLINE

Using the list you have prepared, see if you can prepare a scratch outline made up of the three main reasons you liked or did not like the job.   *Answers will vary.*

_____ was the best (or worst) job (or chore) I ever had.

Reason 1: _____

Reason 2: _____

Reason 3: _____

STEP 3 WRITING THE FIRST DRAFT

When you do a first draft, be prepared to put in additional thoughts and details that didn't emerge in your prewriting. And don't worry if you hit a snag. Just leave a blank space or add a comment such as "Do later," and press on to finish the paper. Also, don't worry yet about grammar, punctuation, or spelling. You don't want to take time correcting words or sentences that you may decide to remove later. Instead, make it your goal to develop the content of your paper with plenty of specific details.

Here are a few lines of Michael's first draft:

First Draft

> There are some changes our country needs. Everyone should pay their fair share of taxes. Rich people take tax deductions for all kinds of stuff. Some dont even pay much inkome tax at all, like the boss I read about who pays less than his secritery. And their are some companies that dont pay any taxes. Also people should be less rude. You hear them talking loud on their cell phones, others push ahead in line, or they drive to slow or to fast, which can cause an aksident . . .

Practice 7: FIRST DRAFT

Now write a first draft of your paper. Begin with your topic sentence stating that a certain job (or chore) was the best or worst one you ever had. Then state the first reason why it was the best or the worst, followed by specific details supporting that reason. Use a transition such as *First of all* to introduce the first reason. Next, state the second reason, followed by specific details supporting that reason. Use a transition such as *Secondly* to introduce the second reason. Last, state the third reason, followed by support. Use a transition such as *Finally* to introduce the last reason.

Don't worry about grammar, punctuation, or spelling. Just concentrate on getting down on paper the details about the job.

STEP 4 REVISING

Revising is as much a stage in the writing process as prewriting, outlining, and doing the first draft. **Revising** means that you rewrite a paper, building upon what has been done, to make it stronger and better. One writer has said about revision, "It's like cleaning house—getting rid of all the junk and putting things in the right order." A typical revision means writing at least one or two more drafts, adding and omitting details, organizing more clearly, and beginning to correct spelling and grammar.

Here is Michael's second draft.

Second Draft

> There are three changes that could make our country a better place. On the national level, everyone should pay their fair share of taxes. Many rich people pay less income tax than they should because of deductions and write-offs. Some companies dont pay any taxes at all. We need to be more democratic. Another welcome change would be on the social level. People should be less rude and more kind. Some of them interrupt each other while talking, or they talk loud on their cell phones. Others drive too slow or too fast, which can cause an accident. You see rudeness in restaurants as well with children allowed to run around everywhere. In our daily lives we need to stop watching so many stupid commercials on TV. People are shown to act so happy about a mattress or furniture sale or a cereal or a car purchase that they seem like idiots.

Notice that in redoing the draft, Michael has refined his topic sentence. Also, he added phrases ("On the national level" and "on the social level") to clearly set off two of his supporting points. Finally, he provided more details about each of his points.

Michael then went on to revise and further expand the second draft. Since he was doing his paper on a computer, he was able to print it out quickly. He double-spaced the lines, allowing room for revisions, which he added in longhand as part of his third draft, and eventually the paragraph on page 212 resulted. (Note that if you are not using a computer, you may want to skip every other line when writing out each draft. Also, write on only one side of a page, so that you can see your entire paper at one time.)

Practice 8: REVISING THE DRAFT

Ideally, you will have a chance to put the paper aside for a while before doing later drafts. When you revise, try to do all of the following:

- Omit any details that do not truly support your topic sentence.
- Add more details as needed, making sure you have plenty of specific support for each of your three reasons.
- Be sure to include a final sentence that rounds off the paper, bringing it to a close.

STEP 5 EDITING

Editing, the final stage in the writing process, means checking a paper carefully for spelling, grammar, punctuation, and other errors. You are ready for this stage when you are satisfied that your point is clear, your supporting details are good, and your paper is well organized.

At this stage, you must read your paper out loud. Hearing how your writing sounds is an excellent way to pick up grammar and punctuation problems in your writing. Chances are that you will find sentence mistakes at every spot where your paper does not read smoothly and clearly. This point is so important that it bears repeating: *To find mistakes in your paper, read it out loud!*

At this point in his work, Michael read his latest draft out loud. He looked closely at all the spots where his writing did not read easily. He used a grammar handbook to deal with the problem at those spots in his paper, and he made the corrections needed so that all his sentences read smoothly. He also used his dictionary to check on the spelling of every word he was unsure about. He even took a blank sheet of paper and used it to uncover his paper one line at a time, looking for any other mistakes that might be there.

Practice 9: EDITING

When you have your almost-final draft of the paper, edit it in the following ways:

- Read the paper aloud, listening for awkward wordings and places where the meaning is unclear. Make the changes needed for the paper to read smoothly and clearly. In addition, see if you can get another person to read the draft aloud to you. The spots that this person has trouble reading are spots where you may have to do some revision and correct your grammar or punctuation mistakes.

- Using your dictionary (or a spell-check program if you have a computer), check any words that you think might be misspelled.

- Finally, take a sheet of paper and cover your paper so that you can expose and carefully proofread one line at a time. Use this grammar book to check any other spots where you think there might be grammar or punctuation mistakes in your writing.

Final Thoughts

When you have a paper to write, here in a nutshell, is what to do:

1 Write about what you know. If you don't know much about your topic, go onto the Internet and use the helpful search engine Google. You can access it by typing **www.google.com**.

A screen will then appear with a box in which you can type one or more keywords. For example, if you were thinking about doing a paper about why students drop out of school, Google "why students drop out of school," and you will find millions of articles on that topic. Just reading and reflecting on some of the articles listed on the first or second Google page will help you think about the topic and develop your own ideas about it.

Keep in mind that you do not want to take other people's words—that would be **plagiarism**, which is stealing. Rather, your goal is to use other people's information and thoughts as a springboard for your own words and ideas about a topic.

2 Use prewriting strategies to begin to write about your topic. Look for a point you can make, and make sure you have details to support it.

3 Write several drafts, aiming all the while for three goals in your writing: a clear point, strong support for that point, and well-organized support. Use transitions to help organize your support.

4 Then read your paper out loud. It should read smoothly and clearly. Look closely for grammar and punctuation problems at any rough spots. Check this grammar book or a dictionary as needed.

Writing Assignments

Writing is best done on topics about which you have information and in which you have interest. To ensure that you have a choice of topics, following are twenty writing assignments. With your instructor's guidance, decide which of the topics you will write about during the course, and whether you'll be writing a paragraph or an essay. In general, the assignments proceed from simpler, first-person topics to more difficult, third-person ones.

1 Getting Around

Explain in detail what means of transportation you have relied upon to get from one place to another in your life. To make your writing more interesting, be sure to include descriptive details about each method of transportation you've used. Your paragraph or essay should be arranged in a time order, from your childhood to your teenage years to the present.

2 Your Room

Describe in detail the room where you sleep. You might order your details by proceeding in a left to right sequence around the room. Or you might describe the largest items in the room first and then go on to the smaller ones. Or you might present a dominant impression about your room (for example, "My room is a very cluttered/neat/comfortable/small/multi-purpose—*or some other quality*—place"). Whatever organization you choose, be sure to include plenty of vivid details to make your description come alive.

3 Eating Habits

Describe in detail what you typically eat, when you eat, and how your eating habits have perhaps changed over the years. Be sure to mention individual favorite foods. Include a closing sentence or two about ways you might want to improve your eating habits.

Here is one student's response to this assignment:

Eating Habits

When it comes to eating, I have very specific habits, some of which may not be the best. To begin with, when I eat is often based more on my emotions than on any actual need to eat. If I'm having a really stressful morning at work, I'll often start snacking on something as early as ten o'clock and keep on eating right up to lunch. It doesn't matter that I'm not hungry; I'll eat to calm myself down. On the other hand, if I'm having a good and productive day, I might completely forget to eat and then be totally starved by mid-afternoon. At that point, I'll eat way too much all at once. Furthermore, the foods I choose to eat could not always be called the best choices. Because I have to be at work so early, I typically have nothing more than a couple cups of coffee for breakfast. Lunch during the week is nearly always something from one of the nearby restaurants. Most of these restaurants are either fast food or some other kind of takeout where the emphasis is, of course, on cheap, quick food as opposed to nutritious food. Dinnertime is the only time that I actually pay some attention to healthy choices and include a salad and some fruit. Finally, however, I often cancel out dinner's health with my worst eating habit. By about nine or ten o'clock, I tend to get a little hungry, and if I'm watching TV or a movie, I end up eating something sugary and fattening. Naturally, since my attention is on what I'm watching, I don't watch how much I eat. I've been known to eat an entire quart of fudge ice cream in one sitting! I know that many of these old habits could be changed by making just a few simple adjustments like eating a good breakfast and packing my own lunch (and staying out of the kitchen after dinner). There is probably no better time than right now to start breaking old eating habits.

4 Technology in Your Life

When Abraham Lincoln was a boy, he expanded his world through reading books by the light of a log fire. In contrast, you have access to all kinds of technology, including television, smartphones, tablets, and computers. Explain in detail how technology has been an influence in your daily life. How has it been of value to you? What has it made possible for you? Include a closing thought about whether all this technology has been more of a help or a hindrance.

5 Hometown

If a friend wrote to you asking whether your hometown would be a good place for him or her to move to, what would be your response? Write a one-paragraph letter to your friend explaining the advantages or disadvantages of living in your hometown. Begin your remarks with a specific recommendation to your friend; it will serve as the topic sentence of the paragraph. Cover such matters as employment, recreation, housing, schools, and safety. Be sure your details are as specific and descriptive as you can make them. To connect your ideas, use transitions such as *in addition, furthermore, on the other hand,* and *however.*

6 Best or Worst Childhood Experience

Some of our most vivid memories are of things that happened to us as children, and these memories don't ever seem to fade. In fact, many elderly people say that childhood memories are clearer to them than things that happened yesterday. Think back to one of the best or worst experiences you had as a child. Try to remember the details of the event—sights, sounds, smells, textures, tastes.

You might begin by freewriting for ten minutes or so about good or bad childhood experiences. That freewriting may suggest to you a topic you will want to develop.

After you have decided on a topic, try to write a clear sentence stating what the experience was and whether it was one of the best or worst of your childhood. For example, "The time I was beaten up coming home from my first day in fifth grade was one of my worst childhood moments."

You may then find it helpful to make a list in which you jot down as many details as you can remember about the experience. Stick with a single experience, and don't try to describe too much. If a week you spent at summer camp was an unpleasant experience, don't try to write about the entire week. Just describe one horrible moment or event.

When you write the paper, use a time order to organize details: first this happened, then this, next this, and so on.

As you write, imagine that someone is going to make a short film based on your paragraph. Try to provide vivid details, quotations, and pictures for the filmmaker to shoot.

Here is one student's response to this assignment:

It may not sound that exciting, but one of the best childhood experiences that I can remember was visiting a big farm with my grandfather. The visit began in the early morning when we went out to a huge pen and fed a dozen or more pigs. To an eight-year-old who was unusually crazy about pigs, this was probably the high point of my entire life! My grandfather held me up on his shoulders and let me throw corn and old bananas to the pigs. In addition to getting to throw rotten bananas in the air, I was thrilled to have an audience of grunting pigs all staring at me eagerly. Next, my grandfather led me into a giant barn that was filled with all sorts of animals that I was allowed to pet, brush, and even ride. A pen full of goats ate feed out of my hands and made me laugh with their curious expressions as I petted their scruffy heads. My grandfather let me brush a small pony's mane, and then he lifted me up onto the pony's back and let me ride in a small circle inside the barn. Finally, the farm's owner, a friend of my grandfather's, took me for a ride out into the cornfield on a huge red tractor. The tractor cut down all the old cornstalks and made a tremendous roar as we moved along. It kicked up so much dust that it seemed like we were moving through a cloud. That tractor ride surpassed any carnival ride I had ever been on by a mile! And that visit to a farm, simple as it may have been, surpassed most of my childhood experiences.

7   Adults and Children

It has been said that the older we get, the more we see our parents (or other influential adults) in ourselves. Indeed, any of our habits (good and bad), beliefs, and temperaments can often be traced to a parent or other significant adult in our life.

Write a paper in which you describe three characteristics you have "inherited" from an adult. You might want to think about your topic by asking yourself a series of questions: "How am I like my mother (or father or uncle or mentor or guardian)? "When and where am I like her (or him)?" "Why am I like her (or him)?" Be sure to include examples for each of the characteristics you mention.

One student who did such a paper used as her topic sentence the following statement: "Although I hate to admit it, I know that in several ways I'm just like my mom." She then went on to describe how she works too hard, worries too much, and judges other people too harshly. Another student wrote, "I resemble my grandfather in my love of TV sports, my habit of putting things off, and my reluctance to show my feelings."

Here is one student's response to this assignment:

Adults and Children

Although everyone says I look just like my mother, I am beginning to realize that I am more like my dad in a few unusual ways. To begin with, my dad and I are the only ones in our family that really like to watch football. You would think my two older brothers would be more interested in football than their younger sister is, but I'm always the one sitting with Dad in front of the television on Sundays, cheering and yelling. My mom kind of rolls her eyes at our obsession, but Dad and I understand each other. Second, just like my dad, I've always loved winter more than any other season. Dad and I prefer really cold weather, and we can't wait for the first snowfall. The rest of the family lives for summer and hides away inside during the winter, but Dad and I have always particularly enjoyed skiing, sledding, and wild snowball fights. While everyone else celebrates the end of winter, Dad and I are both always a little sad when the last of the winter snow and ice melts. Finally, like my dad, I've always liked math and numbers. My mother prefers words and writing, and she generally seems confused or bored when it comes to dealing with numbers. However, Dad and I both enjoy mathematical puzzles and mysteries. One time, we spent an entire afternoon working on a particularly baffling math equation—and we enjoyed it! I may have my mom's eyes and nose, but when it comes to certain characteristics, I am definitely more like my dad.

8 Best or Worst Job or Chore You Ever Had

Most people, at some point in their lives, have had to deal with a job or a chore that was a challenging one. Perhaps you worked in a restaurant where the boss was nasty or the hours were very inconvenient or the customers were rude. Perhaps you had a babysitting job with a difficult child. Perhaps you were responsible for taking care of a pet that required more time than you could give. Or perhaps the work turned out to be a valuable and fulfilling learning experience. Whatever the job or chore, see if you can provide three reasons why it was a worst—or best—one. And be sure to provide details for each of the reasons you cite. See also the prewriting activities on pages 218–223.

Here is one student's response to this assignment:

My Worst Job

Many people might think working as a lifeguard would be a dream job, but it turned out to be one of the worst jobs I've ever had. To begin with, this lifeguarding position was not exactly on a beautiful beach or at a lake. I was in charge of an old public pool that was, basically, in the middle of a big parking lot. My view was of a strip mall and the back of an old apartment building. Two restaurant dumpsters were downwind from the pool, so there was always the smell of garbage in the air to add to this unpleasant location. Secondly, I spent way more time doing disgusting chores than I did actually lifeguarding. My boss was too cheap to hire anyone to do maintenance, so I had to clean the bathrooms, mop up spilled drinks around the pool, and even clean out all the gross stuff that collects in a pool. On a bad day, I might have to remove band aids and hair from the filters three or four times. On a very bad day, I might have to order everyone out of the wading pool section while I fished out a diaper that had fallen off a baby. Finally, I was required to wear a really ridiculous red and white tank top and a matching red cap while I was working. My boss thought it was important for a lifeguard to stand out. I definitely did. I had thought that my being a lifeguard might impress the girls around the pool and lead to some dates. However, thanks to that clown-like uniform, the girls giggled at me more than anything else. I'm sure that being a lifeguard can be a glamorous experience, but my first (and last!) lifeguarding job had no glamour to it at all.

9 Being One's Own Worst Enemy

"A lot of people are their own worst enemies" is a familiar saying. We all know people who hurt themselves. Write a paragraph describing someone you know who is his or her own worst enemy. In your paper, introduce the person and explain his or her hurtful behaviors. You may wish to conclude your paragraph with suggestions for that person. A useful way to gather ideas for this paper is to combine two prewriting techniques—outlining and listing. Begin with an outline of the general areas you expect to cover. Here's an outline that may work:

— Introduce the person
— Describe the hurtful behavior(s)
— Suggest changes

Once you have a workable outline, then use list making to produce specific details for each outline point. For example, here are one person's lists for the points in the outline:

Person
— Vanessa
— Just graduated high school
— Works at a department store
— Wants to go to college, but needs money

Hurtful behaviors
— Just moved into own apartment, which takes much of monthly income—could have stayed at home
— Spends a lot of money on clothing
— Makes no effort to find financial aid for school

Changes
— Stop spending so much and start saving
— Get information from school financial aid offices

10 A Helpful Experience

Write an account of an experience you have had that taught you something important. It might involve a mistake you made or an event that gave you insight into yourself or others. Perhaps you have had school problems that taught you to be a more effective student, or you have had a conflict with someone that you now understand could have been avoided. Whatever experience you choose to write about, be sure to tell how it has changed your way of thinking.

11 Dealing with a Problem

M. Scott Peck states that the only way to solve a problem is to solve it—in other words, to take responsibility for the problem and find a solution. When did you accept the responsibility for a problem in your own life and figure out a solution for it? Write about what happened. Be sure to answer the following questions:

● How was the problem affecting my life?
● When did I realize that I was (in part) responsible for the problem?
● What solution for the problem did I come up with?
● What happened after I put my solution to work?

In selecting a topic for this assignment, think about various kinds of problems you may have experienced: problems getting along with other people, money problems, relationship problems, problems completing work on time, difficulties in self-discipline, use of alcohol or other drugs, and so on. Then ask yourself which of these problems you have accepted responsibility for and solved. Once you have thought of a topic, you might begin with a statement like one of the following:

- This past year, I began to take responsibility for my continuing problems with my mother.

- I recently faced the fact that I have a self-discipline problem and have taken steps to deal with it.

- After years of spending my money on the wrong kinds of things, I've acted to deal with my money problems.

This statement could then be supported with one or more examples of the problem, a description of how and when you realized the problem, and a detailing of the steps you have taken to deal with the problem.

12 Making the World a Better Place

What are three ways in which our country could be made a better place? Describe one change on the national level, one change on the social level, and one change on the personal level. Note there are examples of student responses to this assignment on pages 212–213. In your paper, do not use any of the three changes cited in the student models; instead, provide your own suggested changes. You may find it helpful to first Google "making the world a better place" and to read and reflect on some of the information you find.

13 Why Students Drop Out of School

Google "why students drop out of school." Read and reflect on the information you find, and use it to write a paragraph or an essay on three reasons why students drop out of school.

NOTE Do not use someone else's words in writing your paper. That would be plagiarizing—in a word, stealing. Use other people's ideas only as a springboard for developing your own thoughts about a topic.

14 Harmful Habits

Google "harmful habits." Read and reflect on the information you find, and use it to write a paragraph or an essay on three harmful bad habits in people's lives.

NOTE Do not use someone else's words in writing your paper. That would be plagiarizing—in a word, stealing. Use other people's ideas only as a springboard for developing your own thoughts about a topic.

15 Parenting Styles

Google "parenting styles." Read and reflect on the information you find, and use it to write a paragraph or an essay on the advantages and drawbacks of different parenting styles. In your conclusion, you may want to state which parenting style seems the most effective, and why.

NOTE Do not use someone else's words in writing your paper. That would be plagiarizing—in a word, stealing. Use other people's ideas only as a springboard for developing your own thoughts about a topic.

16 Adult Children at Home

Google "adult children living at home." Read and reflect on the information you find, and use it to write a paragraph or an essay on three reasons why it is or is not a good idea for adult children to live with their parents.

NOTE Do not use someone else's words in writing your paper. That would be plagiarizing—in a word, stealing. Use other people's ideas only as a springboard for developing your own thoughts about a topic.

17 Characteristics of Bullies

Google "characteristics of bullies." Read and reflect on the information you find, and use it to write a paragraph or an essay on three characteristics that bullies often have in common.

NOTE Do not use someone else's words in writing your paper. That would be plagiarizing—in a word, stealing. Use other people's ideas only as a springboard for developing your own thoughts about a topic.

18 Improving Health and Wellbeing

Google "improving health and wellbeing." Read and reflect on the information you find, and use it to write a paragraph or an essay on three lifestyle changes that would improve the health and wellbeing of many children and adults. In your conclusion, stress the importance of these changes to living a long and healthy life.

NOTE Do not use someone else's words in writing your paper. That would be plagiarizing—in a word, stealing. Use other people's ideas only as a springboard for developing your own thoughts about a topic.

19 Student Stress

Google "student stress." Read and reflect on the information you find, and use it to write a paragraph or an essay on three kinds of stress that students often encounter in everyday life.

NOTE Do not use someone else's words in writing your paper. That would be plagiarizing—in a word, stealing. Use other people's ideas only as a springboard for developing your own thoughts about a topic.

20 People of Courage

Google "people of courage." Read and reflect on the information you find, and use it to write a paragraph or an essay on three people who displayed remarkable courage in their lives.

NOTE Do not use someone else's words in writing your paper. That would be plagiarizing—in a word, stealing. Use other people's ideas only as a springboard for developing your own thoughts about a topic.

35 Proofreading Techniques

Basics about Proofreading

An important step in becoming a good writer is learning to proofread. When you **proofread**, you check the next-to-final draft of a paper for grammar, punctuation, and other mistakes. Such mistakes are ones you did not find and fix in earlier drafts of a paper because you were working on content.

All too often, students skip the key step of proofreading in their rush to hand in a paper. As a result, their writing may contain careless errors that leave a bad impression and result in a lower grade. This chapter explains how to proofread effectively and suggests a sequence to follow when proofreading. The chapter also provides a series of practices to help you improve your proofreading skills.

HOW TO PROOFREAD

1 Proofreading is a special kind of reading that should not be rushed. Don't try to proofread a paper minutes before it is due. If you do, you are likely to see what you intended to write, not what is actually on the page. Instead, do one of the following:

   ● Read your writing out loud.

   ● Alternatively, do the reading "aloud" in your head, perhaps moving your lips as you read.

   In either case, listen for spots that do not read smoothly and clearly. You will probably be able to hear where your sentences should begin and end. You will then be more likely to find any fragments and run-ons that are present. Other spots that do not read smoothly may reveal other grammar or punctuation errors. Take the time needed to check such spots closely.

2 Read through your paper several times, looking for different types of errors in each reading. Here is a good sequence to follow:

   ● Look for sentence fragments, run-ons, and comma splices.

   ● Look for verb mistakes.

   ● Look for capital letter and punctuation mistakes.

   ● Look for missing words or missing -s endings.

   ● Look for spelling mistakes, including errors in homonyms.

   This chapter will give you practice in proofreading for the above mistakes. In addition, as you proofread your work, you should watch for problems with pronoun and modifier use, word choice, and parallelism.

SENTENCE FRAGMENTS, RUN-ONS, AND COMMA SPLICES

Sentence Fragments

When proofreading for sentence fragments, remember to look for the following:

- Dependent-word fragments
- Fragments without subjects
- Fragments without a subject and a verb (-*ing* and *to* fragments, example fragments)

In general, correct a fragment by doing one of the following:

1 Connect the fragment to the sentence that comes before or after it.

2 Create a completely new sentence by adding a subject and/or a verb.

To further refresh your memory about fragments, turn to pages 27–38.

Run-On Sentences and Comma Splices

When proofreading for run-on sentences and comma splices, keep the following definitions in mind:

- A **run-on sentence** results when one complete thought is immediately followed by another, with nothing between them.

- A **comma splice** is made up of two complete thoughts that are incorrectly joined by only a comma.

To correct run-on sentences and comma splices, do one of the following:

1 Use a period and a capital letter to create separate sentences.

2 Use a comma plus a joining word (such as *and, but,* or *so*) to combine the two complete thoughts into one compound sentence.

3 Use a dependent word (see page 45) to make one of the complete thoughts dependent upon the other one.

4 Use a semicolon to connect the two complete thoughts.

To further refresh your memory about run-on sentences and comma splices, turn to pages 39–50 and 179–182.

Practice 1

Read each of the following short passages either aloud or to yourself. Each passage contains a sentence fragment, a run-on, or a comma splice. Find and underline the error. Then correct it in the space provided.   *Methods of correction may vary.*

1. <u>That bookcase is too heavy on top it could fall over.</u> Take some of the big books off the highest shelf and put them on the bottom one.

Because that bookcase is too heavy on top, it could fall over. Take some of the big books off the highest shelf and put them on the bottom one.

2. The detective asked everyone to gather in the library. He announced that he had solved the mystery. <u>And would soon reveal the name of the murderer.</u> Suddenly the lights went out.

The detective asked everyone to gather in the library. He announced that he had solved the mystery and would soon reveal the name of the murderer. Suddenly the lights went out.

3. That rocking chair is very old. <u>It belonged to my great-grandfather, he brought it to the United States from Norway.</u> I like to think about all the people who have sat in it over the years.

That rocking chair is very old. It belonged to my great-grandfather, and he brought it to the United States from Norway. I like to think about all the people who have sat in it over the years.

4. <u>Before you leave the house.</u> Please close all the windows in case it rains. I don't want the carpet to get soaked.

Before you leave the house, please close all the windows in case it rains. I don't want the carpet to get soaked.

5. <u>Midori is from Taiwan, she uses the English name Shirley, which is easier for her American friends to say.</u> Everyone in her family has both a Chinese and an English name.

Midori is from Taiwan, but she uses the English name Shirley, which is easier for her American friends to say. Everyone in her family has both a Chinese and an English name.

6. My aunt took a trip on a boat off the coast of California. She wanted to see whales. Whales are always sighted there. <u>At a certain time of the year.</u>

My aunt took a trip on a boat off the coast of California. She wanted to see whales. Whales are always sighted there at a certain time of the year.

7. For vacation this year, we are going to rent a cabin. <u>It is on a lake in the mountains we can swim, fish, and sunbathe there.</u> Everyone in the family is looking forward to that week.

For vacation this year, we are going to rent a cabin. It is on a lake in the mountains, so we can swim, fish, and sunbathe there. Everyone in the family is looking forward to that week.

8. Rosalie went to the beauty salon on Friday. <u>To get her long hair trimmed just a little.</u> However, she changed her mind and had it cut very short.

Rosalie went to the beauty salon on Friday to get her long hair trimmed just a little. However, she changed her mind and had it cut very short.

9. The Webbs put a white carpet in their living room. Now they feel that was a foolish choice. Every bit of dirt or spilled food shows on the white surface. <u>And is nearly impossible to get rid of.</u>

The Webbs put a white carpet in their living room. Now they feel that was a foolish choice. Every bit of dirt or spilled food shows on the white surface and is nearly impossible to get rid of.

10. That waiter is quick and hard-working, he is not friendly with customers. For that reason he doesn't get very good tips. His boss tells him to smile and be more pleasant, but he doesn't seem to listen.

Although that waiter is quick and hard-working, he is not friendly with customers. For that reason he doesn't get very good tips. His boss tells him to smile and be more pleasant, but he doesn't seem to listen.

COMMON VERB MISTAKES

When proofreading, look for the following common verb mistakes:

- The wrong past or past participle forms of irregular verbs (pages 9–14)
- Lack of subject-verb agreement (pages 15–20; 153–159)
- Needless shifts of verb tense (pages 171–172)

Practice 2

Read each of the following sentences either aloud or to yourself. Each contains a verb mistake. Find and cross out the error. Then correct it in the space provided.

_____swam_____ **1.** The girls ~~swimmed~~ all the way to the raft.

_____wear_____ **2.** The rock climbers ~~wears~~ safety ropes in case they fall.

_____did_____ **3.** Because my brother studied hard, he ~~does~~ very well on the exam.

_____grew_____ **4.** The strange-looking puppy ~~growed~~ up to be a beautiful dog.

_____is_____ **5.** Neither of our cars ~~are~~ working right now.

_____answered_____ **6.** The phone rang twenty times before someone ~~answers~~ it.

_____are_____ **7.** The public swimming pools in the city ~~is~~ not open yet.

_____slept_____ **8.** Somehow, I ~~sleeped~~ through last night's loud thunderstorm.

_____is_____ **9.** There ~~are~~ poison ivy growing all over that empty lot.

_____claims_____ **10.** Gerald tells everybody it's his birthday and then ~~claimed~~ he doesn't want presents.

CAPITAL LETTER AND PUNCTUATION MISTAKES

When proofreading, be sure the following begin with **capital letters**:

- The first word in a sentence or direct quotation
- The word *I* and people's names
- Family names
- Names of specific places and languages
- Names of specific groups
- Names of days of the week, months, and holidays (but not the seasons)
- Brand names
- Titles
- Names of specific school courses
- Names of historical periods and well-known events
- Opening and closing of a letter

When proofreading, be sure **commas** are used in the following places:

- Between items in a series
- After introductory material
- Around words that interrupt the flow of a sentence
- Between complete thoughts connected by a joining word
- Before and/or after words of direct address and short expressions
- In dates, addresses and letters

When proofreading, be sure **apostrophes** are used in the following:

- Contractions
- Possessives (but not in plurals or verbs)

When proofreading, look for quotation marks around direct quotations. Eliminate any quotation marks around indirect quotations.

Finally, remember to also watch for problems with colons, semicolons, hyphens, dashes, and parentheses.

To further refresh your memory, turn to "Capital Letters," pages 75–80 and 207–210; "Commas," pages 51–56 and 183–188; "Apostrophes," pages 57–62 and 189–194; "Quotation Marks," pages 63–68 and 195–199; and "Punctuation Marks," pages 89–95.

Practice 3

Read each of the following sentences either aloud or to yourself. Each sentence contains an error in capitalization, an error in comma or apostrophe use, or two missing quotation marks. Find the mistake, and correct it in the space provided.

_____ sauce, _____ **1.** I loaded up my low-fat frozen yogurt with fudge sauce peanuts, cherries, and whipped cream.

_____ Bob's _____ **2.** Bobs uncle is an actor in a soap opera.

_____ yelled, _____ **3.** The deli clerk yelled "Who's next?"

_____Chicago_____ **4.** Our flight to chicago was delayed two hours because of mechanical problems.

_____"Please . . . Tom,"_____ **5.** Please call me Tom, our business instructor said.

_____summer_____ **6.** I dread the Summer because I get hay fever so badly.

_____doesn't_____ **7.** A person doesnt have to be great at a sport to be a great coach.

_____character,_____ **8.** Although he's only a cartoon character Mickey Mouse is loved by millions.

_____watermelons_____ **9.** The fresh watermelon's in the supermarket look delicious.

_____question," . . . "I_____ **10.** "I'd like to ask you a question, Marvin told June. I hope you don't think it's too personal."

MISSING -S ENDINGS AND MISSING WORDS

Since you know what you meant when you wrote something, it is easy for you not to notice when a word ending or even a whole word is missing. The following two sections will give you practice in proofreading for such omissions.

Missing -s Endings

When you proofread, remember the following about noun and verb endings:

● The plural form of most nouns ends in *s* (for example, two *cups* of coffee).

● Present tense verbs for the singular third-person subjects end with an *s*.

To further refresh your memory about the present tense, turn to pages 161–162.

Practice 4

Read each of the following sentences either aloud or to yourself. In each case an *-s* ending is needed on one of the nouns or verbs in the sentence. Find and cross out the error. Then correct it in the space provided, being sure to add the *s* to the word.

_____telephones_____ **1.** All of the pay ~~telephone~~ are being used.

_____looks_____ **2.** You should check your front left tire because it ~~look~~ a little flat.

_____jokes_____ **3.** My uncle is always telling terrible ~~joke~~.

_____barns_____ **4.** Most ~~barn~~ are painted a dark red color.

_____makes_____ **5.** Ella ~~make~~ new friends quite easily.

_____speaks_____ **6.** Luis got his job because he ~~speak~~ Spanish and English equally well.

_____closes_____ **7.** The drugstore ~~close~~ at nine o'clock, but the other mall stores stay open till ten.

_____grows_____ **8.** The grass always ~~grow~~ faster whenever we have a heavy summer rain.

_____cans_____ **9.** There are two ~~can~~ of soda hidden on the shelf of the refrigerator.

_____freckles_____ **10.** Many red-haired people have ~~freckle~~ on their skin and also get sunburned quickly.

Missing Words

When you proofread, look for places where you may have omitted such short words as *a, of, the,* or *to.*

Practice 5

Read each of the following sentences either aloud or to yourself. In each sentence, one of the following little words has been omitted:

a   **and**   **by**   **of**   **the**   **to**   **with**

Add a caret (∧) at the spot where the word is missing. Then write the missing word in the space provided.

Example   ____of____   My new pair∧jeans is too tight.

____of____   **1.** Several pieces∧this puzzle are missing.

____to____   **2.** When she went to the grocery store, Louise forgot∧buy bread.

____of____   **3.** Some∧the programs on TV are too violent for children.

____with____   **4.** That orange shirt looks great∧the black pants.

____a____   **5.** I didn't think I had a chance of winning∧prize in the contest.

____and____   **6.** Paul plays both the piano∧the bass guitar.

____the____   **7.** Sandra became tired while climbing up∧steep hill.

____by____   **8.** Everyone was surprised∧the school principal's announcement.

____with____   **9.** Do you drink your coffee∧cream or just sugar?

____to____   **10.** It's hard∧pay attention to a boring speaker.

HOMONYM MISTAKES

When proofreading, pay special attention to the spelling of words that are easily confused with other words.

To refresh your memory of the homonyms listed in this book, turn to pages 69–74 and 200–206.

Practice 6

Read each of the following sentences either aloud or to yourself. Each sentence contains a mistake in a commonly confused word. Find and cross out the error. Then correct it in the space provided.

____too____   **1.** We left the beach early because there were ~~to~~ many flies.

____your____   **2.** It's ~~you're~~ own fault that you missed the deadline.

____whose____   **3.** No one knows ~~who's~~ sweatshirt this is.

____you're____   **4.** If ~~your~~ hungry, fix yourself something to eat.

____its____   **5.** I can't get close enough to the stray dog to read the tag on ~~it's~~ collar.

_____they're_____   **6.** My cousins have promised that ~~their~~ coming here soon for a visit.

_____two_____   **7.** I can think of ~~too~~ practical reasons for staying in school: to improve your skills and to prepare for a better job.

_____their_____   **8.** These greeting cards have pictures on ~~they're~~ covers, but there's no message inside.

_____it's_____   **9.** Although ~~its~~ tempting to keep the money, you should return it to the man whose name appears in the wallet.

_____passed_____   **10.** As we waited in the emergency room to hear whether our sick friend would be all right, time ~~past~~ slowly.

A Note on Making Corrections in Your Papers

You can add minor corrections to the final draft of a paper and still hand it in. Just make the corrections neatly. Add missing punctuation marks right in the text, exactly where they belong. Draw a straight line through any words or punctuation you wish to eliminate or correct. Add new material by inserting a caret (ᴧ) at the point where the addition should be. Then write the new word or words above the line at that point. Here's an example of a sentence that was corrected during proofreading:

- Some Hondas are made in ~~japan~~ ^{Japan}, but others are made ⁱⁿ this country.

Retype or recopy a paper if you discover a number of errors.

Practice 7

Here are five sentences, each of which contains **two** of the types of errors covered in this chapter. Correct the errors by crossing out or adding words or punctuation marks, as in the example above.

1. Helena is taking two ~~english course~~ ^{English courses} in school this semester.

2. I feel sorry for ~~Donnas dog, it~~ ^{Donna's dog. It} lost a leg in a car accident.

3. Rusty cans,ᴧplastic bags,ᴧand scraps of wood washed up on ᴧ^{the} deserted beach.

4. My mother ~~take~~ ^{takes} night classes at college, ~~wear~~ ^{where} she is learning to use a computer.

5. When the power came back ~~on. All~~ ^{on, all} the digital clocks in the house began to blink,ᴧ^{and} the refrigerator motor started to hum.

Name _____   Section _____   Date _____

Score: (Number right) _____ x 10 = _____ %

Proofreading: TEST 1

Read the following passage either aloud or to yourself, looking for the following **ten** mistakes:

1 irregular verb mistake
2 sentence fragments
1 missing comma after introductory material
1 apostrophe mistake
2 missing sets of quotation marks
2 homonym mistakes
1 faulty parallelism

Correct the mistakes, crossing out or adding words or punctuation marks as needed.

Parents Who Care

¹Carla was talking to her best friend, Sara, about things her parents did that annoyed her.
²She said, "My parents drive me crazy. ³No matter what I do, it never seems to be enough." ⁴Carla
complained that her mother was always telling her to try to get a better job. ⁵One that required
job, one
more skill than working as a waitress. ⁶Her father always pushed her to study harder, ~~not be~~
to not eat
~~eating~~ junk food, and to keep herself informed by reading. ⁷He often ~~bringed~~ home books and
brought
piled them on the dresser in ~~Carlas~~ bedroom. ⁸Both her parents always seemed to be nagging her
Carla's
to save more money for the future. ⁹Finally, Carla asked Sara if her parents were the same way.
¹⁰After a long pause and a sad smile, Sara just shrugged and said, "~~Accept~~ for telling me that I'd
Except
better not flunk out of school, my parents never really seem to care ~~weather~~ I do better or not."
whether
¹¹Carla was ~~surprised.~~ ¹²~~To~~ see that Sara looked a little embarrassed. ¹³Suddenly, it occurred to
surprised to
Carla that the reason her parents pushed her was simply that they loved her.

Name _____   Section _____   Date _____

Score: (Number right) _____ x 10 = _____ %

Proofreading: TEST 2

Read the following passage either aloud or to yourself, looking for the following **ten** mistakes:

1 irregular verb mistake
1 sentence fragment
1 run-on sentence
1 comma splice
1 missing comma between items in a series
1 apostrophe mistake
2 missing quotation marks
1 homonym mistake
1 faulty parallelism

Correct the mistakes, crossing out or adding words or punctuation marks as needed.

Learning a Lesson

¹A lot of important learning take's [takes] place outside of school. ²We were at Universal Studios in Florida, ³Waiting [waiting] to be seated for a movie. ⁴We knew the wait would not be too long and stood there fairly content, munched [munching] Good Humor ice cream bars and watching people. ⁵My eye was drawn to a tall older woman in her fifties near the front of the line. ⁶She were [was] flashily dressed, with a bright pink jacket, white pants, and white blonde hair teased and curled like cotton candy. ⁷Her makeup looked painted on, [and] she seemed to me like a clown as she smiled and talked to someone near her.

⁸"That woman near the front has no idea of how ridiculous she is," I commented to my friend. ⁹"She should act her age."

¹⁰Then the line started to move, and I noticed that the woman walked with a crutch. ¹¹It was hooked up under one arm and supported what was obviously a very weak leg. ¹²She moved more slowly than other people. ¹³And then I realized that while she had been talking to people in line, she was alone. ¹⁴She found a seat by herself as we past [passed] her by. ¹⁵The show started, but I didn't pay much attention [because] I realized that the joke was on me. ¹⁶I judged that woman as preposterous and stupid, and I was the one who was preposterous and stupid. ¹⁷And I thought about how all through our lives we pile up pluses and minuses—moments when we are kind and moments when we are cruel. ¹⁸I had just scored another minus.

Name _____ Section _____ Date _____

Score: (Number right) _____ x 10 = _____ %

Proofreading: TEST 3

Read the following passage either aloud or to yourself, looking for the following **ten** mistakes:

1 sentence fragment   **2** homonym mistakes

1 run-on sentence   **1** capital letter mistake

2 missing commas in a series   **1** shift in verb tense

2 missing apostrophes in contractions

Correct the mistakes, crossing out or adding words or punctuation marks as needed.

Balancing Act

¹Sometimes Carl feels like ~~hes~~ *he's* being pulled in five different directions all at once. ²It's an unsettling and often nerve-wracking sensation, but it's one that thousands of young people are accustomed to feeling.

³"I'm just trying to make my life better," Carl explains, "but it's not easy."

⁴Carl attends school part time, works two part-time jobs, and constantly lives with the stress of wondering whether or not ~~their~~ *there* will be enough money to pay rent. ⁵Even though Carl shares a small apartment with two other ~~roommates.~~ *roommates, he's* ⁶~~He's~~ never entirely certain that the money will come together.

⁷"Minimum wage just ~~doesnt~~ *doesn't* cut it," Carl says. ⁸"But right now, that's all I can get. ⁹That's why I'm in school—so that I can get a better job one day."

¹⁰Carl's day begins at 4 a.m. ¹¹He ~~worked~~ *works* at a fast food restaurant until 10:00, and then he attends classes until mid-afternoon. ¹²After a quick bite to eat and whatever studying he can cram in, Carl works evenings cleaning office buildings. ¹³Back home after 10:00, Carl often studies until ~~midnight then~~ *midnight. Then* after he is back up before daylight and back at it all over again.

¹⁴"~~it's~~ *It's* a real balancing act," Carl says with a tired laugh. ¹⁵"If one little thing goes wrong, like I get sick or my beat-up old car breaks down, it throws everything off. ¹⁶It's tough sometimes, but I know I can get ~~threw~~ *through* it."

¹⁷How does Carl know? ¹⁸He knows because he watched his own mother juggle a ~~job school~~ *job, school,* and a child twelve years ago. ¹⁹Several years of nonstop juggling paid off. ²⁰Carl's mom now works as a dental technician and makes good money.

²¹"Back when I was ten years old, I couldn't understand why my mom worked so hard and why we never had any extra money to do fun things. ²²I didn't get it," Carl says. ²³"But I get it now."

Name _____   Section _____   Date _____

Score: (Number right) _____ x 10 = _____ %

Proofreading: TEST 4

Read the following passage either aloud or to yourself, looking for the following **ten** mistakes:

1 irregular verb mistake   **1** apostrophe mistake

1 sentence fragment   **1** missing quotation mark

1 run-on sentence   **1** homonym mistake

2 comma splices   **1** missing word

1 missing comma

Correct the mistakes, crossing out or adding words or punctuation marks as needed.

Being There When a Friend Needs You Most

¹Courtney and Karen had been close friends since middle school, they knew all of each ~~others~~ *other's* [*and* inserted]

secrets. ²Then all of a sudden, Karen stopped calling Courtney and kept making excuses for why she

couldn't do things with her.

³"I couldn't understand it," Courtney said. ⁴"She had moved in with her boyfriend, Ron, so I

knew I'd see less of her, but I didn't think I'd totally lose her as a friend."

⁵Then, one day, Courtney ~~runned~~ *ran* into Karen and Ron at the supermarket. ⁶Karen had *a* bruise on

her cheek. ⁷When Courtney asked what had happened, Karen looked scared and didn't say anything,

Ron laughed and told Courtney that Karen was just clumsy. ⁸But Courtney had a bad feeling. ⁹She

called Karen at work the next day and told her they had to talk.

¹⁰"She kept saying everything was okay, but then she began crying," Courtney explained. ¹¹"Ron

had been abusing her for months. ¹²She was ~~to~~ *too* scared to tell anyone. ¹³She felt trapped."

¹⁴Courtney then did the most important things a friend can do for a friend who's being abused.

¹⁵First, she didn't judge or give advice; she just listened. ¹⁶Next, Courtney let Karen know that Karen

deserved to be treated well and loved by someone who really cared about her. ¹⁷Finally, Courtney

offered Karen a place to ~~stay.~~ *stay where* ¹⁸~~Where~~ she'd feel safe and have someone to talk to. ¹⁹Karen was truly

relieved to move in with Courtney. ²⁰After about six months with Courtney, Karen was back on her

feet both emotionally and financially. ²¹She was ready for a fresh start on life.

²²"People always say they don't know what to do when a friend is being abused," Courtney says.

²³"It's pretty simple—just be there for that friend."

Name _____   Section _____   Date _____

Proofreading: TEST 5

Read the following passage either aloud or to yourself, looking for the following **ten** mistakes:

1 mistake in subject-verb agreement
2 sentence fragments
1 comma splice
1 run-on sentence
1 missing comma
1 apostrophe mistake
1 homonym mistake
1 capital letter mistake
1 missing question mark

Correct the mistakes, crossing out or adding words or punctuation marks as needed.

Better with Age

[1]When I returned to school at the age of 38, [2]I thought it was going to be a serious nightmare. [3]I knew I needed a ~~College~~ *college* degree in order to get a better job and earn a better salary, but I was really worried. [4]In my mind, college was all about young people who were right out of high school with their futures wide open. [5]Here I was, almost old enough to be their mother and with 20 years of my working life already behind me. [6]I was going to really stick out. [7]There wouldn't be anyone older ~~then~~ *than* I was. [8]However, I was wrong, *because* in my very first class, I met a student who was 53! [9]Nobody looked twice at him or me. [10]Nobody cared. [11]There ~~was~~ *were* a lot of older students. [12]Nonetheless, I was still nervous. [13]What if I had forgotten how to study after so many years out of school*?* [14]Because I hadn't done any homework in nearly 20 ~~years.~~ *years, I* [15]~~I~~ was sure I wouldn't have a clue how to study. [16]Again, I was wrong. [17]All my years of working had kept my brain sharp and my organizational and focusing skills even sharper. [18]If anything, I was better at studying than my younger classmates. [19]That brings me to my final worry. [20]I had thought that the younger students would ignore me or even laugh at me because of my age. [21]Instead, it was just the opposite. [22]Many of my ~~classmate's~~ *classmates* respected me for returning to school. [23]They had a lot of questions about the "real world" and about working in an office. [24]I actually made a lot of new friends. [25]Despite all my worry, returning to school was far from a serious ~~nightmare it~~ *nightmare. It* was a dream come true!

Name _____   Section _____   Date _____

Score: (Number right) _____ x 10 = _____ %

Proofreading: TEST 6

Read the following passage either aloud or to yourself, looking for the following **ten** mistakes:

1 mistake in subject-verb agreement
2 sentence fragments
2 comma splices
1 missing comma in a series
1 missing comma after an introductory word
2 capital letter mistakes
1 faulty parallelism

Correct the mistakes, crossing out or adding words or punctuation marks as needed.

Why Sugar Is Not So Sweet

¹Everyone craves something sweet from time to time, ˄*and* there's a good reason for that. ²Our bodies need sugar for energy. ³We store sugar in the form of glucose so that we have a quick and powerful source of energy when we need it. ⁴So, when our body signals that it wants something sugary, it's not necessarily a bad ~~thing. ⁵Except~~ *thing—except* when we start responding to that signal too often. ⁶That's when sugar becomes an addiction, and then it can become a very bad thing. ⁷How much is too much sugar? ⁸Most ~~americans~~ *Americans* take in about 22 teaspoons of sugar a ~~day. ⁹Which~~ *day, which* is more than twice as much as we should consume! ¹⁰And all this sugar is ruining the health of millions of us. ¹¹Excess sugar has been blamed for tooth decay, skin problems, premature wrinkles, moodiness, ulcers, gallstones, and even arthritis. ¹²However, the most severe and dangerous problems caused˄ by consumption of too much sugar ~~is~~ ˄*are* obesity and diabetes. ¹³It is estimated that more than a third of the people in our country are now ~~obese, many~~ *obese. Many* of them have gotten that way through one common poison: sugar. ¹⁴Obesity has many dangers of its own, and one of the worst and deadliest is diabetes. ¹⁵People with diabetes can't convert sugar into energy. ¹⁶So the sugar stays in the bloodstream. ¹⁷This can cause shock and, if untreated, death. ¹⁸The good news, though, is that avoiding all these health problems is as simple as cutting back on sugar intake. ¹⁹Many ~~Doctors~~ *doctors* recommend no more than six to nine teaspoons of sugar a day. ²⁰Since many foods already have added sugars, we need to avoid eating most desserts, sodas, and ~~the eating of~~ candy. ²¹An occasional treat is fine, but be careful. ²²You don't want to find yourself on the bitter side of sugar.

Name _____ Section _____ Date _____

Score: (Number right) _____ x 10 = _____ %

Proofreading: TEST 7

Read the following passage either aloud or to yourself, looking for the following **ten** mistakes:

1 irregular verb mistake
1 sentence fragment
2 run-on sentences
1 comma splice
2 missing commas around interrupting words
1 missing apostrophe
1 capital letter mistake
1 shift in verb tense

Correct the mistakes, crossing out or adding words or punctuation marks as needed.

The Night I Woke Up

¹I always used to blame everyone else for anything that went wrong in my life. ²When I didn't make good grades in high ~~school.~~ ³I blamed my teachers for being too boring. [*school, I*] ⁴When all I could get was an uninspiring, low-paying job after high school, it was my parents' fault. ⁵If they'd only ~~lended~~ me a little money, I said to myself, I could have had more time to look for a [*lent*] good job. ⁶Then, later on, when I got fired from that job for slacking off, I blamed my ~~Boss.~~ [*boss*] ⁷In my mind, it was her fault for being so demanding and picky. ⁸I continued on this path of taking no responsibility for my life for several years, then something woke me up: my baby son. [*and*] ⁹Somehow, a wonderful woman had fallen in love with me in spite of my lack of ambition and self-responsibility. ¹⁰The night our son was born, I took my first look at him, and a light ~~switches~~ [*switched*] on in my ~~head for~~ the first time in my life, I was responsible for someone else. [*head. For*] ¹¹I might have been able to fool myself with my excuses in the past, but that wouldn't cut it now. ¹²Suddenly, all my years of blaming others for my mistakes came back to me in a shameful rush. ¹³The very next morning I went to our local community college and signed up for ~~classes today,~~ I'm working [*classes. Today*] during the day and studying accounting at night. ¹⁴By this time next year, I hope to have a good job that will provide a good life for my son. ¹⁵Sometimes, I'm exhausted, but it's okay. ¹⁶It feels pretty good to know that, one day, when ~~Ive~~ achieved my goals, I'll have only myself to blame! [*I've*]

Name _____   Section _____   Date _____

Score: (Number right) _____ x 10 = _____ %

Proofreading: TEST 8

Read the following passage either aloud or to yourself, looking for the following **ten** mistakes:

1 mistake in subject-verb agreement

1 sentence fragment

2 comma splices

1 missing comma after introductory material

1 apostrophe mistake

1 homonym error

1 faulty parallelism

1 missing question mark

1 missing word

Correct the mistakes, crossing out or adding words or punctuation marks as needed.

Helping Others

¹Do you think that you would be less likely to help others when it's cloudy outside? ²What if you were in a big city~~,~~ ?³Studies show that environment has a big ~~affect~~ *effect* on whether we help *others* ~~other's~~ in need. ⁴In one study that was conducted outdoors,people were approached and asked to help a local charity by filling out a quick questionnaire. ⁵The researchers discovered that people were much more likely to help when the day is sunny and mild than ~~in~~ cloudy and cool ~~weather~~ *when it is*. ⁶In a second study, it was found that customers left bigger tips when the sun was ~~shining, it~~ *shining. It* was also discovered that the size of a city has an effect on people's willingness to help. ⁷The common stereotype is that big cities are less friendly than small towns, *and* research has supported this theory. ⁸Strangers are more likely to be assisted in small towns than in large cities. ⁹Furthermore, studies show that even if a person grew up in a small town, he or she is no more likely *to* give help in a big city than someone who grew up there. ¹⁰Finally, population density is one more ~~factor.~~ *factor that* ¹¹~~That~~ determines helping. ¹²The more crowded a city is, the less likely that people in need of help ~~is~~ *are* likely to get it. ¹³Apparently, a little extra elbow room brings out the best in us.

Name _____ Section _____ Date _____

Score: (Number right) _____ × 10 = _____ %

Proofreading: TEST 9

Read the following passage either aloud or to yourself, looking for the following **ten** mistakes:

1 irregular verb mistake
2 sentence fragments
3 comma splices
2 missing commas
2 missing capital letters

Correct the mistakes, crossing out or adding words or punctuation marks as needed.

Justice Not Served

¹"Justice is blind" is a well-known saying. ²Lady Justice is pictured holding a ~~scale, she~~ *scale. She* is also wearing a blindfold. ³What does this pose mean? ⁴It means that the jurors or judge in a trial should be blind to matters of race, wealth, education, status, age, or anything that is not involved with the case. ⁵Decisions should be made solely on the facts presented in the case and nothing else. ⁶Lady Justice, then, is shown weighing her decision without "seeing" anything that might prejudice her judgment.

⁷Keeping this rule in mind, consider the following case. ⁸Several years ago in Fort Lauderdale, ~~florida~~ *Florida*, a 36-year-old white millionaire lost control of his $120,000 Porsche after a night of drinking and partying with his friends. ⁹His car jumped the curb and plowed into two ~~british~~ *British* tourists on the ~~sidewalk.~~ *sidewalk, killing* ~~¹⁰Killing~~ them instantly. ¹¹Instead of stopping, the millionaire ~~drived~~ *drove* off at top speed.

¹²Later, when the driver was apprehended by the police, he lied to ~~them.~~ *them and* ~~¹³And~~ tried to claim that the accident was someone else's fault. ¹⁴He insisted he was no criminal, *but* this was not the driver's first run-in with the law. ¹⁵Previously, he had been charged with possession of ~~cocaine, he~~ *cocaine. He* had also received a string of traffic violations. ¹⁶Sentencing guidelines for a hit-and-run manslaughter conviction call for 20 to 45 years in prison. ¹⁷However, the drunk driver was sentenced to a mere two years of house arrest in a fancy beachfront condo. ¹⁸Although he will remain on probation for ten years, he avoided prison time altogether.

Name _____ Section _____ Date _____

Score: (Number right) _____ x 10 = _____ %

Proofreading: TEST 10

Read the following passage either aloud or to yourself, looking for the following **ten** mistakes:

2 sentence fragments
1 run-on sentence
2 comma splices
1 missing comma after introductory words
1 apostrophe mistake
2 homonym mistakes
1 capital letter mistake

Correct the mistakes, crossing out or adding words or punctuation marks as needed.

Some Truths about Poverty in the United States

¹There are many untrue beliefs about poor people in the United States. ²To begin with, many

people believe that poverty isn't really much of a problem in our country. ³After all, America

is a rich country, right? ⁴In reality, the United States has more ~~poverty.~~ ~~⁵Than~~ *poverty than* the majority of

developed countries in our world. ⁶We rank third poorest, just above Mexico and ~~turkey.~~ *Turkey* ⁷It is

estimated that more than 16 percent of Americans live in ~~poverty.~~ ~~⁸Nearly~~ *poverty—nearly* 50 million people!

⁹Furthermore, one in three children will spend part or all of their ~~childhood's~~ *childhoods* in homes where

there isn't enough to eat. ¹⁰Some people argue that if people are poor, ~~its~~ *it's* because ~~there~~ *they're* lazy

and won't work. ¹¹Nothing could be farther from the truth. ¹²Most poor people work full-

time, *and* many even work two or more jobs. ¹³Because the minimum wage is so terribly low, it is

often impossible for millions of hard workers to move above the poverty line. ¹⁴Finally, many

Americans falsely believe that most poor people are members of minorities living in ghettos

in our big cities. ¹⁵Again, this is wrong. ¹⁶Nearly 50 percent of people living in poverty in the

United States are white, *and* the vast majority of poor American people (close to 75 percent) live in

rural areas and small towns. ¹⁷Still, in spite of the facts, many Americans refuse to believe poverty

is a real ~~problem it~~ *problem. It* is simply easier to cling to comforting myths.

37 Parts of Speech

Words—the building blocks of sentences—can be divided into eight parts of speech. **Parts of speech** are classifications of words according to their meaning and use in a sentence.

This chapter will explain the eight parts of speech:

nouns	**prepositions**	**conjunctions**
pronouns	**adjectives**	**interjections**
verbs	**adverbs**	

Nouns

A **noun** is a word that is used to name something: a person, a place, an object, or an idea. Here are some examples of nouns:

woman	city	pizza	success
Oprah Winfrey	street	diamond	possibility
Stephen Colbert	Miami	Toyota	mystery

Most nouns begin with a lowercase letter and are known as **common nouns**. These nouns name general things. Some nouns, however, begin with a capital letter. They are called **proper nouns**. While a common noun refers to a person or thing in general, a proper noun names someone or something specific. For example, *woman* is a common noun—it doesn't name a particular woman. On the other hand, *Oprah Winfrey* is a proper noun because it names a specific woman.

Practice 1

Insert any appropriate noun into each of the following blanks.   Answers may vary.

1. The shoplifter stole a(n) _____jacket_____ from the department store.

2. _____Randall_____ has been texting me all day.

3. Tiny messages were scrawled on the _____paper_____.

4. A(n) _____baseball_____ crashed through the window.

5. Give the _____job_____ to Elena.

SINGULAR AND PLURAL NOUNS

Singular nouns name one person, place, object, or idea. **Plural nouns** refer to two or more persons, places, objects, or ideas. Most singular nouns can be made plural with the addition of an *s*.

Some nouns, like *box*, have irregular plurals. You can check the plural of nouns you think may be irregular by looking up the singular form in a dictionary.

Singular	Plural
vampire	vampires
turkey	turkeys
exam	exams
truth	truths
box	boxes

For more information on nouns, see "Subjects and Verbs," page 3.

Practice 2

Underline the three nouns in each sentence. Some are singular, and some are plural.

1. Two <u>bats</u> swooped over the <u>heads</u> of the frightened <u>children</u>.

2. The <u>artist</u> has purple <u>paint</u> on her <u>sleeve</u>.

3. The lost <u>dog</u> has <u>fleas</u> and a broken <u>leg</u>.

4. <u>Gwen</u> does her <u>homework</u> in green <u>ink</u>.

5. Some <u>farmers</u> plant <u>seeds</u> by <u>moonlight</u>.

Pronouns

A **pronoun** is a word that stands for a noun. Pronouns eliminate the need for constant repetition. Look at the following sentences:

- The phone rang, and Bill answered the phone.
- Lisa met Lisa's friends at the mall. Lisa meets Lisa's friends there every Saturday.
- The waiter rushed over to the new customers. The new customers asked the waiter for menus and coffee.

Now look at how much clearer and smoother the sentences sound with pronouns.

- The phone rang, and Bill answered **it**.

  The pronoun *it* is used to replace the word *phone*.

- Lisa met **her** friends at the mall. **She** meets **them** there every Saturday.

  The pronoun *her* is used to replace the word *Lisa*. The pronoun *she* replaces *Lisa*. The pronoun *them* replaces the words *Lisa's friends*.

● The waiter rushed over to the new customers. **They** asked **him** for menus and coffee. The pronoun *they* is used to replace the words *the new customers*. The pronoun *him* replaces the words *the waiter*.

Following is a list of commonly used pronouns known as **personal pronouns**:

I	you	he	she	it	we	they
me	your	him	her	its	us	them
my	yours	his	hers		our	their

Practice 3

Fill in each blank with the appropriate personal pronoun.

1. Andrew feeds his pet lizard every day before school. _____He_____ also gives _____it_____ flies in the afternoon.

2. The female reporter interviewed the striking workers. _____They_____ told _____her_____ about their demand for higher wages and longer breaks.

3. Students should save all returned tests. _____They_____ should also keep _____their_____ review sheets.

4. The recorded message told us that _____we_____ would have to wait to speak to a representative. However, _____our_____ call was very important, so we should stay on the line.

5. Randy returned the calculator to Sheila last Friday. But Sheila insists _____she_____ never got _____it_____ back.

There are a number of types of pronouns. For convenient reference, they are described briefly in the box below.

Types of Pronouns

Personal pronouns can act in a sentence as subjects, objects, or possessives.

Singular   I, me, my, mine, you, your, yours, he, him, his, she, her, hers, it, its

Plural   we, us, our, ours, you, your, yours, they, them, their, theirs

Relative pronouns refer to someone or something already mentioned in the sentence.

who, whose, whom, which, that

Interrogative pronouns are used to ask questions.

who, whose, whom, which, what

Demonstrative pronouns are used to point out particular persons or things.

this, that, these, those

NOTE Do not use *them* (as in *them* shoes), *this here, that there, these here* or *those there* to point out.

Reflexive pronouns are those that end in *-self* or *-selves*. A reflexive pronoun is used as the object of a verb (as in *Cary cut **herself***) or the object of a preposition (as in *Jack sent a birthday card to **himself***) when the subject of the verb is the same as the object.

Singular   myself, yourself, himself, herself, itself

Plural   ourselves, yourselves, themselves

Intensive pronouns have exactly the same forms as reflexive pronouns. The difference is in how they are used. Intensive pronouns are used to add emphasis. (*I **myself** will need to read the contract before I sign it.*)

Indefinite pronouns do not refer to a particular person or thing.

each, either, everyone, nothing, both, several, all, any, most, none

Reciprocal pronouns express shared actions or feelings.

each other, one another

For more information on pronouns, see "Pronoun Forms," pages 96–104, and "Pronoun Problems," pages 105–114.

Verbs

Every complete sentence must contain at least one verb. There are two types of verbs: **action verbs** and **linking verbs**.

ACTION VERBS

An **action verb** tells what is being done in a sentence. For example, look at the following sentences:

● Mr. Jensen **swatted** at the bee with his hand.

● Rainwater **poured** into the storm sewer.

● The children **chanted** the words to the song.

> In these sentences, the verbs are *swatted, poured,* and *chanted.* These words are all action verbs; they tell what is happening in each sentence.

For more about action verbs, see "Subjects and Verbs," pages 3 and 146–147.

Practice 4

Insert an appropriate word into each blank. That word will be an action verb; it will tell what is happening in the sentence.   *Answers may vary.*

1. The surgeon _____cut_____ through the first layer of skin.

2. The children _____ran_____ through the supermarket aisles.

3. An elderly woman on the street _____asked_____ me for directions.

4. A man in the restaurant _____called_____ to the waitress.

5. Our instructor _____graded_____ our papers over the weekend.

LINKING VERBS

Some verbs are **linking verbs**. These verbs link (or join) a noun to something that is said about it. For example, look at the following sentence:

● The clouds **are** steel gray.

> In this sentence, *are* is a linking verb. It joins the noun *clouds* to words that describe it: *steel gray.*

Other common linking verbs include *am, appear, become, feel, is, look, seem, sound, was,* and *were.*

For more about linking verbs, see "Subjects and Verbs," page 3, and "More about Subjects and Verbs," pages 147–148.

Practice 5

Into each slot, insert one of the following linking verbs: *am, feel, is, look,* and *were.* Use each linking verb once.

1. The Christmas presents _____ were _____ in a locked cabinet.

2. I _____ am _____ anxious to get my test back.

3. The bananas _____ look _____ ripe.

4. The grocery store _____ is _____ open until 11 p.m.

5. Whenever I _____ feel _____ angry, I go off by myself to calm down.

HELPING VERBS

Sometimes the verb of a sentence consists of more than one word. In these cases, the main verb will be joined by one or more **helping verbs**. Look at the following sentence.

● The basketball team **will be leaving** for their game at six o'clock.

In this sentence, the main verb is *leaving.* The helping verbs are *will* and *be.*

Other helping verbs include *can, could, do, has, have, may, must, should,* and *would.*

For more information about helping verbs, see "Subjects and Verbs," pages 3–4; "Irregular Verbs," pages 9–10; "More about Subjects and Verbs," pages 148–149; "More about Verbs," pages 160–171; and "Even More About Verbs," pages 172–174.

Practice 6

Into each slot, insert one of the following helping verbs: *does, must, should, could,* and *has been.* Use each helping verb once.

1. You _____ should _____ see a doctor about the mole on your forehead.

2. The victim _____ could _____ describe her attacker in great detail.

3. You _____ must _____ rinse the dishes before putting them into the dishwasher.

4. My neighbor _____ has been _____ arrested for drunk driving.

5. The bus driver _____ does _____ not make any extra stops.

Prepositions

A **preposition** is a word that connects a noun or a pronoun to another word in the sentence. For example, look at the following sentence:

● A man **in** the bus was snoring loudly.

  In is a preposition. It connects the noun *bus* to *man*.

Here is a list of common prepositions:

about	before	down	like	to
above	behind	during	of	toward
across	below	except	off	under
after	beneath	for	on	up
among	beside	from	over	with
around	between	in	since	without
at	by	into	through	

The noun or pronoun that a preposition connects to another word in the sentence is called the **object** of the preposition. A group of words that begins with a preposition and ends with its object is called a **prepositional phrase**. The group of words *in the bus*, for example, is a prepositional phrase.

Now read the following sentences and explanations.

● An ant was crawling **up the teacher's leg**.

  The noun *leg* is the object of the preposition *up*. *Up* connects *leg* with the word *crawling*. The prepositional phrase *up the teacher's leg* describes *crawling*. It tells just where the ant was crawling.

● The man **with the black mustache** left the restaurant quickly.

  The noun *mustache* is the object of the preposition *with*. The prepositional phrase *with the black mustache* describes the word *man*. It tells us exactly which man left the restaurant quickly.

● The plant **on the windowsill** was a present **from my mother**.

  The noun *windowsill* is the object of the preposition *on*. The prepositional phrase *on the windowsill* describes the word *plant*. It tells exactly which plant was a present.

  There is a second prepositional phrase in this sentence. The preposition is *from*, and its object is *mother*. The prepositional phrase *from my mother* explains *present*. It tells who gave the present.

For more about prepositions, see "Subjects and Verbs," page 4; "Subject-Verb Agreement," pages 15–20; and "More about Subjects and Verbs," pages 144–145.

Practice 7

Into each slot, insert one of the following prepositions: *of, by, with, on,* and *without.* Use each preposition once.

1. The letter from his girlfriend had been sprayed _____with_____ perfume.

2. Crabgrass and dandelions are growing _____on_____ our lawn.

3. _____Without_____ giving any notice, the tenant moved out of the expensive apartment.

4. Donald hungrily ate three scoops _____of_____ ice cream and an order of French fries.

5. The crates _____by_____ the back door contain glass bottles and old newspapers.

Adjectives

An **adjective** is a word that describes a noun (the name of a person, place, or thing). Look at the following sentence.

● The dog lay down on a mat in front of the fireplace.

Now look at this sentence when adjectives have been inserted.

● The **shaggy** dog lay down on a **worn** mat in front of the fireplace.
The adjective *shaggy* describes the noun *dog*; the adjective *worn* describes the noun *mat*.

Adjectives add spice to our writing. They also help us to identify particular people, places, or things.

Adjectives can be found in two places:

1 An adjective may come before the word it describes (a **damp** night, the **moldy** bread, a **striped** umbrella).

2 An adjective that describes the subject of a sentence may come after a linking verb. The linking verb may be a form of the verb *be* (he is **furious**, I am **exhausted**, they are **hungry**). Other linking verbs include *feel, look, sound, smell, taste, appear, seem,* and *become* (the soup tastes **salty**, your hands feel **dry**, the dog seems **lost**).

NOTE The words *a, an,* and *the* (called **articles**) are generally classified as adjectives.

For more information on adjectives, see "Adjectives and Adverbs," pages 115–124.

Practice 8

Write any appropriate adjective in each slot.   *Answers may vary.*

1. The _____*large*_____ pizza was eaten greedily by the _____*hungry*_____ teenagers.

2. Melissa gave away the sofa because it was _____*old*_____ and _____*worn*_____.

3. Although the alley is _____*dark*_____ and _____*lonely*_____, Karen often takes it as a shortcut home.

4. The restaurant throws away lettuce that is _____*wilted*_____ and tomatoes that are _____*overripe*_____.

5. When I woke up in the morning, I had a(n) _____*slight*_____ fever and a(n) _____*sore*_____ throat.

Adverbs

An **adverb** is a word that describes a verb, an adjective, or another adverb. Many adverbs end in the letters *ly*. Look at the following sentence:

● The canary sang in the pet-store window as the shoppers greeted each other.

Now look at this sentence after adverbs have been inserted.

● The canary sang **softly** in the pet-store window as the shoppers **loudly** greeted each other.
The adverbs add details to the sentence. They also allow the reader to contrast the singing of the canary to the noise the shoppers are making.

Look at the following sentences and the explanations of how adverbs are used in each case.

● The chef yelled **angrily** at the young waiter.
The adverb *angrily* describes the verb *yelled*.

● My mother has an **extremely** busy schedule on Tuesdays.
The adverb *extremely* describes the adjective *busy*.

● The sick man spoke **very** faintly to his loyal nurse.
The adverb *very* describes the adverb *faintly*.

Some adverbs do not end in *-ly*. Examples include *very, often, never, always*, and *well*.

For more information on adverbs, see "Adjectives and Adverbs," pages 115–124, and "More about Subjects and Verbs," page 150.

Write any appropriate adverb in each slot.   *Answers may vary.*

1. The water in the pot boiled _____ quickly _____.

2. Carla _____ carefully _____ drove the car through _____ slowly _____ moving traffic.

3. The telephone operator spoke _____ softly _____ to the young child.

4. The game show contestant waved _____ happily _____ to his family in the audience.

5. Wes _____ rarely _____ studies, so it's no surprise that he did _____ very _____ poorly on his finals.

Conjunctions

Conjunctions are words that connect. There are two types of conjunctions, coordinating and subordinating.

COORDINATING CONJUNCTIONS (JOINING WORDS)

Coordinating conjunctions join two equal ideas. Look at the following sentence:

● Kevin **and** Steve interviewed for the job, **but** their friend Anne got it.

In this sentence, the coordinating conjunction *and* connects the proper nouns *Kevin* and *Steve*. The coordinating conjunction *but* connects the first part of the sentence, *Kevin and Steve interviewed for the job*, to the second part, *their friend Anne got it.*

Following is a list of all the coordinating conjunctions. In this book, they are simply called **joining words**.

and	for	or	yet
but	nor	so	

For more on coordinating conjunctions, see information on joining words in "Sentence Types," pages 21–26, and "Run-Ons and Comma Splices," pages 39–50.

Practice 10

Write a coordinating conjunction in each slot. Choose from the following: *and, but, so, or*, and *nor*. Use each conjunction once.

1. Either my father _____*or*_____ my brother will be making the dessert.

2. I expected roses for my birthday, _____*but*_____ I received a vase of plastic tulips from the discount store.

3. The cafeteria was serving liver and onions for lunch, _____*so*_____ I bought a sandwich at the corner deli.

4. Marian brought a pack of playing cards _____*and*_____ a pan of brownies to the company picnic.

5. Neither my sofa _____*nor*_____ my armchair matches the rug in my living room.

SUBORDINATING CONJUNCTIONS (DEPENDENT WORDS)

When a **subordinating conjunction** is added to a word group, the words can no longer stand alone as an independent sentence. They are no longer a complete thought. For example, look at the following sentence:

● Karen fainted in class.

   The word group *Karen fainted in class* is a complete thought. It can stand alone as a sentence.

See what happens when a subordinating conjunction is added to a complete thought:

● **When** Karen fainted in class

   Now the words cannot stand alone as a sentence. They are dependent on other words to complete the thought:

● **When** Karen fainted in class, we put her feet up on some books.

In this book, a word that begins a dependent word group is called a **dependent word**. Subordinating conjunctions are common dependent words.

Below are some subordinating conjunctions.

after	even if	unless	where
although	even though	until	wherever
as	if	when	whether
because	since	whenever	while
before	though		

Following are some more sentences with subordinating conjunctions:

- **After** she finished her last exam, Joanne said, "Now I can relax."
  After she finished her last exam is not a complete thought. It is dependent on the rest of the words to make up a complete sentence.

- Lamont listens to books on tape **while** he drives to work.
  While he drives to work cannot stand by itself as a sentence. It depends on the rest of the sentence to make up a complete thought.

- **Since** apples were on sale, we decided to make an apple pie for dessert.
  Since apples were on sale is not a complete sentence. It depends on *we decided to make an apple pie for dessert* to complete the thought.

For more information on subordinating conjunctions, see information on dependent words in "Sentence Types," pages 21–26; "Fragments I," pages 27–32; and "Run-Ons and Comma Splices II," pages 45–50.

 Practice 11

Write a logical subordinating conjunction in each slot. Choose from the following: *even though, because, until, when,* and *before*. Use each conjunction once.

1. Sara didn't go to the party _____because_____ she didn't want to risk seeing her former boyfriend.

2. _____When_____ Paula wants to look mysterious, she wears dark sunglasses and a scarf.

3. _____Even though_____ the restaurant was closing in fifteen minutes, customers sipped their coffee slowly and continued to talk.

4. _____Before_____ anyone else could answer it, Carl rushed to the phone and whispered, "It's me."

5. The waiter was instructed not to serve any food _____until_____ the guests of honor arrived.

Interjections

Interjections are words that can stand independently and are used to express emotion. Examples are *oh, wow, ouch,* and *oops.* These words are usually not found in formal writing:

- "**Hey!**" yelled Maggie. "That's my bike."
- **Oh**, we're late for class.

A Final Note

A word may function as more than one part of speech. For example, the word *dust* can be a verb or a noun, depending on its role in the sentence.

- I **dust** my bedroom once a month, whether it needs it or not. (verb)
- The top of my refrigerator is covered with an inch of **dust**. (noun)

Dictionary Use

Owning a Good Dictionary

It is a good idea to own two dictionaries. The first dictionary should be a paperback that you can carry with you. Any of the following would be an excellent choice:

The American Heritage Dictionary, Paperback Edition
The Random House Dictionary, Paperback Edition
Webster's New World Dictionary, Paperback Edition

Your second dictionary should be a full-sized, hardcover edition which should be kept in the room where you study. All the above dictionaries come in hardbound versions, which contain a good deal more information than the paperback editions.

Understanding Dictionary Entries

Each word listed alphabetically in a dictionary is called an **entry word**. Here is a typical dictionary entry word:

> **thun·der** (thŭn′dər) *n.* **1.** The sound that follows lightning and is caused by rapidly expanding air in the path of the electrical discharge. **2.** A loud sound like thunder. —*v.* **1.** To produce a sound resembling thunder. **2.** To express in a loud or threatening way. —**thun′der·ous** *adj.*

SPELLING AND SYLLABLES

The dictionary first gives the correct spelling and syllable breakdown of a word. Dots separate the words into syllables. Each syllable is a separate sound, and each sound includes a vowel. In the entry shown above, *thunder* is divided into two syllables.

 Practice 1

Use your dictionary to separate the following words into syllables. Put a slash (/) between each syllable and the next. Then write the number of syllables in each word. The first one is done for you as an example.

1. g u a r / a n / t e e   __3__ syllables
2. n e w s / p a / p e r   __3__ syllables
3. v o / c a b / u / l a r / y   __5__ syllables
4. c a u / l i / f l o w / e r   __4__ syllables

PRONUNCIATION SYMBOLS AND ACCENT MARKS

Most dictionary entry words are followed first by a pronunciation guide in parentheses, as in the entry for *thunder*:

thun·der (thŭn ′dər)

The information in parentheses includes two kinds of symbols: *pronunciation symbols* and *accent marks*. Following is an explanation of each.

Pronunciation Symbols

The **pronunciation symbols** tell the sounds of consonants and vowels in a word. The sounds of the consonants are probably familiar to you, but you may find it helpful to review the vowel sounds. Vowels are the letters *a, e, i, o, u,* and sometimes *y*. To know how to pronounce the vowel sounds, use the **pronunciation key** in your dictionary. Such a key typically appears at the front of a dictionary or at the bottom of every other page of the dictionary. Here is a pronunciation key for the vowels and a few other sounds that often confuse dictionary users.

Pronunciation Guide

ă hat	ā say	â dare	ĕ ten	ē she	ĭ sit	ī tie, my
ŏ lot	ō go	ô all	oi **oil**	o͝o look	o͞o cool	
th **thin**	*th* **this**	ŭ up	ûr **fur**	yo͞o use	ə ago, easily	

The key tells you, for instance, that the sound of ă (called "short a") is pronounced like the *a* in *hat*, the sound of ā (called "long a") is pronounced like the *ay* in *say*, and so on. All the vowels with a cup-shaped symbol above them are called **short vowels**. All the vowels with a horizontal line above them are called **long vowels**. Note that long vowels have the sound of their own name. For example, long *a* sounds like the name of the letter *a*.

To use the above key, first find the symbol of the sound you wish to pronounce. For example, suppose you want to pronounce the short *i* sound. Locate the short *i* in the key and note how the sound is pronounced in the word *(sit)* that appears next to the short *i*. This tells you that the short *i* has the sound of the *i* in the word *sit*. The key also tells you, for instance, that the short *e* has the sound of the *e* in the word *ten*, that the short *o* has the sound of the *o* in the word *lot*, and so on.

Finally, note that the last pronunciation symbol in the key looks like an upside-down e: ə. This symbol is known as the **schwa**. As you can see by the words that follow it, the schwa has a very short sound that sounds much like "uh" (as in *ago*) or "ih" (as in *easily*).

Practice 2

Refer to the pronunciation key to answer the questions about the following words. Circle the letter of each of your answers.

1. **hic·cup** (hĭk′ŭp)
   The *i* in *hiccup* sounds like the *i* in
   (a.) sit.   **b.** tie.

2. **si·lent** (sī′lənt)
   The *i* in *silent* sounds like the *i* in
   a. sit.   **(b.)** tie.

3. **na·tive** (nā′tĭv)
   The *a* in *native* sounds like the *a* in
   a. hat.   **(b.)** say.

4. **lot·ter·y** (lŏt′ə-rē)
   The *o* in *lottery* sounds like the *o* in
   (a.) lot.   **b.** go.

Practice 3

Use your dictionary to find and write in the pronunciation symbols for the following words. Make sure you can pronounce each word. The first word has been done for you as an example.

1. reluctant   _rĭ-lŭk′tənt_

2. homicide   _hom′ĭ-sīd′_

3. extravagant   _ĭk-străv′ə-gənt_

4. unanimous   _yŏo-năn′ə-məs_

ACCENT MARKS

Notice the mark in the pronunciation guide for *thunder* that is similar to an apostrophe:

thun·der (thŭn′dər)

The dark mark (′) is a bold accent mark, and it shows which syllable has the stronger stress. That means the syllable it follows is pronounced a little louder than the others. Syllables without an accent mark are unstressed. Some syllables are in between, and they are marked with a lighter accent mark (′).

The word *recognize*, for example, is accented like this:

rec·og·nize (rĕk′əg-nīz′)

Say *recognize* to yourself. Can you hear that the strongest accent is on *rec*, the first syllable? Can you hear that the last syllable, *nize*, is also accented but not as strongly? If not, say the word to yourself again until you hear the differences in accent sounds.

Answer the questions following each of the words below.

1. **mol·e·cule**   (mŏl′ĭ-kyōōl′)
   a. How many syllables are in *molecule*?   3
   b. Which syllable is most strongly accented?   First

2. **in·ter·me·di·ate**   (ĭn′tər-mē′dē-ĭt)
   a. How many syllables are in *intermediate*?   5
   b. Which syllable is most strongly accented?   Third

3. **in·her·it**   (ĭn-hĕr′ĭt)
   a. How many syllables are in *inherit*?   3
   b. Which syllable is accented?   Second

4. **con·tra·dic·tion**   (kŏn′trə-dĭk′shən)
   a. How many syllables are in *contradiction*?   4
   b. Which syllable is most strongly accented?   Third

PARTS OF SPEECH

Every word in the dictionary is either a noun, a verb, an adjective, or another part of speech. In dictionary entries, the parts of speech are shown by abbreviations in italics. In the entry for *thunder*, for example, the abbreviations *n.* and *v.* tell us that thunder can be both a noun and a verb.

When a word is more than one part of speech, the dictionary gives the definitions for each part of speech separately. In the entry for *thunder*, the abbreviation telling us that *thunder* is a noun comes right after the pronunciation symbols; the two noun definitions follow. When the noun meanings end, the abbreviation *v.* tells us that the verb definitions will follow.

Parts of speech are abbreviated in order to save space. Following are common abbreviations for parts of speech.

n.—noun	*v.*—verb
pron.—pronoun	*conj.*—conjunction
adj.—adjective	*prep.*—preposition
adv.—adverb	*interj.*—interjection

IRREGULAR VERB FORMS AND IRREGULAR SPELLINGS

After the part of speech, special information is given in entries for irregular verbs, for adjectives with irregularly spelled forms, and for irregularly spelled plurals.

For **irregular verbs**, the dictionary gives the past tense, the past participle, and the present participle. For example, the entry for *blow* shows that *blew* is the past tense, *blown* is the past participle, and *blowing* is the present participle.

blow (blō) *v.* **blew** (bloo), **blown** (blōn), **blowing.**

For **adjectives with irregularly spelled forms**, the comparative (used when comparing two things) and the superlative (used when comparing three or more things) are shown after the part of speech. The entry for *skinny*, for instance, shows that the comparative form of that adjective is *skinnier* and the superlative form is *skinniest*.

skin·ny (skĭn′ē) *adj.* **-ni·er, -ni·est.**

Irregular plural spellings are also included in this spot in an entry. For example, after the part of speech, the entry for *party* tells us that this word's plural ends in *-ies*.

par·ty (pär′tē) *n., pl.* **-ties.**

DEFINITIONS

Words often have more than one meaning. When they do, their definitions may be numbered in the dictionary. You can tell which definition of a word fits a given sentence by the meaning of the sentence. For example, the following are dictionary definitions for the verb form of *surprise*:

1 To take unawares.

2 To attack suddenly and unexpectedly.

3 To astonish or amaze with the unexpected.

Which of these definitions best fits the sentence below?

The soldiers *surprised* the enemy troops, who had bedded down for the night.

The answer is definition 2: The soldiers *suddenly attacked* the enemy troops.

Practice 5

A. Use your dictionary to answer the questions below about *obstinate*.

1. Which syllable in *obstinate* is most strongly accented?   _____First_____

2. How many syllables are in the word *obstinate*?   _____3_____

3. How many *schwa* sounds are in the word *obstinate*?   _____1_____

4. Does the first syllable in *obstinate* have a long or short *o* sound?   _____Short_____

5. Which definition of *obstinate* applies in the following sentence? (Write out the full definition from your dictionary.)   *Wording of definitions may vary.*

    Felicia stayed home all week with an *obstinate* case of the flu.

    Definition: _____ Difficult to alleviate or cure _____

    _____

B. Use your dictionary to answer the questions below about *solitary*.

6. How many syllables are in the word *solitary*?   _____4_____

7. Which syllable in *solitary* is most strongly accented?   _____First_____

8. Does the first syllable in *solitary* have a long or short *o* sound?   _____Short_____

9. Which definition of *solitary* applies in the following sentence? (Write out the full definition from your dictionary.)

    The box of cookies was bought yesterday, and today there's only a *solitary* cookie remaining.

    Definition: _____ Single; sole _____

    _____

10. Which definition of *solitary* applies in the following sentence? (Write out the full definition from your dictionary.)

    Some people like to study in groups, but Sarita prefers *solitary* study.

    Definition: _____ Happening or done alone _____

    _____

This chapter explains the following ways to improve your spelling:

- Use the dictionary and other spelling aids
- Keep a personal spelling list
- Learn commonly confused words
- Learn some helpful spelling rules
    1 *I* before *E* rule
    2 Silent *E* rule
    3 *Y* rule
    4 Doubling rule
    5 Rules for adding *-es* to nouns and verbs that end in *s, sh, ch,* or *x*
    6 Rules for adding *-es* to nouns and verbs ending in a consonant plus *y*

Use the Dictionary and Other Spelling Aids

The single most important way to improve your spelling is to get into the habit of checking words in a dictionary. (As alternatives to using a print dictionary, you might try an online dictionary or simply a Google search for "how to spell _____.") But you may at times have trouble locating a given word. "If I can't spell a word," you might ask, "how can I find it in the dictionary?" The answer is that you have to guess what the letters might be.

Here are some hints to help you make informed guesses.

HINT 1

If you're not sure about the vowels in a word, you will have to experiment. Vowels often sound the same. So try an *i* in place of an *a*, an *e* in place of an *i*, and so on.

HINT 2

Consonants are sometimes doubled in a word. If you can't find your word with single consonants, try doubling them.

HINT 3

In the box below are groups of letters or letter combinations that often sound alike. If your word isn't spelled with one of the letters in a pair or group shown in the box, it might be spelled with another in the same pair or group. For example, if it isn't spelled with a *k*, it may be spelled with a *c*.

Vowels				
ai / ay	au / aw	ee / ea	ou / ow	oo / u
Consonants				
c / k c / s	f / ph	g / j	sch / sc / sk	s / z
Combinations				
re / ri	able / ible	ent / ant	er / or	tion / sion

Practice 1

Use your dictionary and the hints on the previous page to find the correct spelling of the following words.

1.	rilease	release	**11.**	aukward	awkward
2.	diferent	different	**12.**	photografy	photography
3.	sertain	certain	**13.**	asemble	assemble
4.	chearful	cheerful	**14.**	seazon	season
5.	sergery	surgery	**15.**	dependant	dependent
6.	skedule	schedule	**16.**	terrable	terrible
7.	kontrol	control	**17.**	dezign	design
8.	comfortible	comfortable	**18.**	cownty	county
9.	mayer	mayor	**19.**	funcsion	function
10.	paiment	payment	**20.**	awthor	author

In addition to a dictionary, take advantage of a spelling checker on your computer. Also, pocket-size electronic spelling checkers are widely available.

Keep a Personal Spelling List

In a special place, write down every word you misspell. Include its correct spelling, underline the difficult part of the word, and add any hints you can use to remember how to spell it. If spelling is a particular problem for you, you might even want to start a spelling notebook that has a separate page for each letter of the alphabet.

Here's one format you might use:

How I spelled it	Correct spelling	Hints
recieve	rec<u>ei</u>ve	I before E except after C
seperate	sep<u>a</u>rate	There's A RAT in sepARATe
alot	<u>a l</u>ot	Two words (like "a little")
alright	<u>all r</u>ight	Two words (like "all wrong")

Study your list regularly, and refer to it whenever you write and proofread a paper.

Learn Commonly Confused Words

Many spelling errors result from words that sound alike or almost alike but that are spelled differently, such as *break* and *brake*, *wear* and *where*, or *right* and *write*. To avoid such errors, study carefully the list of words on pages 69–74 and 200–204.

Learn Some Helpful Spelling Rules

Even poor spellers can improve by following a few spelling rules.
Following are six rules that apply to many words.

RULE #1
I before E rule

*I before **E** except after **C***
Or when pronounced like **A**, as in *neighbor* and *weigh*.

	I before E	*Except after C*	*Or when pronounced like A*
Examples	belief, chief, field	receive, ceiling	vein, eight

Exceptions to the above rule include: either, leisure, foreign, science, society

Practice 2

A. Complete each word with either *ie* or *ei*.

1. br_ie_f
2. bel_ie_ve
3. dec_ei_ve
4. fr_ei_ght
5. c_ei_ling

6. w_ei_gh
7. pr_ie_st
8. cash_ie_r
9. p_ie_ce
10. r_ei_ndeer

B. In each sentence, fill in the blank with either **ie** or **ei**.

11. I rec_ei_ved some interesting junk mail today.

12. Many of the people in my n_ei_ghborhood are retired.

13. Norma never gave up her bel_ie_f in her husband's innocence.

14. What do you like to do in your l_ei_sure time?

15. There's a lot of traffic now, so don't ignore this y_ie_ld sign.

16. The r_ei_gn of Queen Victoria of Great Britain lasted over sixty years.

17. My parents are working hard to ach_ie_ve their retirement goals.

18. I have never traveled to any for_ei_gn countries.

19. My _ei_ghty-year-old grandfather still does a daily twenty pushups.

20. A th_ie_f broke into Parker's Bakery last night and stole all the dough.

RULE #2
Silent *E* rule

If a word ends in a silent (unpronounced) *e*, drop the *e* before adding an ending that starts with a vowel. Keep the *e* when adding an ending that begins with a consonant.

	Drop the e with endings that start with a vowel	*Keep the e with endings that start with a consonant*
Examples	like + ed = liked	love + ly = lovely
	confuse + ing = confusing	shame + ful = shameful
	fame + ous = famous	hope + less = hopeless
	guide + ance = guidance	manage + ment = management

Exceptions include: noticeable, argument, judgment, truly

Practice 3

A. Write out each word shown.

1.	love + ing	=	loving
2.	hope + ed	=	hoped
3.	have + ing	=	having
4.	desire + able	=	desirable
5.	ridicule + ous	=	ridiculous
6.	sincere + ity	=	sincerity

B. Write out each word shown.

7.	like + ly	=	likely
8.	peace + ful	=	peaceful
9.	advance + ment	=	advancement
10.	noise + less	=	noiseless
11.	large + ness	=	largeness
12.	grace + ful	=	graceful
13.	sincere + ly	=	sincerely

C. Write out each word shown.

14.	write + ing	=	writing
15.	care + ful	=	careful
16.	safe + ly	=	safely
17.	hire + ed	=	hired
18.	active + ist	=	activist
19.	notice + able	=	noticeable
20.	excite + ment	=	excitement

RULE #3
Y rule

When adding an ending, change the final *y* of a word to *i* when both of the following are present:
a The last two letters of the word are a consonant plus *y*. (Keep a *y* that follows a vowel.)
b The ending being added begins with a vowel or is *-ful*, *-ly*, or *-ness*.

Exception   Keep the *y* if the ending being added is *-ing*.

	Change the y to i	*Keep the y*
Examples	happy + ness = happiness	destroy + s = destroys
	lucky + ly = luckily	display + ed = displayed
	beauty + ful = beautiful	gray + ed = grayed
	try + ed = tried	try + ing = trying
	carry + er = carrier	carry + ing = carrying

Practice 4

A. Write out each word shown.

1. pity + ed = _____ pitied _____
2. holy + ness = _____ holiness _____
3. play + ful = _____ playful _____
4. cry + ing = _____ crying _____
5. cry + ed = _____ cried _____
6. plenty + ful = _____ plentiful _____
7. lazy + ness = _____ laziness _____
8. enjoy + ing = _____ enjoying _____
9. angry + ly = _____ angrily _____
10. betray + ed = _____ betrayed _____

B. Write out each word shown.

11. pray + ing = _____ praying _____ pray + ed = _____ prayed _____
12. busy + est = _____ busiest _____ busy + ly = _____ busily _____
13. silly + er = _____ sillier _____ silly + ness = _____ silliness _____
14. employ + ed = _____ employed _____ employ + er = _____ employer _____
15. bury + ing = _____ burying _____ bury + ed = _____ buried _____
16. dry + ing = _____ drying _____ dry + ed = _____ dried _____
17. happy + ly = _____ happily _____ happy + er = _____ happier _____
18. funny + er = _____ funnier _____ funny + est = _____ funniest _____
19. satisfy + ing = _____ satisfying _____ satisfy + ed = _____ satisfied _____
20. annoy + ed = _____ annoyed _____ annoy + ance = _____ annoyance _____

RULE #4
Doubling rule

Double the final consonant of a word before adding an ending when all three of the following are present:

a The last three letters of the word are a consonant, a vowel, and a consonant (CVC). Note that if the last three letters of the word are two vowels and a consonant (VVC), or a vowel and two consonants (VCC), the final consonant is **not** doubled.

b The word is only one syllable (for example, *stop*) or is accented on the last syllable (for example, *begin*).

c The ending being added begins with a vowel.

	One-syllable words that end in CVC	Words accented on the last syllable that end in CVC
Examples	stop + ed = stopped	begin + ing = beginning
	flat + er = flatter	control + er = controller
	red + est = reddest	occur + ence = occurrence

Practice 5

A. First note whether each one-syllable word ends in the CVC pattern or with another pattern (VVC, VCC, etc.), and write the pattern in the first column. Then add to each word the endings shown.

	Word	Pattern of Last Three Letters	Add *-ed*	Add *-ing*
Examples	trip	CVC	tripped	tripping
	growl	VCC	growled	growling
1.	plan	CVC	planned	planning
2.	learn	VCC	learned	learning
3.	slam	CVC	slammed	slamming
4.	wrap	CVC	wrapped	wrapping
5.	fail	VVC	failed	failing
6.	dot	CVC	dotted	dotting
7.	flood	VVC	flooded	flooding
8.	beg	CVC	begged	begging
9.	clip	CVC	clipped	clipping
10.	burn	VCC	burned	burning

B. First note whether each two-syllable word ends in the CVC pattern or with another pattern (VVC, VCC, etc.), and write the pattern in the first column. Then add to each word the endings shown. *If a word ends in CVC, remember to check to see if the final syllable is stressed or not.*

	Word	Pattern of Last Three Letters	Add -*ed*	Add -*ing*
Examples	admit	CVC	admitted	admitting
	recall	VCC	recalled	recalling
11.	expel	CVC	expelled	expelling
12.	perform	VCC	performed	performing
13.	enter	CVC	entered	entering
14.	omit	CVC	omitted	omitting
15.	murder	CVC	murdered	murdering
16.	prefer	CVC	preferred	preferring
17.	occur	CVC	occurred	occurring
18.	explain	VVC	explained	explaining
19.	submit	CVC	submitted	submitting
20.	reason	CVC	reasoned	reasoning

RULE #5
Rules for adding -*es* to nouns and verbs that end in s, sh, ch, or x

Most plurals are formed by adding -*s* to the singular noun, but in some cases -*es* is added. For nouns that end in **s**, **sh**, **ch**, or **x**, form the plural by adding -*es*.

Examples	kiss + es = kisses	coach + es = coaches
	wish + es = wishes	tax + es = taxes

Most third-person singular verbs end in -*s* (he runs, she sings, it grows). But for verbs that end in **s**, **sh**, **ch**, or **x**, form the third-person singular with -*es*.

Examples	miss + es = misses	catch + es = catches
	wash + es = washes	mix + es = mixes

Practice 6

Add **-s** or **-es** as needed to each of the following words.

1. rush _____ rushes
2. fix _____ fixes
3. pitch _____ pitches
4. glass _____ glasses
5. carpet _____ carpets
6. crash _____ crashes
7. box _____ boxes
8. watch _____ watches
9. shine _____ shines
10. business _____ businesses

RULE #6

Rules for adding -es to nouns and verbs that end in a consonant plus y

For nouns that end in a consonant plus **y**, form the plural by changing the **y** to **i** and adding **-es**.

Examples   fly + es = flies   lady + es = ladies
            canary + es = canaries

For verbs that end in a consonant plus **y**, form the third-person singular by changing the **y** to **i** and adding **-es**.

Examples   pity + es = pities   marry + es = marries
            bully + es = bullies

Practice 7

Add **-s** or **-es** as needed to each of the following words. Where appropriate, change a final **y** to **i** before adding **-es**.

1. party _____ parties
2. try _____ tries
3. stay _____ stays
4. hurry _____ hurries
5. attorney _____ attorneys
6. variety _____ varieties
7. chimney _____ chimneys
8. baby _____ babies
9. journey _____ journeys
10. sympathy _____ sympathies

Practice 8

Use the spelling rules in the chapter to write out the words indicated.

A. Complete each word with either *ie* or *ei*.

1. gr_ie_f
2. dec_ei_ve
3. n_ei_ghbor
4. fr_ie_nd
5. retr_ie_ve

B. Use the *silent e* rule to write out each word shown.

6. time + ed = _timed_
7. time + ly = _timely_
8. hope + ful = _hopeful_
9. fame + ous = _famous_
10. abuse + er = _abuser_

C. Use the *Y* rule to write out each word shown.

11. fry + ed = _fried_
12. easy + ly = _easily_
13. stay + ed = _stayed_
14. duty + ful = _dutiful_
15. lonely + ness = _loneliness_

D. Use the *doubling* rule to write out each word shown.

16. join + ing = _joining_
17. pad + ing = _padding_
18. prefer + ed = _preferred_
19. jump + er = _jumper_
20. sad + est = _saddest_

E. Add *-s* or *-es* as needed to each of the following words. Where appropriate, change a final *y* to *i* before adding *-es*.

21. pass _passes_
22. enemy _enemies_
23. country _countries_
24. valley _valleys_
25. porch _porches_

Practice 9

Use the spelling rules in the chapter to write out the words indicated.

A. Complete each word with either *ie* or *ei*.

1. n_ie_ce
2. f_ie_ld
3. sobr_ie_ty
4. v_ei_n
5. con_ei_ve

B. Use the *silent e* rule to write out each word shown.

6. come + ing = _coming_
7. care + less = _careless_
8. desire + able = _desirable_
9. accurate + ly = _accurately_
10. serve + er = _server_

C. Use the *Y* rule to write out each word shown.

11. reply + ed = _replied_
12. pray + ing = _praying_
13. carry + ed = _carried_
14. glory + ous = _glorious_
15. study + ing = _studying_

D. Use the *doubling* rule to write out each word shown.

16. bark + ing = _barking_
17. rob + er = _robber_
18. commit + ed = _committed_
19. mop + ed = _mopped_
20. refer + ing = _referring_

E. Add *-s* or *-es* as needed to each of the following words. Where appropriate, change a final *y* to *i* before adding *-es*.

21. city _cities_
22. branch _branches_
23. subway _subways_
24. dress _dresses_
25. puppy _puppies_

Index